PRAISE FOR *B2B DIGITAL*

'A brilliant, rare and impactful insight into areas to consider when creating a B2B digital marketing strategy. Great guidance on how to think about your customer journey throughout the process, not just in the implementation phases. Highly recommend this read as an essential for all marketers.'
Catherine Dutton, Vice President Marketing, Atos

'Simon Hall has written a B2B Marketing primer for the 2020s, which, by definition, deals with the realities of a digital first world. This is long over-due in the world of B2B Marketing and will no doubt become a standard source for the discipline.

I recognize through my own practice that this digital transformation from "outbound" marketing – or a "tell" approach – to inbound, customer journey-focused marketing, with all of its personalized digital touchpoints and omni-channel focus is today's B2B marketing reality and Simon does a good job of comprehensively covering all of the key elements, from content, to social, SEO, SEM and Web – as well as the enabling infrastructure: martech, data, marketing processes (eg lead nurturing, ABM) and analytics. Simon presents a best-practice approach to each, steeped in personal experience and in that of leading companies in the technology market. He provides theoretical context and practical how-to guidance, with great detail on management and execution across the buyers' journey.

The chapter on digital strategy points to the need for digital to be a clear part of the overall marketing strategy which delivers clear outcomes based on business goals. Too often in my experience, marketing strategy is confused with annual budget and resource planning, so the tools and approach Simon summarizes here are a useful reminder to understand the context of your digital strategy.

This book is a really valuable addition to the B2B marketing armoury and is highly recommended for those who intend to build their career in marketing.'
Ceri Jones, former Vice President, Global Demand Centre and Operations, Basware Oyj

'Digital marketing continues to be a minefield for marketers, especially those in B2B where extended decision-making groups and lengthy sales cycles pervade. Clear, engaging and practical, *B2B Digital Marketing Strategy* helps navigate the complexities of digital marketing.'
Richard Robinson, Chairman, B2B Council, DMA

'This is a well-written book suitable for both beginners and seasoned practitioners on a topic that's very important to business today. The case studies and tips are practical and useful for any business.'
Jayson Gehri, Executive Director, Marketing, IBM

'Whether you are new to digital marketing strategy in general or looking to brush up on a specific topic, this is a very useful read. It's informative, easy to navigate, and gives you the tools to understand and implement a great digital strategy in your company.'
Amalie Lyneborg, Head of Marketing, Sturrock & Robson

B2B Digital Marketing Strategy

*How to use new frameworks and models
to achieve growth*

Simon Hall

KoganPage

First published in Great Britain and the United States in 2020 by Kogan Page Limited

2nd Floor, 45 Gee Street	122 W 27th St, 10th Floor	4737/23 Ansari Road
London	New York, NY 10001	Daryaganj
EC1V 3RS	USA	New Delhi 110002
United Kingdom		India
www.koganpage.com		

Kogan Page books are printed on paper from sustainable forests.

ISBNs
Hardback   978 1 78966 256 6
Paperback   978 1 78966 254 2
eBook   978 1 78966 255 9

British Library Cataloguing-in-Publication Data

A CIP record for this book is available from the British Library.

Library of Congress Cataloging-in-Publication Data

Names: Hall, Simon, 1971- author.
Title: B2B digital marketing strategy : how to use new frameworks and
    models to achieve growth / Simon Hall.
Description: London ; New York, NY : Kogan Page, 2020. | Includes
    bibliographical references and index. |
Identifiers: LCCN 2020009464 (print) | LCCN 2020009465 (ebook) | ISBN
    9781789662542 (paperback) | ISBN 9781789662566 (hardback) | ISBN
    9781789662559 (ebook)
Subjects: LCSH: Internet marketing. | Internet advertising. | Social
    media–Marketing. | Data transmission systems.
Classification: LCC HF5415.1265 H35155 2020 (print) | LCC HF5415.1265
    (ebook) | DDC 658.8/72–dc23

Typeset by Integra Software Services, Pondicherry
Print production managed by Jellyfish
Printed and bound by CPI Group (UK) Ltd, Croydon CR0 4YY

Thank you Laura for your inexhaustible source of positivity and perseverance, as well as your boundless energy, all of which have inspired me in writing this book

CONTENTS

ABOUT THE AUTHOR

Simon Hall is a marketing innovator with 25 years' experience in technology and services marketing. In his former career, he served as UK Chief Marketing Officer for Dell as well as holding many senior European roles at Acer, Microsoft and Toshiba. He is also author of the book *Innovative B2B Marketing*.

In 2016 Simon founded NextGen Marketing Solutions, with the aim to help companies of all sizes capitalize on the latest marketing techniques. He is passionate about pioneering new and exciting initiatives, and sharing his knowledge and experience with the current and next generation of marketers.

In addition to running courses and workshops with companies on various B2B marketing and digital marketing areas, Simon also lectures final-year university students and degree apprentices in strategy and marketing at Pearson Business School.

He is a member of the Chartered Institute of Marketing and the DMA B2B Council, and a Global Thought Leader in B2B Marketing for the ICG Group (a global consulting company).

PREFACE

B2B Digital Marketing Strategies is a clear and practical digital marketing guide which aims to assist B2B companies, marketers and departments in dealing with the most recent challenges surrounding digital marketing.

With rapidly changing B2B customer buying behaviours and the changing dynamics in the industry, there have been substantial changes and step changes in how digital marketing is applied in B2B marketing. The focus of this book is to explain and promote the new B2B digital marketing models and practices which have arisen as a result of these key changes in the marketplace.

You will find a number of case studies throughout the book, spanning different types of sectors as well as company sizes. Some of the best practices come from large enterprises, as well as small and medium businesses. Please use these as practical examples which you can apply in your own company.

This book is perfect for any marketer working in, or interested in building a more in-depth knowledge and understanding of, B2B digital marketing. It is suitable for small and medium-sized business owners and sales and marketing professionals as well as practitioners. I truly hope you benefit from my experience in leveraging these models.

B2B marketers will find new approaches, models, processes and solutions as well as examples of technologies to help them deal with key current B2B digital marketing challenges.

01

The new evolving business landscape

Introduction

The changing business landscape

In less than 100 years we've moved through multiple eras of business and industry, from the production age through to the marketing age, and recently from the globalization era to the era of digital and applications.

We've also seen a number of changes in B2B marketing; in fact, in a recent survey it was found that 76 per cent of B2B marketers feel marketing has changed more in the past two years than in the previous 50 years (Taylor, 2017).

Customers are changing in how they engage with businesses, how they evaluate products and services, and how they respond to marketing and sales efforts.

B2B insights

According to the latest B2B buyer research published by DemandGen Report, the world of B2B marketing is continuing to get more complex, and buyers are becoming more sophisticated. Some of the results from the survey show:

- more than half (56 per cent) of companies have four or more people involved in a purchase decision, while 21 per cent have seven or more stakeholders;

- 75 per cent of buyers said they are spending more time researching purchases, up from 72 per cent in 2018;

- 79 per cent of respondents said the winning vendor's content had a significant impact on their ultimate buying decision.

FIGURE 1.1 The changing B2B landscape

Changing sales		Changing marketing
Changes in technology	The changing B2B landscape	Social organization and social media
Changing customer and buying process		Influences of ethics and legislation

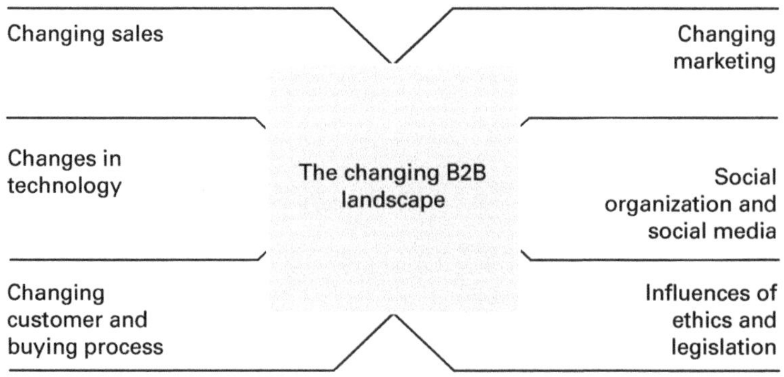

The study also found that buyers are developing a growing reliance on peers. Sixty-one per cent said they agree that they rely more on peer recommendations and review sites (Andersen, 2019).

All the above statistics point to the fact that marketers need to embrace different marketing vehicles, and better tailor their messages and content to the customer. Marketers have the challenging role of influencing buyers more than before, so that when customers are about to purchase, they're already considering the vendors' products or services.

We can summarize the changing B2B landscape across six core areas: marketing, sales, customers, technology trends, the social organization and social media, and ethics and legislation. See Figure 1.1.

Changes to the marketing discipline

With increasingly demanding customers who for a large part of their buying process don't interact with potential vendors, marketing departments need to think more creatively about how to influence the buying process. Due to the indirect and non-interactive nature of the stages of the buying process, B2B marketers need to look to more sophisticated advertising and targeting strategies, improved content marketing approaches, clever SEO strategies and how to leverage marketing partners or third parties. The use of third parties and marketing partners may be referred to as marketing partner development management.

Today we see B2B marketers leveraging partners in different ways to reach customers, nurture customers and improve the customer experience.

As a result, we're seeing the marketing mix – already up to 7Ps – evolve to include an 8th 'P', Partnerships.

Within the marketing discipline, data and data analytics is becoming more critical to support marketing and the business. Skills are needed to analyse the right data, interpret it and develop insights to guide marketing strategies. Data management or analysis-based jobs aren't the obvious focus for people wanting to enter marketing; hence, the industry needs to consider how best to attract those with such skills.

In parallel there are a number of applications online which embed analytics and have developed analytical platforms. Some offer free versions, such as Twitter or Google Analytics. With this explosion of data and data analytics, B2B digital marketers are no longer asking 'Where can I find the data?' but 'How do I use the right data, and in a meaningful manner?'

B2B marketing contribution to business

Undoubtedly the role of B2B marketing has evolved in the past decade: now most B2B marketers are supporting the business and adding value. As mentioned before, one main area is leveraging partners to support marketing and the business. Another area of value-add is providing richer and more detailed insights relating to customers.

We've also seen a general increase in content in the B2B marketing space. Most B2B marketing departments appear to be spending more than half their budget on content creation.

Another change for B2B marketing has been lead-to-revenue management (L2RM), or lead generation as it is often called. Although this has been around for some time, the industry is seeing a greater emphasis on delivering higher-quality leads.

L2RM is about marketing supporting across the entire customer buyer journey through to post-acquisition. Within the discipline of L2RM, business marketers need to prove their value more, and show how they contribute to top-line and bottom-line growth.

Boundary-spanning skills

The ability to work outside the marketing remit with other departments calls for better boundary-spanning skills, as marketers need to collaborate to improve delivery and impact of marketing initiatives. This means working outside the function; understanding how to work across different marketing functions, as well as with people outside the company.

New changes in sales

Changing sales

There has also been a change in marketing and sales dynamics over recent years. As a result of the changing buyer journey, there has been an emphasis on the marketing department supporting the business in different ways. These include nurturing leads and enabling sales through provision of content, and any additional sales enablement activities to allow sales colleagues to nurture the prospect without actively or directly interacting with the customer. Figure 1.2 demonstrates how the sales and marketing roles have changed.

Buyers now want information and knowledge at the touch of a button, and want to find information about prospective vendors when they need it, through the channels they use and in the formats they like. With prospective buyers becoming more demanding, organizations need to make content and information available in different ways through different channels, whilst ensuring consistency of message.

Salesperson 2.0

As marketing has needed to change, so the same is happening with sales. The sales department now carries out different functions, and needs to spend its time differently. Effective salespeople will spend more time identifying and understanding customers' challenges as well as exploring and resolving problems; their focus is to understand the customers' environment and challenges in greater depth.

Sales have also needed to learn how to use social media in different ways to not only engage existing customers, but to share content with prospects.

Changing selling

Those companies that haven't adapted their sales techniques are having a tough time of it. In 2010 a salesperson would need to make three or four cold calls before they could get through to a person; now this is more like 10 calls. This means that sales need to work three times harder just to be able to talk to someone, and this is before we consider reactions from call recipients and whether this converts to sales at all.

Some organizations continue to rely heavily on sales to acquire customers through traditional out-bounding approaches, though the inefficiencies in the process are high.

FIGURE 1.2 Changing sales and marketing in B2B

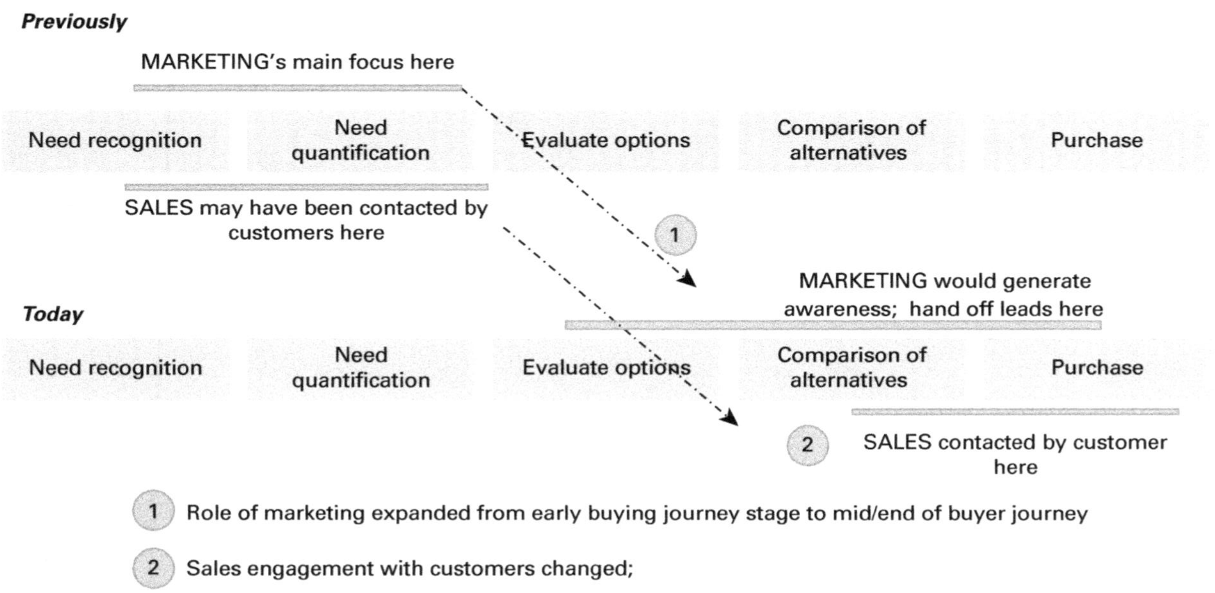

Previously

MARKETING's main focus here

| Need recognition | Need quantification | Evaluate options | Comparison of alternatives | Purchase |

SALES may have been contacted by customers here

Today

MARKETING would generate awareness; hand off leads here

| Need recognition | Need quantification | Evaluate options | Comparison of alternatives | Purchase |

SALES contacted by customer here

(1) Role of marketing expanded from early buying journey stage to mid/end of buyer journey

(2) Sales engagement with customers changed;

The lengthening sales cycle

The lengthening sales cycle has significant consequences for marketing and sales at two key stages. The first issue is that customers take more time to evaluate organizations and prospective purchases, and, secondly, the customer decision process can take much longer between initial engagement with sales and the ultimate purchase of products and services.

In both situations this impacts sales (and marketing). In the first case, it involves doing a better job to find the right prospect, and understanding their various needs. Answering those needs with educational content, and guiding the customer through their buying process is also part of this process.

In the second instance, this requires keeping the prospect warm, making sure their interest in the organization's products and services is kept at its maximum. Though managed by sales, answering customers' questions is again involved. Here the role of sales is to work with marketing in order to:

- share and obtain insights relating to possible next steps;
- obtain content;
- ensure that marketing activities such as webinars, events, email content and templates are in place to support customers.

As sales cycles get longer, the emphasis should be on sales and marketing cooperating better and looking for ways to speed up the customer purchase process.

The new B2B customer

Increased stakeholders in the buying process

Another trend is the increasing number of stakeholders and departments involved in the purchase process. This proves challenging for marketing, as they need to consider more people within the prospective organization and across departments. This means that B2B marketers for a given target customer segment need to think of creating more than one buyer persona, and formulating different messages, marketing vehicles and content.

Certain technologies such as account-based marketing (ABM) have enabled this process to become easier. The question for B2B marketers now is where to stop with B2B buyer personas, and where to create more focus within their marketing efforts.

An interesting question is: what is behind the increase in stakeholders and departments; what is the driving force? Is it caused by customers having more information and data to hand, therefore needing more time to consider options, or is it that customers no longer look for products, but real solutions?

Additionally, with this complexity in solutions, more specialists need to be involved, so this may contribute to the lengthening of the buyer process.

The evolving workforce

Another changing trend is how people work. For many organizations – even large ones – there has been a shift away from office-based working towards more remote working. According to a PGi report, 79 per cent of knowledge workers in a global survey said they work from home (Thomas-Aguilar, 2015).

As a consequence, the working day for B2B customers is no longer nine-to-five, but can be more fragmented as B2B customers juggle business and personal priorities throughout the day. This means that B2B marketers need to rethink how they target prospects, understand prospects in more detail than before, and consider how to reach them.

Also, B2B marketers can no longer take for granted the timings for sending emails and advertisements – although phone calls or other aspects can be planned according to traditional working schedules.

With more remote working, B2B customers are also more distributed geographically, and their company office location may be less relevant as a result. Of course, the great saviour here is mobile marketing, as people always keep their smartphone with them. Alongside this, collaborative software and virtual meets are becoming more used, such as Zoom, Slack, and even WhatsApp, and with that there are new ways of considering marketing or supporting sharing of information.

The changing mix of the workforce

In the past decade we've also seen a big shift in the mix of the workforce, where Millennials start to occupy a large proportion of the workforce. Millennials are generally defined as those people born between 1985 and the early 2000s.

Millennials in the workforce have a significant impact on B2B marketing activities and strategies. One could argue that that is the reason for digital marketing evolving so quickly, though digital marketing has been playing an increasingly important part of the marketing mix for some time to target decision makers from different generations. However, a Millennial buyer persona may influence marketing in different ways, such as types of digital channels and digital content formats used.

By 2020, Millennials are expected to make up 50 per cent of the work-force. There are two angles to consider here: one is to ensure Millennials factor more into the shaping of B2B digital marketing. The other is to consider the remaining 50 per cent of the workforce who may have very different needs and react differently. This mix of generations varies by industry and by role. From recent interactions with companies, some still leave decision-making in the hands of Baby Boomers.

How customers buy

Previously, businesses in the early stages of needing recognition would tend to reach out to vendors or potential suppliers they knew, and from that point would be guided through the buying process.

Today, this has changed dramatically, with most prospective buyers going through 60–75 per cent of the buying process before they actually interact with or contact the vendor. As a result, more departments need to cooperate to provide a better customer experience before and after their initial purchase.

Customer experience has changed

Customer experience also has become an increasingly important topic for digital marketers. Customer experience refers to a customer's interactions with a brand and the touchpoints they have with it.

These touchpoints can be marketing-owned, marketing-influenced or co-owned between marketing and other organizational departments.

Legislation and ethics

Legislation, privacy and data

As data about people and behaviours has multiplied, there has been increasing concern about privacy and protecting individual interests. These two seem-ingly opposing trends force companies to think differently regarding data and data management. The introduction of the EU General Data Protection Regulation (GDPR) and, in the UK, the passing of the Data Protection Act on

25 May 2018, was a clear prompt for companies to think more carefully about how they use data, if they weren't already.

As well as GDPR, there are various legal aspects impacting privacy, such as the EU ePrivacy Regulation. These mean companies need to think how they secure marketing permissions from customers, and understand how they manage and use data. Privacy impacts direct marketing and digital marketing directed at particular individuals; as B2B marketing is aimed at multiple individuals within organizations, it has particular relevance here.

Some companies are proactively thinking about how to reassure customers regarding data collection, management, and use. Those companies are also benefiting from using customer insights and data to optimize digital marketing.

Ethics – transparency affecting communication

B2B brands are becoming more transparent with their customers: their behaviours are publicly discussed, or even scrutinized by buyers. As consumers, 81 per cent of us care about the companies we buy from (CPG, FMCG and Retail, 2018), but 100 per cent of buyers are consumers – so B2B companies need to find a balance between company objectives, profit targets and managing marketing and messages to customers.

How companies conduct themselves is therefore becoming increasingly important. Rather than relying solely on marketing, they need to ensure that any messages related to ethical and sustainable behaviours is actually backed up by how companies operate. Any lack of coherence between what a company claims and what they actually do can quickly surface through social media and online applications, and could affect public perceptions and, consequently, sales.

Technologies and influence

Artificial intelligence (AI) in marketing has been around since the early 2000s. Programmatic applications now automate the media buying and placement process, and were arguably among the first applications for AI in marketing. Since then AI has been applied in other areas such as marketing automation, email management, personalization marketing and predictive or prescriptive analytics.

AI can be particularly interesting when it emulates human sales or marketing behaviour well, as it deals with the resource gaps or challenges encountered by some organizations.

Personalization

In the 1990s and early 2000s, personalization was developing in the consumer marketing space. Colour was probably one of the main personalization possibilities used in product design; one of the main examples of personalization in technology was by Nokia when they introduced the first removable phone covers. Today, personalization means many different things in B2B marketing and comes in different forms.

With AI, organizations have the ability to deal with personalized conversations in bulk, but there are also interesting automated applications allowing companies to personalize web greetings, schedules for customers visiting events, emails, social media and so on.

The improvement in smartphone technology

In the last decade, smartphone and wireless technology has advanced to the point that it now offers a similar or better experience compared to desktop in receiving and viewing information, watching videos and switching between applications. Today, smartphone and tablet technology is more widely available than ever before, which means that users have access to information almost anywhere

With the ability to access more and view more, the challenge for B2B marketers is using more mobile channels and mobile technologies as part of their channel mix to reach and engage B2B customers.

Advanced analytics in B2B

As companies collect huge volumes of customer data, there are greater possibilities in segmentation without conducting a primary search. Some digital technologies allow companies to more easily merge data from different platforms and provide a means to gain a more holistic view of the customers.

With larger data volumes to manage comes the need to have more advanced analytics; simply viewing and crunching numbers in a spreadsheet is no longer good enough. Customer-centric companies today can implement a much better data governance approach through digital technologies which support data capture, data merge, data deduplication, data interpretation and insights.

The social organization

Marketers now also need to understand the full scope of social media: how it can be used across all areas of the customer lifecycle in terms of marketing, but also how marketing can work better with sales and other departments to capitalize on social media.

Social selling

In more forward-thinking organizations, sales has not only been encouraged to use social media, but has been provided tools and training to use it in the most effective way. This is sometimes known as social selling, allowing people to connect, engage, nurture customers and prospects. Social selling differs from traditional approaches to selling, as it places greater emphasis on building long-lasting relationships.

Many sales professionals are seeking to understand more about social selling. Fifty-three per cent of salespeople want help in understanding social selling better, and 80 per cent believe their salesforce would be more effective and efficient if they could leverage social media (Kunsman, 2018).

Social procurement

Another recent phenomenon is that of social procurement; that is, purchasing managers and departments leveraging social media channels to support purchasing activities. One community platform spearheading in this area is Procurious: the first procurement industry organization to launch an online community platform. The platform now has a membership of more than 5,000 followers.

Social media in the finance industry

Those institutions that recognized that social media is important and has an impact on business and marketing have come out all the better for it. Bank of America has one of the largest Twitter followings in the finance sector (spread across multiple accounts such as Tips, News, Help and Careers), and has a Twitter-focused customer service team to match.

Another good example is Amex, who launched 'Open Forum' in 2007 and still today offer an online and social media platform for small business to discuss financial and financially related challenges.

Social media maturity

Social media 10 years ago was very much in its infancy: LinkedIn was founded in 2002, Facebook in 2004, and Twitter in 2006. As the functionality and usage of these platforms has become more pervasive over time – LinkedIn is adding an average of two members a second, and Facebook membership has grown from 100m active users in 2008 to 2.2bn today – their ability to support different marketing and even organizational and customers roles has supported greater adoption in business.

In the last five years in particular, they have matured and evolved from platforms to networks, to be used for PR or to recruit people to a fully fledged business tool. Now, some social media networks pride themselves on 'full funnel' marketing.

Platforms like LinkedIn, Facebook and Twitter offer greater advertising possibilities and advertising targeting possibility, as well as lead generation.

References

Andersen, B, 2019 [accessed 16 January 2020] The 2019 B2B Buyers Survey Report, *DemandGen Report* [online] www.demandgenreport.com/resources/research/the-2019-B2B-buyers-survey-report (archived at https://perma.cc/4M28-TD59)

CPG, FMCG and Retail (2018) [accessed 3 August 2019] Global consumers seek companies that care about environmental issues, *Nielsen* [online] www.nielsen.com/uk/en/insights/article/2018/global-consumers-seek-companies-that-care-about-environmental-issues/ (archived at https://perma.cc/R375-MZLK)

Kunsman, Todd (2018) [accessed 17 October 2019] 25 Social Selling Statistics that Matter for Sales Teams and Beyond, *EveryoneSocial* [online] https://everyonesocial.com/blog/social-selling-statistics/ (archived at https://perma.cc/BM6M-S7HP)

Taylor, H (2017) [accessed 16 January 2020] 5 Steps, Questions and Actions for Thinking Different in B2B Marketing, *B2B Marketing* [online] www.b2bmarketing.net/en-gb/resources/blog/5-steps-questions-and-actions-thinking-different-b2b-marketing (archived at https://perma.cc/RDC7-TA8E)

Thomas-Aguilar, B (2015) [accessed 24 January 2020] PGi Global Telework Survey Reveals Surprising Telecommuting Trends & Worker Demands, *PR Newswire* [online] www.prnewswire.com/news-releases/pgi-global-telework-survey-reveals-surprising-telecommuting-trends–worker-demands-300103241.html (archived at https://perma.cc/4DCU-3358)

Further reading

Matthews, K (2017) [accessed 16 January 2020] 4 B2B Content Marketing Trends to Watch in 2018, *convince&convert* [online] www.convinceandconvert.com/content-marketing-research/b2b-content-marketing-trends/ (archived at https://perma.cc/RM8F-2MTX)

O'Brien, S (2015) [accessed 16 January 2020] PGi's New Survey Reveals the Latest Global Telework Stats, *PGi* [online] https://uk.pgi.com/blog/2015/06/pgi-global-telework-survey/ (archived at https://perma.cc/X68F-Q2CR)

Vivid Fish (2017) [accessed 16 January 2020] 75% of customers say they use social media as part of the buying process, *Vivid Fish* [online] www.vividfish.co.uk/blog/75-of-customers-say-they-use-social-media-as-part-of-the-buying-process (archived at https://perma.cc/CH74-FBJS)

Developing the B2B digital strategy

Digital marketing and digital marketing technologies have evolved in recent years to provide increased value-add in supporting organization goals and objectives. Part One looks at the key elements of identifying, creating and evaluating B2B digital marketing strategies.

We'll be focusing on the B2B customer by exploring customer journeys, customer journey maps, customer insights and methods.

Related to better tailoring marketing to customers is personalization, which is all about better tailoring messages and marketing to specific customer segments or customers themselves. We'll also be covering B2B personalization marketing within this part.

02

B2B digital marketing strategy

WHAT YOU WILL GAIN FROM THIS CHAPTER

After reading this chapter, you will understand:

- how to assess the market environment;
- how to identify strategic options;
- how to achieve strategic alignment;
- how to evaluate strategic options.

Introduction

Digital marketing strategy

When marketing strategy is referred to, it usually relates to a plan of action for marketing that contributes to long-term organizational success. With that in mind, a marketing strategy should shape longer-term marketing activities, as well as provide the direction for marketing.

A first step in crafting a marketing strategy is understanding who the main owner of the marketing strategy is. If this is fragmented across various people or even departments, who will be the 'acting' owner of the strategy and the subsequent plan? Many organizations still exist with marketing ownership divided up between different areas, such as digital marketing teams, PR, lead generation, and product marketing, the result being that the creation of one holistic and coherent marketing strategy for the company is challenging.

Ownership of marketing strategy

Ownership of the marketing strategy can differ depending on industry and organization. Whoever takes the lead, there should only be one owner of the marketing strategy and plan. The marketing efforts should reflect the market to better support customers in their customer journeys.

In B2B marketing there is often a mix between offline and digital activities, so understanding how these interact is key to providing a better omnichannel marketing experience.

The increasing importance of digital marketing

If we consider possible business strategies, we think of how to develop products for existing markets and how to penetrate those markets. There are also opportunities to enter new segments or new geographies, or to create new products or services for new markets.

This is summarized in the matrix below, adapted from the Ansoff matrix.

For each segment, the bundle and mix of digital marketing activities and technologies will differ, but as will be demonstrated, digital marketing and digital technologies now open up new possibilities to support these business directions.

FIGURE 2.1 The Ansoff matrix applied

	EXISTING CUSTOMERS	NEW CUSTOMERS
EXISTING MARKETS	Share of wallet increase – in retention customers	Business development Identifying new customers in the same market for existing product propositions
NEW MARKETS	Where customers operate in different geographical markets, this involves penetrating the account for new geographies	Using new products to go after new target customers

Bhasin, 2019

The digital marketing strategy matrix

One way to view digital marketing strategy is to consider strategic directions of the company and possible routes to developing the business. We can divide these into four core areas using the adaptation of the Ansoff matrix in Figure 2.1.

Existing markets, existing customers

This refers to increasing share of wallet with existing customer bases. Share of wallet is a metric used to calculate the percentage of a customer's spending on a type of product or service that goes to a particular company. Share of wallet can be increased in different ways, including customers buying more of a product or buying a larger portfolio of the products which organizations offer, or both of these.

To increase share of wallet, a company should first understand the customer in more detail. What are the dynamics within the buyer's organization? How do they move through their buying process and the various touchpoints they have with your company?

Digital marketing and digital technologies can help find answers to these questions, and so increase this share of wallet with existing customers. They can identify touchpoints, and analyse the experience of those touchpoints, insights which can then be used to provide more personalized experiences throughout the buyer's journey.

Digital technologies can deliver insights on how customers interact with channels, and use data analytics to better interpret customer behaviour. Leveraging account-based marketing allows organizations to treat customers as organizations, and to track messages content engagement across the account.

Existing markets, new customers

In looking at existing markets and new customers, we are talking about expanding presence in the existing market through greater market penetration and growing share. In terms of market penetration, digital marketing allows us to create better advertising and to carry out more targeted advertising by advertising to the right and most suitable prospects.

Through digital technologies, we can also identify the most suitable prospects through understanding how they search and what keywords they use.

Digital technologies and integrated digital marketing allow us to nurture prospects from early lead through to conversion. Examples of digital technologies could be those technologies which allow us to improve lead nurturing, such as content management and tracking technologies, and those which allow us to monitor marketing by specific customer or account.

New markets, existing customers

In this quadrant, we are interested in new geographies and markets. This could be a new region within a country or a new country itself. Existing customers here refers to organizations who have a footprint in more than one country, and the objective with this strategy would be to increase the business to other geographies where existing customers are present.

For this, technologies such as account-based marketing and data analytics can be invaluable depending on the B2B customer's company's size, footprint and potential.

There are a number of ways that applying digital marketing will also support this strategic direction. One would be identifying those prospects with multiple geographical footprints using CRM technologies or customer insights information. Another would be improving awareness through social media or other digital marketing approaches.

Employing better targeted advertising or using influencer marketing may provide organizational targeting benefits, or can facilitate reach beyond the current geography.

New markets, new customers

Approaching new markets and new customers is the method that involves most risk for acquiring customers. Reasons for taking this approach may include an expansion of the product portfolio into a new area, requiring a search for completely new customers. It is important, therefore, to employ all of the aspects of digital marketing in identifying, engaging, nurturing and acquiring customers, which will be explored throughout this book.

As seen above, marketing strategy can encompass many things such as identifying best customer fit, understanding needs, implementing marketing, reaching customers more efficiently, engaging them and nurturing them. All these activities can be conducted better today than 10 years ago because of digital marketing and technology.

This book will help you to identify the right bundle of activities for different strategic approaches. Combined use of the digital strategy matrix and digital strategy SWOT analysis will help you think more carefully about what to consider as you go forward and implement.

The digital marketing strategy is also the process allowing the organization to focus on available resources and utilize them in the optimum way to boost sales and gain competitive advantage. Digital B2B marketers need to consider where and how to define and use synergies with other departments to support the overall value chain of the organization as well as value in the ecosystem.

Defining the digital strategy – first steps

Why create a digital marketing strategy?

Essentially the digital marketing strategy is the blueprint and roadmap for all marketing and digital marketing teams. These strategy outlines become particularly important today as marketing departments are more disparate than before.

The digital marketing strategy should provide direction and improve cohesion. The challenge with digital marketing strategies is the ability to adapt them and to understand the ever-changing market environment.

Strategy development and key stages – the 3As of audit, assimilation and aims

Strategy development can be broken into the following key areas:

- **Audit:** Within this step, there are two elements: the company-level (or micro-environment) audit, and the macro-environment audit.
- **Assimilation:** Here, the audit takeaways are interpreted to provide an overview of possible paths forward, in terms of opportunities to take and/or threats and weaknesses to mitigate.
- **Aims and strategy definition:** The third step in strategy development is to define aims and provide the outline to the strategy.

The micro-environment audit

A company-level audit is about identifying strengths and weaknesses in marketing, and how approaches support or work against organizational strategy. Companies can also look at reviewing their portfolio of resources to understand if there are any gaps to support current or past strategic directions, and consider the digital marketing assets.

Micro-environment audits may involve reviewing how the company uses advertising, uses lead generation and measures content and engagement.

Some questions you may ask at this stage include:

- How is the organization performing digitally?
- Are there any areas where it is weak or open to threat?
- What are the organization's strengths, and could these be used in a digital marketing strategy?
- What digital technologies does the company use today?
- How are the different digital channels performing?
- How is the content performing?
- What are the strongest (and weakest) marketing and digital marketing competencies?

The macro-environment audit

The next part of the audit is to look at the external environment. For this we can use a tool known as PEST analysis, which covers political and legal, economic, social and cultural and technological considerations.

The key point is to not only capture aspects of the external environment, but to rate them in terms of impact and influence on the customer. Let's take a look at possible trends which could influence a digital marketing strategy.

POLITICAL AND LEGAL

It's important to understand legislation which relates to the industry and product changes, such as price setting. Other legislation to consider is that which impacts the marketing discipline and customer interaction, such as data usage and data privacy.

Political aspects may relate to how digital technologies are used or promoted – eg in China, the country promotes Baidu as the main search engine as it is provided by a Chinese-based company.

ECONOMIC

Economic aspects can refer to business confidence, GDP growth of a country or a specific region's economic stability These may affect messaging within a region or the focused products or services used; for example, in an economic downturn, the best approach may not be to push high-value products and services to companies, but to instead offer more economical alternatives.

Other economic influences could be related to industry seasonality, as some industries can have sharp movements in buying patterns: a large proportion of purchases in the education sector occur in the second quarter of the year, so B2B marketing teams need to consider whether to align lead generation to that.

SOCIAL AND CULTURAL

This doesn't just impact consumers, but businesses as well. Points of consideration include social or cultural dynamics, and the use of social media. In a digital marketing context, this can relate to how images are used in content marketing – where some logos, icons, images may fit with the culture and others may not, or may even cause offence.

It can also relate to generations within the workplace and how companies need to accommodate for them.

TECHNOLOGICAL

If a technology has been adopted by most competitors in an industry, this should be factored in as a threat to a company's strategy and digital strategy. Technology can also include things such as AI or 5G, which may have an impact on customers and digital marketing strategy.

PEST analysis helps to define the top influences by category. The second part of this exercise would be to understand the impact level of the influence – if it is more of a trend which impacts some customers, or legislation which impacts 100 per cent of companies, then the latter would be rated as having a higher impact.

Once rating has been carried out, the high-impact influences would then be reviewed to understand which ones could be addressed by the company as opportunities to leverage in marketing to customers, in terms of products, services and solutions which relate to the new trend or mitigate a potential risk in the market.

FIGURE 2.2 PEST analysis

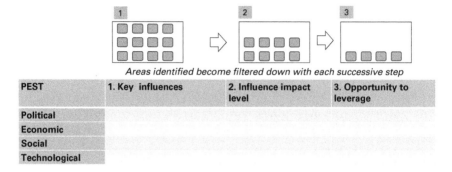

PEST	1. Key influences	2. Influence impact level	3. Opportunity to leverage
Political			
Economic			
Social			
Technological			

Competition audit

Another audit type to mention here is the competition audit, which may be incorporated within the macro-level audit, but may also require a much broader analysis. For the purposes of this book, the focus will be on competitor marketing activities, rather than competitor strategy.

Competitive marketing activities could relate to how competitors operate, how they position themselves within the market, how many audiences they target, how they communicate their messages, and their future focus areas. It may also include how they bid on terms and any keywords they use, as this may have a bearing on digital marketing messaging, content, and target customer group.

Drilling down further in researching competition, there are a number of approaches we can use to understand better competition such as tracking competition through their social media activity, or reviewing their online content library, usually in the PR or Investor Relations sections of their website. Additionally there are also technologies such as Similarweb, which can be used to find information on competitors' website traffic volumes, referral sources, including keyword analysis, and website 'stickiness', among other features.

By doing some of the above, one can view competitors through a customer's eyes and thus have a different perspective in analysis to provide clues around segmentation, campaigns, messaging and positioning.

Assimilation

Following the micro- and macro-level audits, the next stage is to assimilate the findings into one place. Listing these is one option, but a better tool to use would be the dynamic SWOT, as per Figure 2.3.

FIGURE 2.3 The dynamic SWOT

	Opportunities	Threats
Strengths	S-O strategies How can we leverage the company's strengths to maximize opportunities identified?	S-T strategies How can we leverage the company's strengths to minimize the threats identified?
Weaknesses	W-O strategies How can we minimize weaknesses using the identified opportunities?	W-T strategies How can we avoid threats identified by minimizing weaknesses?

Adapted from Agarwal, Grassland and Pahl, 2012

The dynamic SWOT does more than just list strengths, weaknesses, opportunities and threats. It goes one step further by asking us to think about combinations of these areas, and turns aspects of the SWOT into actionable strategies. Strengths and weaknesses refer to internal aspects of the organization, and threats and opportunities refer to external aspects; strengths and weaknesses will come from the company audit above, and the external aspects will come from the PEST analysis.

S-O strategies aim to leverage strengths to pursue opportunities. Examples could be where a company uses their strengths in branding to approach new customers. This approach is sometimes known as the attack strategy: depending on strengths, a number of different attack strategies can be formulated.

W-O strategies aim to mitigate or minimize weaknesses by using the opportunities identified. These could be partnerships you could use to minimize a brand perception weakness, or opening up new channels to market to improve reach and engage a particular customer segment.

S-T strategies involve using company strengths to minimize threats. An example could be where the company has a large established customer base. One way to deal with potential threats of new aggressive marketing tactics would be to use customer loyalty tactics and customer referrals to improve customer loyalty as well as engage new customers.

Finally, the W-T approach is about reducing both the impact and risk of weaknesses in the company and external threats through better leveraging of strengths and weaknesses, so one could combine some of the above strengths and opportunities.

Aims and objectives

Based on the audit and assimilation information, we now decide on the key objectives according to the key strategies or strategic options which have been decided upon. Essentially the digital marketing strategy will likely fall along the lines of penetrating the customer, developing the market, and expanding into new markets in terms of the directions which the digital marketing strategy will take.

In defining objectives, one could use the SMART acronym to improve the specificity of the objective, where SMART stands for Specific, Measurable, Acceptable, Realistic and Time-bound.

Alignment: achieving strategic alignment

Why the need for alignment?

Misalignment between your digital strategy and the perspective of key stakeholders within your organization can undermine your efforts, or even dilute or halt your strategy. Getting key stakeholders on board is critical to success. This book will show that digital transcends functional boundaries and others both inside and outside of the company. Getting alignment in this new world will mean greater impact from strategic implementation.

Stage 1: Alignment as a marketing function

Before looking outside marketing, it's important to understand what happens within marketing. For many companies today, the overall marketing mix of product solutions, pricing, promotions, offers, PR and other things is not owned by one single person or department. Therefore, understanding who could be impacted by a digital strategy and who could support it across what is sometimes a fragmented area is key.

Where do we start? Essentially, it is about sharing the strategic goals and the digital strategy. To ensure alignment within the function, there should be a lead who is bringing the marketing mix together. That person can be the head of the department, or 'act' as the lead.

Stage 2: Alignment outside of marketing

For this we can use Mendelow's power-interest grid (Bourne and Walker, 2005). This grid can help us understand which stakeholders have both

FIGURE 2.4 Mendelow's grid

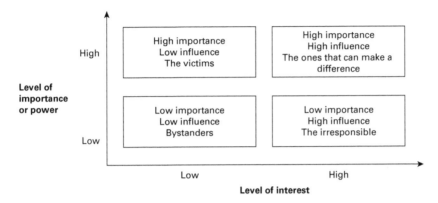

power and interest or influence over the digital strategy, both positively and negatively. Which people have a stake in this digital strategy?

Let's say, for example, the digital strategy is to penetrate a finance sector with digital marketing of professional services. Internal stakeholders might include sales, business development managers and the head of marketing. External stakeholders might include a PR agency, financial market bloggers, trade industry associations and so on.

These would then be plotted on a grid, such as in Figure 2.4. As you can see, there are four main areas: the stakeholders within each area of the grid need to be managed in a different manner. Those with high power and interest should be more formally approached and included; their approval and buy-in to the strategy is critical.

Once this grid is complete, you can see which stakeholders to engage with most or least. This will form part of the development and implementation sections later in this book.

Evaluating and selecting strategies

Often once the different stages of strategy development have been explored, there is a range of possible strategies to choose from. Faced with that situation, it's time to evaluate and select the best strategy or strategies.

One great tool to use is the SAF model (Johnson, Scholes and Whittington, 2010) which looks at suitability, acceptability and feasibility of strategies:

- Suitability refers to whether the strategy leverages strengths, addresses the best goal or objective, and can overcome potential difficulties.

- Acceptability of the strategy includes its value for any financial or resource investment – would it render the best return, or any return? This would also cover how easily the strategy would be adopted by other departments in the organization.
- Feasibility of the strategy would encompass such things as resources in place, including financial, technological, and marketing which would be used to support the strategy. Can the organization feasibly implement the strategy based on current resources, or can resources be put in place in time?

With the SAF model, the strategic options would be evaluated, ranked or rated as in Table 2.1 (Johnson, Scholes and Whittington, 2005). In this example, we can see that options 1 and 4 are the best according to the criteria.

TABLE 2.1 Evaluating your strategy

Perspective/ question	Option 1	Option 2	Option 3	Option 4	Option 5	Option 6
Suitability						
Does the strategy leverage strengths?	8	8	9	9	8	5
Does the strategy address objectives and goals?	9	9	8	9	7	4
Does the strategy overcome the difficulties identified?	9	8	8	8	7	4
Total	26	25	25	26	22	13
Feasibility						
Can the option be financed?	7	6	6	7	5	9
Are there resources to support strategy?	6	7	6	7	6	8
Aptitude and abilities to implement and support strategy	8	6	7	7	6	6
Total	21	19	19	21	17	23

(continued)

TABLE 2.1 (Continued)

Perspective/ question	Option 1	Option 2	Option 3	Option 4	Option 5	Option 6
Acceptability						
Are the risks acceptable in terms of spend?	9	7	6	9	6	8
Would the strategy be accepted by other departments?	9	9	7	9	7	7
Would the return or benefits justify the strategy implementation?	8	9	7	9	7	5
Total	26	25	20	27	20	20
Final scores	73	69	64	74	59	56

Digital marketing strategies

There have been a number of themes evolving and developing over the past years regarding digital strategies, which can be broken down into the key strategic areas of marketing shown in Figure 2.5. This breakdown of strategic types is also reflected in the book, to allow you to deep-dive into key areas of interest.

Customer insights and experience involves leveraging data, insights and improving customer experience. It is about understanding customer journey and marketing accordingly, which can be greatly enhanced through different types of personalization marketing.

Strategies for the early buying journey stage may revolve around channel usage but also refer to approaches to maximize awareness. Digital strategies for lead generation and nurturing are more aligned to the mid- to late buyer journey, capturing leads, and nurturing them through to acquisition.

Campaign management and integration strategies are all about better management of campaigns, improving planning and integration of digital marketing and technologies, not only within marketing but within organizations as well. It also entails better measuring digital marketing activities, and creating response and reaction measures where needed.

FIGURE 2.5 Digital marketing strategy framework

Retention-based digital strategies relate to better usage of digital marketing and technologies to market to existing customers, improve loyalty and satisfaction, as well as to develop better business with them.

The final strategy space is about how to better understand and embrace social media. As social media is evolving so fast and is so pervasive, there are many ways it can be used and integrated into overall digital strategy, or even be the leading part of the strategy in certain instances.

EXERCISE

Put it into practice

1 Review your current marketing or organization objectives, and plot the key objectives according to the adaptation of the Ansoff matrix.
2 According to the objectives, discuss with a colleague where digital marketing and technologies could add value.
3 Create a power/interest grid, and plot the key stakeholders for your digital marketing strategy.

References

Agarwal, R, Grassl, W and Pahl, J (2012) Meta-SWOT: introducing a new strategic planning tool, *Journal of Business Strategy*, **33** (2), pp 12–21

Bhasin, H (2019) [accessed 1 August 2019] Ansoff Matrix Theory Examples of Business Strategies for Future Growth, *Marketing91* [online] www.marketing91.com/ansoff-matrix/ (archived at https://perma.cc/78CM-L4SY)

Bourne, L and Walker, D (2005) Visualising and mapping stakeholder influence, *Management Decision*, **43** (5)

Johnson, G, Scholes, K and Whittington, R (2005) *Exploring Corporate Strategy* (4th edn), Financial Times / Prentice Hall

Johnson, G, Scholes, K and Whittington, R (2010) *Exploring Corporate Strategy* (10th edn), Pearson Education

03

B2B customer journeys and the customer experience

WHAT YOU WILL GAIN FROM THIS CHAPTER

After reading this chapter, you will understand:

- customer journeys;
- customer touchpoints;
- customer journey mapping;
- identifying and evaluating touchpoints.

Introduction

Strategy and customer journeys

In the previous chapter we discussed different forms of strategies using the strategy matrix. As we see from each of the strategic options, understanding our customers better is one of the starting points in developing a strategy. One way to better get to grips with customers are customer journeys.

So, what is a customer journey? It is the sequence of steps a customer goes through fulfil a particular goal, and there can be various journeys which customers follow throughout their interactions with a vendor. Customer journeys are very much aligned to different needs or activities which customers carry out in the pre-purchase and post-purchase phases.

One customer journey is the buyer journey, and depending on how you scope this, it can feature in the pre-purchase phase as well as post-purchase. The buyer journey is arguably the biggest of the customer journeys, encompassing multiple sub-journeys, sometimes called micro journeys.

Macro and micro journeys

Macro journeys typically refer to the larger customer journey or buying process; they are the all-encompassing journeys which usually span multiple phases. Micro journeys are the smaller journeys within this. In the post-purchase stage of the buyer journey, for example, micro journeys can include things like searching for information regarding a purchased product or service, looking to expand purchases, needing to resolve an issue, or trying to understand how to implement the product or service previous purchased.

So how are digital marketing or applications used? The fact is that more and more of these tasks are being enabled through digital, and they can be tracked and monitored by digital technologies.

Customer journeys and maps

According to Salesforce, 80 per cent of senior-ranking marketers state that a cohesive customer journey is absolutely critical for success (Young, 2014).

One of the first tasks B2B marketers should consider doing is to create a customer journey map, an outline of the customer journey across the touchpoints they use for a given stage or set of stages. This provides an understanding of the sequence of touchpoints or steps the customer undertakes for a particular task, as well as which digital channels and related content are used.

By understanding the sequence of the steps, ways to optimize the flow or the touchpoints themselves may be identified. For example, if search or SEO is an initial step, followed by prospective customers going to a vendor's website and visiting the vendor's social media pages, organizations can ensure they include necessary website links in SEO content and that social media links are on the suitable website pages.

A customer journey map proved to be so effective in companies that the Gartner Group predicted that 60 per cent of large organizations would contain in-house customer journey mapping abilities by 2018 (Digital Marketing Institute, 2018).

The buyer journey

The buyer journey is the journey to describe the buying process before and after a customer's purchase. We can define the full buyer journey by looking at six main stages:

1 **Need recognition:** The prospective customer recognizes a potential need. Recognition of the need can come from an individual or a group of people within the business and may be the output from a study or other outside stimuli such as vendors and partners. Typically, the need is resolved by purchasing a product, a service, or a portfolio of products.

2 **Need quantification and research:** Once a need is identified, the next step is to gain commitment to fulfilling the need. In larger businesses, this can be a department persuading stakeholders to release capital to pay for a product or service.

3 **Evaluation:** During this stage, the people involved in the buying process seek out information and search for vendors who could supply potential solutions for their needs. Most buyers start their search online, which can then be followed up with attendance of seminars, trade shows or further search online. Both small and large business may use contacts as sources of inputs for information.

4 **Comparison of alternatives:** The potential suppliers are then evaluated and compared. Typically, buyers will compare vendor alternatives based on a set of purchasing criteria. Each organization will interpret the various parts of a proposal differently, depending on their goals and the products they purchase: price may be an important factor for some, whereas others may place an emphasis on service and service level agreements. Larger business customers have a more structured process to tender for vendors through a request for proposal (RFP).

5 **Purchase:** Based on vendors' input during the evaluation phase, a customer selects a vendor or vendors, and proceeds to order. The ordering of the products or services can be structured within a longer-term agreement such as in the public sector for larger companies, or may be a simple transaction.

6 **Post-purchase:** Following the purchase, the customer proceeds in one of different ways either to repurchase from the vendors, to move to a new vendor for purchasing or revert to a previous vendor, or to increase purchasing activity.

FIGURE 3.1 Customer journey maps

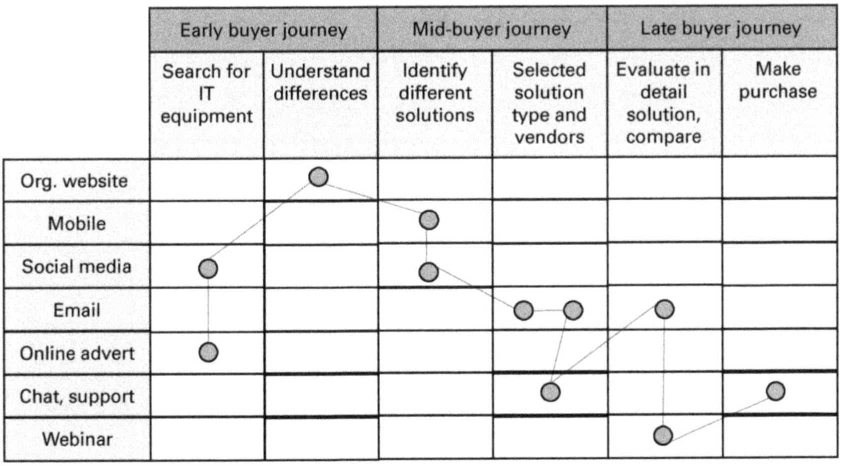

	Early buyer journey		Mid-buyer journey		Late buyer journey	
	Search for IT equipment	Understand differences	Identify different solutions	Selected solution type and vendors	Evaluate in detail solution, compare	Make purchase
Org. website		○				
Mobile			○			
Social media	○		○			
Email				○ ○	○	
Online advert	○					
Chat, support				○		○
Webinar					○	

Stages one to five may be separated into early buyer journey (stages one and two), mid-buyer journey (stages three and four) and late buyer journey (stage five).

Figure 3.1 illustrates an example of a customer's buyer journey.

Benefits of customer journey maps

Although customer journey mapping can be a lengthy and detailed task, it provides a number of benefits. It can help to improve marketing efficiencies with better knowledge of customer segmentation and personas, which enables organizations to create or pay for content, and understand which channels to use according to the customer.

Detailed knowledge of customer journey maps also allow us to better understand our customers as we can better understand the journeys they go through per task, as well as any sub-journeys and related activities.

By understanding journeys, we can identify areas to optimize and improve the experience, which in turn will mean a greater likelihood that customers stay with us. Finally, they can also bridge the gap between sales, marketing and operations as all parties begin to understand exactly how the customer journey is in reality. This can also help shape expectations about customers' touchpoints and activities, and correspondingly the timing of periods for the different stages of the buyer journey.

Customer experience

As noted above, customer journey maps go a long way towards improving customer experience. Customer experience is the product or result of an interaction between an organization and a customer over a period of time. It is also the collection of interactions which can come from different departments – customers service, operations, sales, marketing and more.

Interestingly, it is the digital B2B marketer today that either owns or has the greatest visibility into the majority of these touchpoints.

How customers perceive value

One model or framework which can be applied here is customer perceived value (Hitesh, 2018), which looks at the overall experience related to purchasing a product. Within this, there are the negatively perceived values called 'costs', and positive perceived values known as 'benefits'.

During the purchase of a product or service, the costs cause customers pain and benefits help or even delight customers. This model compares the two sides to understand whether the costs or the benefits outweigh each other.

Costs experienced by the customer include:

- **monetary costs**: this is not only the price of the product or service purchased, but any additional costs associated with the running of the product such as insurance;
- **time costs**: these are associated with finding information, reading and understanding it, as well as the time spent resolving queries;
- **energy costs**: these can relate to travelling to purchase a product or costs associated with electricity, or to paying for an internet connection;
- **psychological costs**: these are the emotional experiences within the purchase process, including any frustration in finding information.

Benefits can be broken down into the following categories:

- **product benefits**: the specific benefit which the product or service delivers;
- **service benefits**: the benefits from additional services such as customer service and the quality of this;
- **personnel benefits**: these include the quality of staff and of the service, or quality of advice given by people representing the company;
- **image benefits**: these relate to the emotional benefits from using the brand.

FIGURE 3.2 Negative and positive touchpoints re CPV

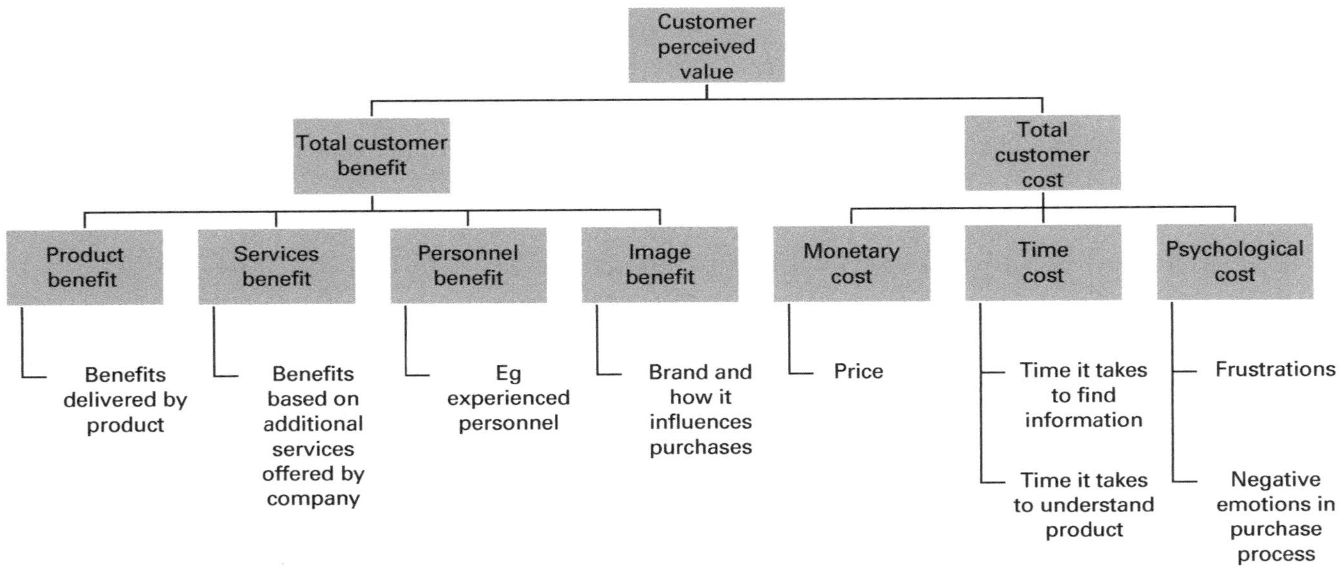

```
                          Customer
                          perceived
                            value
                               |
        ┌──────────────────────┴──────────────────────┐
        |                                              |
  Total customer                                Total customer
     benefit                                          cost
        |                                              |
┌───────┼───────┬───────────┐            ┌─────────────┼─────────────┐
|       |       |           |            |             |             |
Product Services Personnel  Image     Monetary       Time      Psychological
benefit benefit  benefit    benefit     cost         cost          cost
|       |        |          |           |             |             |
Benefits Benefits Eg        Brand and   Price    Time it takes   Frustrations
delivered based on experienced how it             to find
by product additional personnel influences        information
         services         purchases                   |
         offered by                              Time it takes   Negative
         company                                to understand   emotions in
                                                   product       purchase
                                                                 process
```

The idea of customer perceived value is that where the costs heavily outweigh the benefits, the purchase experience and overall experience of the brand is negative and may impact whether the initial purchase is concluded. Even if a purchase is made, a negative experience could have consequences later if there is further business to be sought.

The customer perceived value model is one of the starting points in thinking about customers and customer experience, and can help us start to understand touchpoint mapping and why we take care of touchpoint experiences; we can see this illustrated in Figure 3.2.

In brand terminology, ZMOTS (zero moments of truth) are the points in a customer journey when a key event occurs and an opinion about the brand is formed. These are more than just touchpoints, as they represent critical 'events'.

Customer touchpoints

So, let's take a closer look at touchpoints. A touchpoint is simply any interaction that a customer has with your product, brand, business or service. In marketing, we're more interested in anything related to our marketing messages and content, but any form of interaction – whether it is with customer services, sales, or another team – is a touchpoint.

Some touchpoints are directly influenced by B2B marketing, some we have a good degree of control over, and some we need to see how we indirectly impact through third-party marketing partners or other organizational departments such as sales, customer service and operations.

Customers experience these touchpoints in different ways. Where the experience of a touchpoint is suboptimal or doesn't meet expectations, it becomes a negative touchpoint. In consideration of the costs mentioned previously, this may be closely aligned to time and psychological costs. Examples can be inability to find information, or being given information at the wrong time. Response times – or the lack of response – are also factors.

In some cases, customers can't find a way to get answers to their queries, or when they do, are then overwhelmed with emails they don't need. Other aspects of negative touchpoints include the worsening of a previous experience – the dilution of a positive experience.

Good experiences of a touchpoint where the expectations were exceeded can be called positive touchpoints. Understanding where experiences of touchpoints are at or above expectations can help develop strategies to make sure these are maintained or optimized further.

It's also a good indication to not remove the touchpoint itself. If you know most customers search social media pages for information on the company and would then go to a specific webpage to read more, ensuring links to these are included in articles can support a positive experience. Another example might be offering chat services – rapid responses to queries can take away the need to search through a website.

Finally, experiences that matched expectations may be referred to as neutral touchpoints. As the experience was neither good nor bad, neutral touchpoints indicate that further insights are needed to understand what a good experience of that area is.

The increasingly digital nature of touchpoints

A winning approach to touchpoints is providing seamless connections between them whilst also ensuring consistency in messages. There has been a gradual shift over the past 10–15 years of touchpoints moving to digital or being enabled through digital technologies. One of the first shifts was print advertising moving to digital in the 2000s, but even this has developed in multiple forms in the past decade to include mobile and social media.

Content creation and distribution has since shifted to digital, and lead nurturing and techniques in the purchase stage are becoming more digitized. Lead nurturing and retargeting techniques are expanding to social media, and digital chat technologies and dynamic websites are supporting query resolution.

In marketing, if a customer sees one message on social media and a very different one through SEO, this may work against the purpose of what an organization is trying to achieve. Aside from this, the look and tone should be consistent so that it is recognizable: in the current digital age, customers are consuming and engaging with multiple touchpoints from many brands in a short space of time.

Organizations need to put themselves into the shoes of the customers and consider what it feels like to be receiving the different pieces of content and messaging on different channels, and whether this is a good, neutral or poor experience.

Touchpoint mapping

Touchpoint mapping adds further detail to the customer journey. As mentioned above, the process of mapping touchpoints depends on the goal of the mapping as well as the scope.

There are a number of discrete steps in creating a touchpoint map. This starts with the segmentation of personas, and assumes that there is a focused target customer segment.

(We'll look at segmentation and buyer personas in the next chapter, but for the purposes of this exercise, let's assume there is already a target customer segment and buyer persona in place.)

The steps to conducting the touchpoint map are detailed in Figure 3.3.

Step 1: Touchpoint map goals

What is the goal behind the touchpoint map exercise? Is it to improve loyalty, or lead-nurturing and conversion? Or is the aim broader, to understand the entire pre-purchase journey that the customer makes?

The more defined the goal is, the easier the touchpoint map exercise becomes, particularly when defining the scope. For example, if the purpose of the touchpoint map is to improve lead conversion once a lead is captured, the scope of the touchpoint map is to look at all the steps the customer takes post-lead capture.

Step 2: Identify the touchpoints

Based on the segment, the buyer persona and the scope or objectives of the exercise, you can now start to identify the different interactions from the

FIGURE 3.3 The touchpoint mapping process

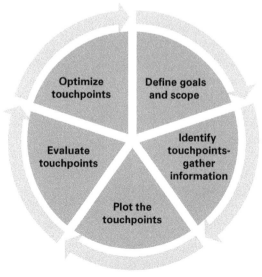

start of the customer journey through to the final outcome or touchpoint. Touchpoints may include marketing, sales, customer service, operations, and within marketing may involve both digital and non-digital ones.

In this example here, you might identify that within one stage of the journey the customer uses social media, webinars, email and marketing events, as well as chat, and various website pages. These are the touchpoints to focus on for this stage of the target customer segment's journey.

Step 3: Plot the touchpoints

It's then necessary to understand the sequence of touchpoint steps the customers goes through. The sequence includes the steps before or after the touchpoint, as well as the sequence (and desired sequence) which a prospective customer uses in conducting a task. This may help later in digital channel selection set-up.

Identifying the sequence of touchpoints can be done by employing different methods, including analysing where traffic comes from to the web pages, identifying sequences by looking at other digital channels or by surveying prospects.

Understanding sequences of touchpoints in the considerations, purchase stages or mid-buyer and late buyer journey is usually easier than in the very early stages, as there is more direct interaction with the prospect. For the early buyer journey, we need to rely on surveys and polls as well as third-party information.

Step 4: Evaluate touchpoints

So now you know the customer journey stages and touchpoints and the sequence of those touchpoints. This provides only part of the story. To get a full understanding of the customer journey, an evaluation of the touchpoints is necessary to understand whether the experience of those touchpoints is a positive, negative or neutral one.

To understand this, let's look at some potential touchpoints and what a positive, negative or neutral experience would be.

Touchpoints which are positive can be defined by being simple and easy to use, adding value (ie they actually help the customer), meeting or over-delivering against expectations (ie they don't disappoint), and finally being context-relevant (ie the channel and content is relevant to requirements at that stage of the journey).

Other ways to understand a good or poor experience include identifying whether the customer moved to the next step of the buying process. Are the right customers being targeted, but a percentage of these being lost partway through the journey? This might indicate a poor experience at one particular touchpoint, and so allow for re-focusing of attention to this stage.

Ad tracking tools can tell you which campaigns, media and advertisements receive the most calls or clicks, and which ones resonate best with customers.

Potential touchpoints could be your website, social media channels, email messages, and webinars, and the content on those could be videos, banners, articles, downloadable content on the website or webinar content. In terms of experience, there are two or three ways to think about this; the actual comment or result provided back from the customer, or the background to that experience illustrated by types of metric and level of metrics.

Figure 3.4 is an example of a template which could be used, where in one snapshot you can see the stages and emotions relating to the touchpoint and whether goals are achieved or not. For example, if a customer is searching for more detailed information about a product or service but only finds short-form content or no content, then this would be rated as a negative touchpoint.

WEBSITE

Where the experience of the website is poor, we may see high bounce rates on certain pages or low click rates on heatmaps. These types of metrics can

FIGURE 3.4 Evaluating touchpoints

demonstrate that the customer didn't find what they were looking for, or that they tried clicking on things which weren't clickable.

Another way to gain more detail is to ask customers for feedback to provide context on the digital experience.

SOCIAL MEDIA

A good social media experience will be observed through the feedback a customer provides (always remember to define which social media channel or channels are being considered). Metrics on social media which provide insights to the experience may be direct interactions such as likes, retweets and shares.

These may indicate whether the content we are providing is relevant and compelling. Other metrics might be traffic or impressions on a tweet or a LinkedIn advertisement.

EMAIL

Open rates can be used to observe whether we are speaking to the right audience in the most appropriate manner. A low open rate might mean the wrong messages are being delivered, or the message is being sent to the wrong audience. Low clickthrough rates mean the content of the email hasn't caught their interest.

Unsubscribe rates are probably the final indicator that the audience is not interested or hasn't been given the right experience.

BENCHMARKING RESULTS

Above we've described the type of metrics but not how to benchmark them. In the evaluation stage, it is important to have an idea of what you would consider good, OK, or bad experiences. Before starting evaluation, therefore, you should understand how to read KPIs.

There are different ways to benchmark or read the KPIs. This can be through a baseline and comparison of findings to it; what were the email open rates, clickthrough rates or other metrics in the original analysis, and have they changed since adapting or adjusting the email according to understanding the customer journey more? Another method could be capturing industry benchmarks related to your industry – some media agencies or companies can help provide these.

Alternatively, it may be beneficial to conduct a more qualitative approach to the metrics through a survey or poll. For example, questions relating to website experience might be:

- How was your experience of our website?
- Did you find what you needed?
- If not, do you want to talk to our people – via chat or call?

CONTEXT AND INTENT

With different segments, models and customer types, the aim is to understand context and use that context to shape digital marketing efforts. In most situations, it will be trying to understand the type of information required, the type of content needed, whether to deliver directly or indirectly, and which messages and phrases should be used to really engage and connect with the customer to help them progress through their journey.

One way to understand the customer's intent in the different stages of the journey or touchpoints is by identifying keywords and key phrases. Although we talk a lot about keywords and key phrases in the early stages of the buyer journey and for PPC search, these are important to understand at all stages in the journey to help shape the right content.

Step 5: Optimizing the customer journey

The final stage in the touchpoint mapping exercise is in optimizing the customer journey. How do we turn a negative or a neutral experience of a touchpoint into a positive? It involves understanding the differences between the ideal customer journey and the customer journey as it is actually experienced, connecting and mapping customer interactions across multiple touchpoints, in order to direct or influence the end-to-end experience.

Based on the evaluation above, there are a number of ways to proceed:

- Optimize within the touchpoint: on the website or on social media, for example by optimizing within the touchpoint, the structure, level of personalization, and the content can be adapted.
- Optimize between touchpoints: if it's been identified that customers are lost at certain stages, facilitating movement between channels is a good area to focus on. Techniques to optimize the movement between touchpoints can be embedding links, enhancing the experience, having 'easy to share' buttons or paying for additional functionality, eg on social media channels.
- Remove touchpoints: some touchpoints might be superfluous and non-utilized, and it might better to remove these altogether. There may be excessive touchpoints within one stage of the journey, such as too many retargeted emails or sending customers to a different channel unnecessarily.

- Offering fast-track possibilities: this would involve offering opportunities for customers to engage, chat, call, or leave their details at any point should they want to move faster along the decision process. There may be a number of reasons why customers want these fast-track possibilities: if they've already done their research and want to talk about specific queries, or they have a particular urgency in getting answers to a question or to purchase.

These are illustrated in Figure 3.5.

Touchpoint mapping benefits

So, what are the benefits of touchpoint mapping, and is it really necessary? The first benefit is that brands can understand how many touchpoints or interactions shape an experience. The second benefit is that by understanding the sequence of touchpoints marketers can better plan and integrate marketing to facilitate the touchpoint journey. Finally, establishing the ideal scenario in touchpoints allows B2B marketers to understand exactly how much content and what types of content are required per segment and buyer persona, which in turn improves efficiency in spend or content produced.

To answer the point of whether touchpoint is necessary, we only need to look to the number of questions we have as B2B marketers – which digital channels should we use, which content should we produce and how should we implement channels and content. Touchpoint mapping brings clarity to how to conduct marketing and how to make investments in digital marketing.

FIGURE 3.5 Optimizing the customer journey

- Facilitating journey, eg adding links
- Shortening journey

Journey-based

Optimization

Channel-based
- Relevant channels
- Right number of channels

Content-based
- Relevant content
- Timely content
- Easy-to-use content
- Accessible – easy to find

Final considerations

Technology enablers and customer experience

As we start to dig into the touchpoints and the collection of touchpoints which shape customer experience, we can use a number of technologies. For example, in understanding the customer we can use CRM systems, search engine analytics, data on the person or journey mapping analytics. As we consider difficulty of interaction, we can track this through sentiment, customer service analytics via social media, Net Promoter Score (NPS), analysis of chat, and so on.

Here is where digital marketing and technology can really help us get to the root of the issue and resolve it. This will be discussed in more detail later in the book.

Nonlinearity of the customer journey

Good customer journey and touchpoint maps highlight a degree of interaction and overlap on touchpoints and channels used. Over the course of the past 10 years, what might have been a more linear and easy-to-follow journey in purchasing goods and services become a maze of channels.

This is a clear challenge for B2B marketers, but by understanding buyer personas and producing detailed customer journey maps, we can start to unravel the mystery of the customer journey.

Inbound and outbound views of customer journeys

Another way to structure the thinking around customer journeys is to think in terms of inbound and outbound marketing and channels. Is the base of the touchpoint a piece of inbound marketing, or is it followed up with outbound marketing?

Inbound marketing is engaging a customer through compelling and well-placed content, good SEO strategy and timing. Outbound channels or marketing activity initiates a conversation and potentially interrupts a customer while they are doing something else. Both approaches have benefits and challenges; some say inbound marketing works better, as traditional outbound marketing can be regarded as a nuisance.

For particular types of customer, the thinking and application will be very different: inbound marketing activities may work very well for a small business owner, but for a CEO of a large conglomerate, there may be a need to trigger interest, engage and intercept customer attention.

The B2B environment is often a mix of outbound and inbound marketing activities, depending on the segment and journey stage, each serving a different purpose.

Omnichannel messaging

Another way to look at customer experience is to optimize content and messages based on consistency and coherence across multiple channels. If a customer is interacting with a brand and comes across different, even conflicting messages on different channels, this risks confusing or even frustrating them.

One way to think about improving the experience of visual and text-based content is to take care of both coherence (do they relate to each other?) and consistency (are they saying the same thing?). This doesn't mean using the exact same words and phrasing, but words, phrases, messages and visual content which support or complement each other, ideally using an overarching theme or message.

A good example this would IBM and their 'Smarter Planet' campaign which ran for around four years. Not only were they delivering consistent messages at any given time, but there was a general consistency to the message and how they delivered the campaign over the four-year period.

EXERCISE
Put it into practice

1 Pick one step or area of a buyer journey and interview some customers – with their buyer persona in mind – to understand what content and marketing channels they use. Once you've conducted the interview, plot the touchpoints according to their feedback.

2 Consider a recent purchase experience. Which aspects would you say were negative and which were positive? Summarizing the negative and positive touchpoints, was the overall experience a positive or negative one?

References

Digital Marketing Institute (2018) [accessed 1 August 2019] How to Create a Customer Journey Map, *Digital Marketing Institute* [online] https://digitalmarketinginstitute.com/en-gb/blog/how-to-create-a-customer-journey-map (archived at https://perma.cc/UJE4-XJ8Y)

Hitesh, B (2018) [accessed 6 March 2020] Customer Perceived Value, CPV, *Marketing91*, 4 May [online] https://www.marketing91.com/customer-perceived-value-cpv/ (archived at https://perma.cc/SD35-XSBQ)

Young, H (2014) [accessed 1 August 2019] 86% of Senior-Level Marketers Agree on the Importance of Creating a Cohesive Customer Journey, *Salesforce* [online] www.salesforce.com/blog/2014/12/86-of-senior-level-marketers-agree-on-the-importance-of-creating-a-cohesive-customer-journey.html (archived at https://perma.cc/X6AX-58Y3)

Further reading

Araujo, C (2013) [accessed 1 August 2019] Moments of truth, the customer experience, *ThinkHDI* [online] www.thinkhdi.com/~/media/HDICorp/Files/SupportWorld/Promo/SW_NovDec13_Araujo_Moments.pdf (archived at https://perma.cc/7FS7-DFQG)

Deloitte (2016) [accessed 1 August 2019] The Deloitte Consumer Review CX marks the spot: Rethinking the customer experience to win, *Deloitte* [online] www2.deloitte.com/content/dam/Deloitte/uk/Documents/consumer-business/deloitte-uk-consumer-review-customer-experience.pdf (archived at https://perma.cc/D32A-B4GM)

KPMG Nunwood Consulting (2017) [accessed 1 August 2019] B2B Customer Experience: Winning in the Moments that Matter, *KPMG* [online] https://home.kpmg/content/dam/kpmg/uk/pdf/2017/05/b2b-customer-experience-report.pdf (archived at https://perma.cc/4RN4-JF7G).

McKinsey (2017) Customer Experience: New capabilities, new audiences, new opportunities, *McKinsey* [online] www.mckinsey.com/~/media/mckinsey/featured%20insights/customer%20experience/cx%20compendium%202017/customer-experience-compendium-july-2017.ashx (archived at https://perma.cc/6C93-UB7A)

04

B2B personalization marketing and buyer personas

WHAT YOU WILL GAIN FROM THIS CHAPTER

After reading this chapter, you will understand:

- B2B personalization marketing;
- types of personalization marketing;
- buyer personas and how to create them;
- progressive profiling.

Introduction

What is personalization?

As we move on from customer journeys and customer journey mapping, one area which is becoming important in B2B is personalization marketing. Personalization (broadly known as customization) consists of tailoring a service or a product to accommodate specific individuals, groups or market segments. This has its history in product personalization in the consumer space with use of colour to personalize cars, mobile phones and even computers, and of course long before that with clothing.

Personalization marketing is about using persona-specific information to create or improve bespoke experiences through marketing. It involves individualizing content or parts of content for target customers through collecting and analysing data. In an era where digital marketing is increasing and customers use or consume more marketing channels within shorter times, the demands on personalization have also increased.

Why personalize?

So why personalize within the B2B area? The answer is that people buy from people, and the personal touch is still important. Let's not forget that B2B marketing is sometimes called B2B relationship marketing, as the main focus is to market to organizations whilst building relationships.

According to McKinsey, 'Personalization can reduce acquisition costs by as much as 50 per cent, lift revenues by 5 to 15 per cent, and increase the efficiency of marketing spend by 10 to 30 per cent' (Gregg *et al*, 2016).

Additionally, the data presented in Figure 4.1 below shows personalization's impact on conversion for 2016–17, and suggests that personalized marketing does work to improve uplift for almost all marketing channels. The highest uplift here is around 40 per cent for search engine marketing, and for email and social media the range is around 30 per cent.

Personalization allows B2B marketers to improve response rates as well as conversion rates from marketing channels, improving the relationship-building process from lead generation through to lead nurturing.

Personalization marketing and the buyer journey

Personalization marketing can play different roles depending on the buyer journey stage:

- Generating awareness: Here, personalization marketing is less about personalizing to the specific individual (as we don't know them yet), and more about tailoring to sectors, segments or even buyer personas.

FIGURE 4.1 The impact of personalization on conversion

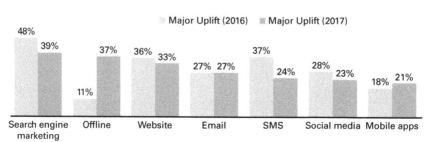

SOURCE Marketing Charts

Additionally, tailoring marketing to better meet needs in the early buyer stage is a form of personalization marketing.

- Generating and nurturing leads: As we move from the early stage of the buyer journey to the mid- and late buyer journey stages, personalization marketing can help in developing connections with the customer through relevant channels, through content, as well as through responding more specifically to questions as customers proceed through different steps of their buyer journey. By understanding the buyer journey and the stages, we can then look to better personalizing content, channels, messages, etc.

- Post-purchase phases: This is a retention marketing strategy which can be used to improve engagement, increase satisfaction and hence improve customer loyalty. During the post-purchase phases, we have the ability to actually understand more specifically customers' needs and to develop better relationships through personalization marketing.

Benefits of personalizing

As mentioned, personalization can help build better relationships through adapting content, messages, and interactions to better speak to prospective or current customers.

As the benefits of personalization have become evident in improved ROI, reduced acquisition costs, and revenue increase, attention should be paid to how to adopt and integrate this into B2B marketing efforts (Steers, 2019). Not using personalization in your marketing could be a major disadvantage as competitors embrace it and approach customers with tailored messaging.

Personalization can help drive sales and enhance understanding of customer segments as well as grow the business. Personalization marketing is still evolving in B2B and will be specific to your industry, product/service type, and even country – hence the need to test.

Types of B2B personalization

Personalization in B2B marketing can come in many forms. Essentially, it's about tailoring content to individual customer preferences, needs and characteristics. Understanding the individual through solid buyer personas is key.

Personalization considerations in B2B include the marketing channel, such as email, social media or website, 'how' the personalization is done (using buyer behaviour information such as how often the prospect or customer uses content), and use of technology, as in account-based marketing.

Levels of B2B personalization

There are also different levels of personalization in B2B marketing: one should remember that there are degrees of personalization, and not all personalized marketing is fully tailored or comprehensively detailed to a person. See Figure 4.2, which illustrates the different forms of B2B marketing personalization:

- Sector-based personalization: This correlates to the industry or sector the organization or the person works in, eg oil and gas, finance or insurance. The personalization can come in the form of content, or the requirements of organizations or individuals working within that sector.

- Segment- or account-based personalization: These can be sub-segments within the sector or groupings of accounts based on geography or other segmentation criteria. Marketing to specific types of organization, or organizations located within a region, may benefit from tailored messaging, for example.

- Persona-based personalization: In this case, the marketing is tailored to the specific buyer persona so content and information are adapted accordingly.

- Stage-based personalization: This is marketing in which content, messaging and techniques are chosen based not only on the buyer persona but a specific stage in the customer journey.

- One-to-one-based personalization: This final version is where the marketing is tailored to the specific individual.

Use of digital in personalization

Digital technologies can make personalization easier by automating some tasks required in the background, for example dynamic or adaptive websites. Such technology supports recognition of customer interest, and provides tailored messages and content accordingly, a process that would not be scalable or feasible without digital means. Hence digital technologies and digital marketing go hand in hand with many forms of personalization.

FIGURE 4.2 Types of B2B personalization

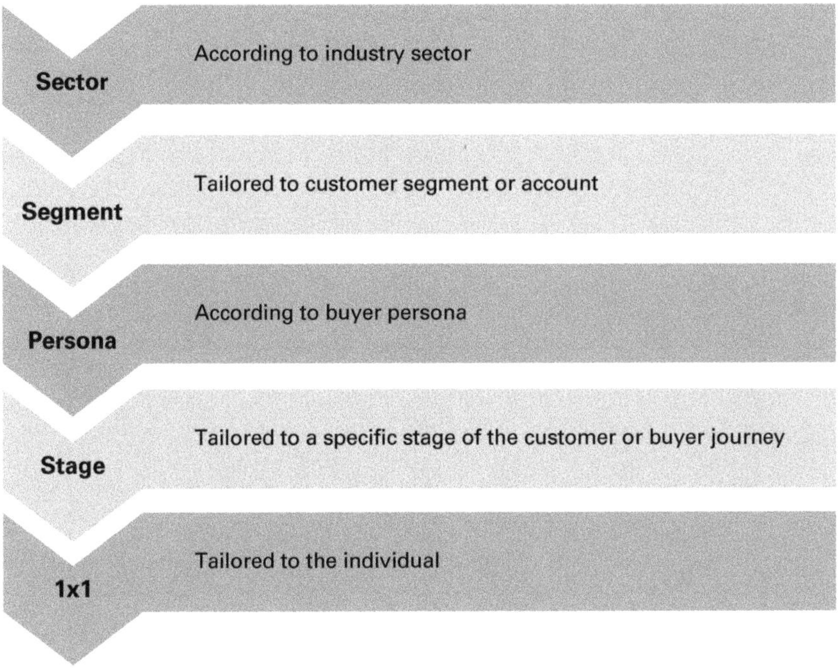

Sector	According to industry sector
Segment	Tailored to customer segment or account
Persona	According to buyer persona
Stage	Tailored to a specific stage of the customer or buyer journey
1x1	Tailored to the individual

Other areas where technologies support personalization are the use of email preference centres to allow for recipients to register their interests and preferences in terms of when and how often they receive emails.

Who to personalize for?

In B2B marketing, it's pertinent to ask who marketing should be personalized for. When organizations are targeted, encounters mainly occur with the decision-making unit (DMU). As shown in in Figure 4.3, this may be made up of a number of people. Studies demonstrate that on average, four to five departments are involved in purchasing products through B2B channels, and around six to seven people – so selecting which people to personalize for is the challenging question (LinkedIn, 2016).

Preceding but linked to the DMU and stakeholder selection is segmentation. Segmentations allow B2B marketers to create customer-specific digital marketing channels like websites and social media accounts, and produce segment-specific content and information. These approaches can improve metrics through repeat visits and greater time spent on websites.

FIGURE 4.3 The DMU

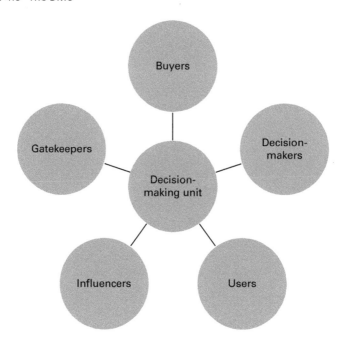

B2B personalization by channel

Let's take a look at some of the way to personalize based on marketing channel.

Website personalization

One way to personalize is via your website. Websites are critical channels to engage customers, and so including a more personal touch can help. According to statistics, 66 per cent of buyers indicated that the vendor's website was important when making their purchase decision (Tirico, 2018). However, a significant challenge is to understand which segments and personas to adapt your website for.

So, what do we mean by website personalization – how do you start and what is it you personalize?

Below are some of the ways you may begin to think about for your organization.

PERSONALIZED URLs

Personalized URLs (PURLs) may be used for targeting customers through personalized web pages or even entire websites, providing respondents with unique, tailored content. Content is usually based on previously stated preferences, information from the database or prior surveys. PURLs can be created based on personas and customer profiles, and can be done as standard or in accordance with a campaign.

A good example of this was a recent campaign by Avios, an air miles company, where they targeted senior decision makers. Customers or prospects were sent a personalized direct mail which consisted of a transparent Perspex box. Within the box was a blister pack with a PURL for each recipient, which when used would take them to a video greeting them personally (Gryg, 2018).

ADAPTIVE OR DYNAMIC WEB CONTENT

Sometimes also known as smart content, this is where a webpage changes content based on the interests and past behaviour of site visitors. Dynamic content can come in the form of website forms, landing pages, and emails which change based on the viewer.

Smart content can also come in the form of calls to actions (CTAs) depending on behaviour or past interactions with the website from the visitor.

REFERRAL-BASED PERSONALIZATION

Another interesting development is referral-based personalization, which alters content according to how visitors arrive at your website, ie the source or channel they're using.

The channel they use to come to your website can indicate a different level of intent: for example, visitors who arrive at your website based on viewing your social media pages would show a greater intent than one who is viewing some SEO content on a third-party site.

With differing consumer intents and stages of the buyer's journey, it is prudent to tailor content accordingly. For example, those who are still in the exploration or self-education stage would likely be more interested in informative articles about trends and challenges, rather than specific named product solutions.

B2B email personalization

Email personalization involves targeting emails to specific recipients using data and information about them. As was discussed with levels of B2B personalization, it can come in different forms:

- **Basic email personalization:** The basic level in email personalization can be as simple as personalizing the header with something related to the person's interests or concerns, which is certainly a suitable strategy in B2B.

- **Intermediate email personalization:** The next level is to also personalize the content to the segment, sector or company you're targeting, including having themes or tailoring content further according to specific department (eg finance, technical).

- **Advanced-level email personalization:** This can be broken down into context and behaviours. Context is using wording and key phrases in the email according to the person's profession and business interests. Email personalization based on behaviours could mean the generation of a specific email if the prospect interacts with a particular page on the website, for instance.

PRACTICAL TIP

How to segment based on email behaviours

Make sure to segment out your database of customers, as this will allow for a segmented email messaging strategy. Identifying similarities between customer types allows for more tailored emails; for example, you might segment out customers who purchase regularly but haven't purchased in six months, and highlight that you've noticed this and are interested to understand the reasons.

SALES EMAIL OUTREACH

Another aspect of personalizing email is using sales channels. Sales reps can help personalize the experience, not only in delivering emails, but also in how they add content according to the account they sell to.

PRACTICAL TIP

Improving sales email outreach

The following approaches may be useful for improving sales email outreach and personalization:

- provide modular content according to account type/sector type;
- provide modular content according to decision-maker type;
- provide email templates which can be easily populated;
- provide curated content sources, eg case studies, which can be tailored to persona and usage case;
- train sales in using content and templates.

Mobile personalization

With more and more people using mobile devices, there is also a call for mobile personalization. Mobile marketing comes in different forms such as SMS, QR codes, mobile advertising, and mobile email and web platforms, and so personalization marketing can be applied to these areas.

Techniques in mobile personalization include:

- **Push notifications:** These are reminders, or messages which pop up on mobile devices via mobile apps. As mobile devices are often the main companion that people refer to multiple times a day, companies are able to reach their target audience anytime, anywhere with personalized push notifications. In B2B, push notifications are being used with reminders, updates, promotions, and product information to connect with, engage or retain customers.

- **Accommodate local search:** Mobile inquiries are further along the buyer journey than desktop-based searches. With that in mind, it is good to optimize for local searches on mobile. The way people use mobile for searches will be different from desktop-based search – prospects searching on mobile will probably have more immediate needs and want to access things faster. Be sure to facilitate quick search and allow for accessing solutions to problems faster.

- **Geo-targeting to mobile devices:** It can sometimes be the case that messages or marketing content are location-sensitive, and need to be delivered only to recipients in a given location. This is where mobile geo-targeting of advertisements or messages plays a role. Geo-targeting can be a particularly interesting prospect for event promotion. Datto Inc, a business continuity and disaster recovery solution provider, needed to target recipients according to their nearness to their roadshows. Datto targeted website visitors that were within a hundred miles of a roadshow location, and consequently experienced an up to 12 per cent clickthrough rate and over 500 incremental registrants to their roadshows (Sweet, 2017).

Social media personalization

Using information about the customer to tailor messages and social media communication is also an effective means of personalizing your B2B marketing. Social media personalization can be carried out by targeted messages and advertising on various platforms to specific groups or personas.

To start, you'll have to have a targeted database within the social media platforms. A means to approach this is creating lists – such as on LinkedIn or Twitter – and segmenting those lists for personalized social media marketing, retargeting on social media, or personally addressing individuals with messages.

Targeting advertising according to personas means selecting appropriate social media platforms that have the right advertising and targeting functionalities. The great news for B2B marketers is that most social media platforms now offer these, and can ensure targeting is even aimed at individuals and specific personas; LinkedIn, for instance, allows you to separate out by sector, level, title and region.

Personalizing based on digital behaviours

In some situations, an alternative approach may be to consider digital behaviours across channels instead of personalizing by just one channel.

As demonstrated in Table 4.1, digital behaviours include clicks or time spent on pages of the website, or opening and clicking through on emails. By personalizing according to content clicked on or according to email clicks or opens, we're actually saying that the more digitally engaged the customer, the higher the level of personalization.

TABLE 4.1 Personalization and B2B behaviours

Low engagement on marketing channel	High engagement on marketing channel	Purchase behaviours
Low open rate	High open rate	Purchased many items
Low click-through rate	High click-through rate	Purchases infrequently
High bounce rate, or visits single page	Visits multiple website pages	Hasn't purchased in a while Changes purchase type

Personalization by account

This personalization can often be the most varied. If you're trying to influence a buying unit where stakeholders are very different, then you'll need to think of personalizing based on marketing channel, content and messaging, among other things. Some of these stakeholders may be more into technical blogs, while others may prefer email. As already mentioned, it's therefore important to research and understand key contacts within your accounts to understand these preferences.

Personalization for accounts can often result in higher response rates, and also reduces the cost of acquisition. As stated, according to McKinsey, personalization reduces acquisition costs by as much as 50 per cent and increases revenues by as much as 15 per cent (Gregg *et al*, 2016).

So, if you're concerned about the extra cost or effort involved in personalization of content and messages, consider that it could be outweighed by acquiring a customer and the long-term benefits of having that bigger account on your books.

The B2B personalization marketing pyramid

To understand how to carry out effective B2B personalization, we can use the B2B personalization pyramid in Figure 4.4. This looks at foundations in B2B personalization and illustrates how to build to an increasingly more sophisticated approach to personalization marketing.

An effective way to use the personalization pyramid is to build personalization marketing capabilities by starting with the first layer and gradually build up all the elements:

- **Data and database:** Having good data and a good-quality database is a key foundation of effective personalization. The database can house data

FIGURE 4.4 The personalization pyramid

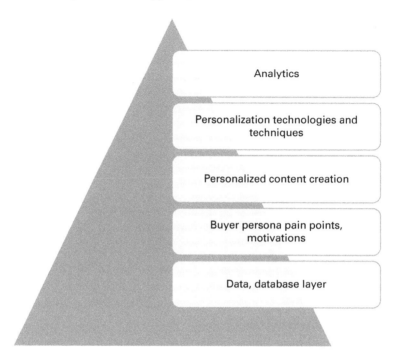

according to buyer persona or customer segment. This part of the exercise is not only about collecting what data you have and organizing it, but understanding key data gaps by doing so. We'll be looking into data and insights more in the next chapter.

- **Buyer persona pain points and motivations:** In the second layer, we start to have an understanding of other aspects such as behaviours, pain points and motivations of the buyer persona. Motivations might be the need for particular types of content or information, or a need to access certain information faster.

- **Personalized content creation:** The third layer is about creating tailored content in some form. This content is channel-agnostic in its creation – the focus is first on the content itself, and later it can be adapted according to the marketing channel used where necessary, eg mobile, email or social media.

- **Personalization technologies and techniques:** Technologies include retargeting technologies, email automation technologies, dynamic web content technologies and dynamic content functionalities on social media.

- **Analytics:** Whether using specific technologies or those included within the platforms you use, use of analytics and applying the insights gained means personalization can be applied relatively quickly or even in real time.

The buyer persona

The buyer persona is one of the key digital tools within the B2B digital marketer's toolbox, and is especially important when carrying out effective personalization marketing. As it is a semi-fictional representation of your ideal target customer and formulated according to your key target customer segment, many questions relating to personalization marketing – and digital marketing more widely – can be answered through a comprehensive buyer persona.

What is included in a buyer persona?

Typically, a B2B buyer persona should include stakeholders, attitudes, pain points, motivations, influences, and key media used by them.

More comprehensive B2B buyer personas include media and key words, as well as content preferences and key phrases used according to different stages in the buyer journey. This creates 'a day in the life' of the persona and can help identify why they may buy the respective products and services as well as why they don't buy.

PRACTICAL TIP
Use prospect language

When creating a buyer persona, it's best not to include 'corporate' language that is only used within your business. Rather, create content and messaging based on terms and phrases actually used by the customers.

Otherwise, when the information gets translated into content and marketing campaigns, it may not resonate as well with the intended audience.

Creating buyer personas

Before commencing the creation of a buyer persona, we need to be clear on the customer segment to which the buyer persona is aligned; poorly defined customer segments will only mean our buyer persona will suffer.

With a well-defined customer segment, finding similarities between the buyers will be easier, and therefore will enable the creation of a more effective buyer persona. Although there is no mathematical rule, generally speaking the majority of the information and answers to questions which support creation of the buyer persona should be similar (some say more than 70 per cent similar). Where there is only a small portion of information similar in the answers, this causes subsequent problems in the creation marketing campaigns, messages and content.

Once you have a well-defined customer segment, you can search customers according to that segment, for example by using a match technique to identify existing customers in organization records and databases which fit the segment criteria. Once these matched customers are identified, start collecting information from CRM data, the account manager, and other areas to form the buyer persona.

Typically, once a B2B buyer persona is created, the work doesn't need to be repeated for some time. Ideally, B2B marketers should continue to monitor sample customers and prospects from the segment to understand if anything has changed. In that way the buyer persona can be tweaked and modified on a regular basis to ensure that personalization is most effective.

The buyer persona should become a living document and essential part of the toolkit for any B2B marketer. It provides a good foundation and reference to support B2B marketers for any of their activities, and provides context for business owners and salespeople.

Example of a B2B buyer persona

Figure 4.6 is a template for a buyer persona. Buyer personas should ideally be presented on one single page, with a more in-depth view of the persona provided in additional, more detailed documents.

PRACTICAL TIP

Applying and using buyer personas

Make sure to create buyer personas with the end in mind: what types of information will you need as a B2B marketer to conduct really effective marketing? For example if you're planning your keywords and phrases research for SEO content, you will want to reference and understand what keywords, key phrases the buyer persona uses and include those, in the same words they used.

FIGURE 4.5 Buyer persona template

Persona context	Goals	Buying process	Buyer needs	Why they buy
Who are they? What is their experience? What are their areas of focus? What are the roles ?	Business goals? Personal goals? Organizational goals affecting buyer behaviour?	What's their buying process? How does procurement play a part?	What is driving their buying need? What are their pain points?	How do buyers make choices? Risk affecting buying choices
What's a day in the life of the person?	Initiatives Projects today? Projects next financial year?	Timing Seasonal patterns of buyers	Buyer view of brands How do they view you as a brand? How do they view other competing brands?	Why they don't buy What are their deal-breakers? Are there any negative opinions of your organization? Have they heard of you?
Influencers, stakeholders, Who are key stakeholders? Who participates in marketing decisions? Who are internal influencers? External influencers? Who participates in approval process?		Content, channels Difference in content consumption between stages in customer journey Differences in use of marketing channels across customer journey		Keywords, key phrases What keywords are being used by persona

Progressive profiling

Progressive profiling is a less invasive method than some of the longer-form profiling surveys which customers are sometimes asked to complete. Progressive profiling is a marketing technique that enhances lead generation and qualification efforts by gradually gathering demographic and preference data over a longer period of time, and across various customer touchpoints.

Progressive profiling can be more effective than surveys or polls as it captures data using short forms, which require customers to fill out much fewer fields. As a result, conversions and response rates are typically higher. With progressive profiling, the questions are asked once, logged and then added up over time. One example can be seen in Figure 4.6, but progressive polling can also be based on capturing information through email rather than forms being filled out.

Progressive profiles work on the idea of two-way conversations between customers and marketers as brands gradually poll customers over time with personalized messaging.

How progressive profiling works

Progressive profiling is based on dynamic web forms; you can find these via marketing automaton platforms such as HubSpot. When a customer is re-engaged to request further information, the background system looks for information already provided so it doesn't duplicate the requests. At the

FIGURE 4.6 Progressive profiling: one method

Step 1	Step 2	Step 3
First name	First name	First name
Last name	Last name	Last name
Email	Email	Email
	Company	Company
	Requirements	Requirements
		Communication preference
		Role
A user visits website and is required to fill out a few fields to download something	A user returns to the website and is asked for additional information when downloading an additional piece of content	When they return the following time again, additional information is asked for

same time, it adds information to the customer's profile so it can gradually build a more complete view over time.

Figure 4.6 illustrates the different stages of progressive profiling.

CASE STUDY
CSC

The Computer Sciences Corporation (CSC) is an IT service company that provides infrastructure, consulting, and custom solutions. One of their key challenges was to better engage and target customers, and to deal with this challenge they used reverse-IP look-up technologies in setting up advertising campaigns.

Reverse-IP look-up allowed them to identify named accounts and then retarget them with personalized content across multiple marketing channels. This approach helped them target 245 companies and engage almost half of them. Among many improvements, they saw a 58 per cent increase in page views.

CSC also use technologies such as Adobe Analytics to create customer profiles, which are in turn used to update billboards and personalize banners to ensure visitors see relevant information and articles according to their interest (Peterson, 2015; Adobe, 2015).

EXERCISE
Put it into practice

1   Review the top three stakeholders in a DMU from one of your key customer segments.

2   Review which marketing channels you use today to personalize your marketing: email, website, mobile, social media, etc.

3   If you apply the personalization pyramid, to what extent does your personalization go? If you needed to move this to the next level in the pyramid, what would you need to do?

4   Review your organization's current buyer persona relating to a marketing activity or campaign. Which elements are useful for your marketing programmes? Which elements are missing? Can these be updated to remove some of the guesswork in creating marketing programmes and campaigns?

References

Adobe (2015) [accessed 16 January 2020] CSC engages B2B customers 1:1, *Adobe* [online] www.adobe.com/content/dam/acom/en/customer-success/pdfs/csc-case-study.pdf (archived at https://perma.cc/WBB7-K84P)

Gregg, B *et al* (2016) Marketing's Holy Grail: Digital personalization at scale, *McKinsey* [online] www.mckinsey.com/business-functions/mckinsey-digital/our-insights/marketings-holy-grail-digital-personalization-at-scale (archived at https://perma.cc/8584-AKMU)

Gryg, O (2018) [accessed 1 August 2019] Awards case study: Why Avios' decision to sprinkle a little magic on its direct mail led to a 58% response rate, *B2B Marketing* [online] www.b2bmarketing.net/en-gb/resources/b2b-case-studies/awards-case-study-why-avios-decision-sprinkle-little-magic-its-direct (archived at https://perma.cc/E2X4-DQEV)

LinkedIn (2016) [accessed 1 August 2019] Rethink the B2B Buyers Journey, *SlideShare* [online] www.slideshare.net/LImarketingsolutions/which-departments-wield-the-most-influence-over-purchase-decisions-in-your-B2B-industry-61624782 (archived at https://perma.cc/5DY5-WC39)

Peterson, A (2015) [accessed 16 January 2020] 3 Killer Examples of Personalized B2B Marketing, *TechnologyAdvice* [online] https://technologyadvice.com/blog/marketing/3-killer-examples-personalized-B2B-marketing/ (archived at https://perma.cc/UX73-FJ5R)

Steers, R (2019) [accessed 1 August 2019] B2B Personalization: What Do Customers Really Want? *Step Change* [online] https://blog.hellostepchange.com/blog/b2b-personalisation (archived at https://perma.cc/2UMR-JG92)

Sweet, K (2017) [accessed 09 November 2019] Examples of B2B Personalization from 4 Leading Demand Gen Marketers, *Evergage* [online] www.evergage.com/blog/examples-B2B-personalization-4-leading-demand-gen-marketers/ (archived at https://perma.cc/TV2T-QAL4)

Tirico, K (2018) [accessed 9 November 2019] 2018 B2B Buyers Survey Report, *DemandGen Report* [online] www.demandgenreport.com/resources/reports/2018-B2B-buyers-survey-report (archived at https://perma.cc/6USR-J5ZV)

Further reading

Behling, E, (2017) [accessed 1 August 2019] 10 Personalization Statistics You Need to Know: Why Personalized Marketing is the Way to Go, *RR Donnelley* [online] https://thoughts.rrd.com/blog/10-personalization-statistics-you-need-to-know-why-personalized-marketing-is-the-way-to-go (archived at https://perma.cc/L6DU-4AKV)

Eres, I (n. d.) [accessed 1 August 2019] What Happens When Content Personalization Meets the B2B Funnel?, *convince&convert* [online] www.convinceandconvert.com/content-marketing/content-personalization-meets-B2B-funnel/ (archived at https://perma.cc/TZQ8-NZDT)

Even, A (2015) [accessed 1 August 2019] Personalization: The Pillar of the Mobile User Experience, *UX Mag* [online] https://uxmag.com/articles/personalization-the-pillar-of-the-mobile-user-experience (archived at https://perma.cc/J8NC-4CK8)

05

B2B customer insights and data management

Introduction

Customer insights and data management

To support customer journey mapping, personalization marketing and strategies, we need to have a firm grasp of customer insights and a well-structured approach to managing and interpreting data. In fact, for any marketing activity we would probably need to revert to customer insights and data analytics.

This chapter looks at how to develop a 360-degree view of customers and how to capture customer insights, as well as customer data and data management in a marketing context.

What are customer insights and why are they needed?

Customer insights analysis should be a starting point – possibly *the* starting point – in marketing, as understanding customers can help to create better strategies.

Customer insights are information sets, and the analysis of them typically helps identify behaviours and patterns about customers which can be used to improve business operations and marketing.

Insights differ from research in that people can conduct research in all different scales and forms. The research can lead to extracting good insights or not; research sometimes may not lead to anything conclusive in terms of real insights.

Where to start with customer insights – the 3As process

The 3As of gathering customer insights are as follows:

1 **Assemble:** Assuming there is a focus area to research, information should be collected through research, assembling data around a topic using a variety of sources. Research as a packaged one-project approach may not work here.

2 **Analysis and interpretation:** After collecting the data, an analysis should be undertaken, potentially with help from analytics platforms and technologies. As part of this stage, the data is interpreted – this is where the magic really happens. Data interpretation is not a skill every marketer has, so finding the right people to do this can be as impactful as the analytics tools themselves.

3 **Apply:** Finally, the insights are applied; in this case the insights are used to improve marketing activities. For example, an insight highlighting the type of content to use to help customers in their mid-buyer journey can subsequently be used to improve the content mix within a lead nurture campaign.

Customer insights framework

To build a set of insights relating to customers, marketers need a framework. Figure 5.1 shows the main areas of customer insights, starting with segment characteristics. Insights relating to customer segment include retention vs

FIGURE 5.1 Customer insights framework

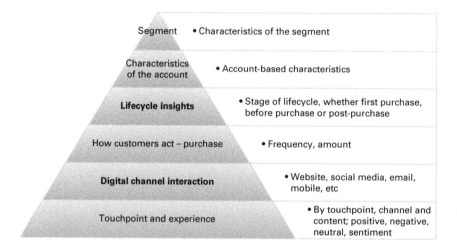

acquisition, industry sector, and any other form of criteria by which customers share common characteristics.

Following segment-based information, the next set of information relates to account-level insights such as organization growth and account size.

Further areas relating to building a comprehensive view of customers are purchase behaviours, digital channel interaction and touchpoint insights, as well as overall experience, which can be positive, negative or neutral.

Methods for gathering customer insights in B2B

There are multiple routes to gathering customer insights. Let's first break these into quantitative and qualitative techniques.

Quantitative research and analytics

Quantitative research is used to compute areas of research through creating numerical data or data that can be transformed into usable statistics.

Advantages of quantitative analytics methods are that larger sample sizes allow for greater generalization of the results. It can also be cheaper as technologies can be used to capture and analyse data, and even to extract insights, rather than relying on skilled researchers. Some of the cons are its lack of detail sometimes, as well as context.

QUANTITATIVE ANALYTICS IN B2B MARKETING

The following are the main areas of quantitative analytics in B2B:

- behavioural analytics: analysing how customers act;
- demographic segment analytics: understanding the characteristics of the segment or of the person;
- insights on attitudes: tools to give a better idea of customer sentiment;
- website analytics: using analytics tools to analyse data relating to websites;
- social media analytics: analysing activity on or between social media channels;
- account analytics: this relates to analytics of companies and includes aspects such as purchasing power, business growth and propensity to buy.

Qualitative research and analytics

With qualitative research, we're researching customers' thoughts – what they think and why they think it. This type of research is typically less structured and facilitates freer thinking and responses.

The advantages of qualitative research are that it provides detailed information and results through exploration. The research allows for freer responses by encouraging discussion and enabling recipients to expand on their answers.

The disadvantages include that due to it being more in-depth, the sample size is usually smaller. Also, the responses being freer makes them more difficult to categorize or generalize, and analysis does rely on more skilled researchers.

QUALITATIVE ANALYTICS IN B2B MARKETING

Examples of qualitative customer insights methods are in-depth interviews, focus groups, customer advisory councils or panels, and any form of moderated group discussions.

The pros and cons of qualitative and quantitative analytics are summarized in Tables 5.1 and 5.2.

TABLE 5.1 Pros and cons of quantitative insight methods

Pros	Cons
Less time-consuming	Data integrity issues
Reliable	Potentially questions are misinterpreted
Easy to carry out	Needs larger sample size
Easy to compare findings	

TABLE 5.2 Pros and cons of qualitative insight methods

Pros	Cons
Richer data	More expensive
More personal	Difficulty to interpret
	More time-consuming
	Difficulty in comparing findings

Quantitative customer insight methods

As mentioned above there are different types of quantitative analytics. We can also break them down according to the digital marketing channel of focus, eg by website, social media or email.

Insights on attitudes

Customer attitudes are something we are particularly interested in as B2B marketers, as this area of insights includes customer satisfaction and customer experience.

Tools one could use include sentiment analysis which trawls online sites and social media platforms for sentiment relating to keywords or organizations. Examples of quantitative technologies that measure attitude and interest are Hootsuite and Sprout Social.

You could also use Net Promoter Score (NPS): though it may be considered qualitative, it is mostly captured in a quantitative manner. The NPS can capture key customer perspectives of the organization in terms of whether the customer is happy with the products and services, whether they would recommend the vendor's goods to a friend and many other areas relating to customer satisfaction.

Behavioural analytics

These analytics observe different behaviours across purchasing, digital channel interaction and device usage, among other aspects of the customer journey. One would typically use any customer or account-level data to identify purchasing behaviours.

CRM tools today equip businesses with the ability to easily manage data and to extract insights relating to this, whether it is historical, predictive or prescriptive analytics. Digital interaction behaviours will be covered later in the website and social media section.

Device usage covers how desktop, mobile and tablet devices are used in relation to the consumption of content or using digital channels.

Demographic and segment analytics

Demographic or segment analytics are particularly useful in B2B marketing. Even though B2B marketing is about marketing to businesses, we need to remember that it is people who influence decisions with companies – so identifying and analysing data relating to buyer persona(s) and customer segments is invaluable.

To gather demographic or segment information one can use social media analytics (see below) which can provide information on customer segment, the role a person has within an organization, location and other characteristics. Other off-the-shelf tools can also be used, such as Nielsen's MyBestSegments where a company can understand the most suitable ways to reach specific audiences and thus narrow this down to prospective customers.

In addition to these tools, organizations can capture key segment or demographic information through CRM technologies such as SAS, Salesforce or Microsoft Dynamics.

Website analytics

Website analytics is about analysing traffic coming to your website, as well as how customers interact with its content. Through these analytics, it's possible to understand what type of traffic is coming to the website – is it based on a campaign, or from a social media channel? We can also understand when they visit, where from, where they go on the website, how long they stay and a number of other great insights to use for digital marketing.

The most used website analytics tool is Google Analytics. It's free for anyone who has a website, and you can obtain a lot of information through this. There are however some limitations with Google Analytics, such as understanding mobile website engagement, but these limitations can be rectified through plugins and additional software.

Other examples of website analytics technologies are Hotjar, Heap Analytics, and Piwik PRO.

Social media analytics

There are great deal of options for social media analytics today. Some tools are cross-platform, such as Sprout Social and Klipfolio, while social media platforms including Twitter, Facebook and LinkedIn offer analytic technologies of their own.

TWITTER ANALYTICS

Twitter offer free analytics within their platform, and can offer information such as demographic data, tweet-based analytics, engagement rates, and some behavioural data.

There are also some Twitter-based analytics platforms which offer a broader range of data such as SocialPilot and Followerwonk. Most of these additional platforms offer a basic version for free.

LINKEDIN ANALYTICS

LinkedIn offer their own analytics functionality. You'll find LinkedIn analytics within your company LinkedIn profile under the dropdown menu from your individual view.

LinkedIn analytics offer some limited free data such as visitor traffic and job functions, and more recently have improved their service to offer content suggestions based on company, sector, interest and position. Where you conduct a marketing campaign via LinkedIn, you can use LinkedIn analytics to measure the impact of ads as well as conversions.

FACEBOOK ANALYTICS AND INSIGHTS

Facebook also include their own analytics platform for free. You can find Facebook analytics through the dashboard, though you'll need Facebook Pixel. With this installed you can produce all sorts of analytical data such as performance of your business's page.

Through Facebook insights you can track likes, page views, reach and many other metrics, allowing you to understand who your audience is and who is engaging the most with your page.

INSTAGRAM

Instagram is becoming increasingly used by B2B companies. Although as recently as three years ago it wasn't seen as a viable B2B marketing social media platform, now more and more businesses are considering it; according to statistics, 71 per cent of US businesses use Instagram (Clarke, 2019).

In a recent study of around 100 companies, about one in three were considering using or were using Instagram already for B2B marketing purposes (West, 2019).

Instagram analytics can track followers, their age, gender, location, even languages spoken. You can also track follower growth rates.

As well as Instagram's own analytics tool, technologies such as Quintly, Brandwatch and Socialbakers allow you to analyse data from the platform.

ACCOUNT ANALYTICS

These can be carried out by CRM, or a marketing automation platform, depending on the type of analytics, or can be purchased as a service from Equifax, D&B or Experian.

Valuable forms of information gained from account analytics include the size of business, their ability to purchase or purchasing power, sector, and growth trends to understand which businesses are growing more than others.

SENTIMENT ANALYSIS AND ITS VALUE

Sentiment analysis is a method to research text, extracting information to provide an indication of social sentiment, opinion and emotional reaction. Largely used on social media networks, sentiment analysis is based on natural language processing (NLP) technology which analyses social conversations online to determine context of information in terms of topics, themes, tone and brand.

In a B2B context, sentiment analysis can help brands understand how customers or prospects perceive a brand in relation to various topics and themes, and inform their future strategy for engaging with these customer segments.

Sentiment analysis can be used in the following manner:

- to analyse posts on social media networks to see the sentiment of particular audiences;
- to run analyses on social media mentions related to your brand;
- to gain deeper insight into sentiment towards brands in relations to specific topics or themes.

Qualitative customer insight methods

Qualitative market research is any research conducted using observation or unstructured questioning. With the increased sophistication of digital technologies, a lot of qualitative research can be conducted without being physically in front of the customer, or sometimes without the customer present. Examples include individual interviews, online focus groups, advisory boards and opinion leader research.

Individual interviews

As well as the more traditional formats such as in-person and phone interviews, the availability of conferencing software and video applications such as Skype allow people to conduct interviews easily and remotely. Some also offer functionalities such as whiteboards and Q&A software.

As the purpose of interviews is to ask questions related to individuals, this form of research could be particularly interesting regarding customer journeys, or to improve understanding of the buyer persona.

Online focus groups

Though similar in format, online focus groups are easier to set up and less costly than in-person ones, as rooms and venues are not required. It is also easier for customers themselves to participate as they don't need to travel and can take part from their desk. Using collaborative conferencing software can still create the feeling of being in a group.

Customer advisory boards

Customer advisory boards are usually conducted face-to-face, although some companies may decide to set up customer advisory panels or boards online in which they invite customers to review a business area or discuss a business topic. These types of insights methods can be powerful in a number of respects, by providing to the customer an unfiltered manner to engage, respond, provide opinions and for companies to capture direct input on topics.

Another interesting approach is a face-to-face and online mix, where an advisory board agree to be recorded or agree to be put online for other customers to view and potentially participate.

Opinion leader research

This form of research allows organizations to identify who is shaping thoughts or opinions on particular specialist topics, and hence who is influencing customer opinion. This can be valuable to understand for strategic direction, or to explain the shifts in customer behaviour.

Online forums

Online forums are great ways to capture qualitative market insights, as it's possible to view current conversations and comments or conduct your own research. Online forums can be paid or unpaid, and can cover multiple topics simultaneously. Participants may be encouraged to share views on topics chosen by the forum organizer or put forward by other participants. Online forums in the business world can be found according to role, specialism or industry, but can also be according to themes.

Some examples of online business forums are Procurious for purchasing functions, Spiceworks for IT decision makers, SERMO for physicians and healthcare practitioners, building.co.uk for the UK construction industry and LexBlog's Reach for lawyers.

Surveys and polls

Surveys can come in various forms on various channels, such as mobile surveys, interview-based, in-depth, email-based surveys, polls and progressive polls, among others. The idea of the survey is to create a series of questions you need answering, and then choose the best and most suitable channels to carry out the survey.

Tools which could be used here include Key Survey and SoGoSurvey.

Customer data management

Behind good-quality customer insights is good-quality data and customer data management. Is your data clean? Is it complete and current? It may be good to remember the 3Cs of customer data management:

- **Clean:** this means lacking any information which may distort analysis. In B2B marketing, the wrong type of organizations or companies may have been filed in a certain category or duplicate records kept. Cleanliness of data allows for better segmentation later if needed.

- **Complete:** do customer records include the all key information, eg email address and phone number? Is the project information detailed? For marketing efforts, crucial information includes social media addresses and specific forms of media they use. Are there any critical information gaps?

- **Current:** how recent is the data? What percentage of the information is from the past year or from previous years? Would updates be beneficial?

Data for marketing

As mentioned, one of the keys to extracting insights is quality data. With digital technologies and the internet, we're seeing more and more information and potentially more data we need to capture and use. Data 'analytics' is the key word rather than data 'capture'; we can capture tons of data, but sorting is the issue.

In marketing there are lots of different types of data we're interested in: internal, external, personal, account-level, sector data and so on. According to the insights methods, we can sort this into opinion-based data, behavioural data, account data, etc.

Types of data in marketing

There are a number of types of data covering individual personal data, organizational data, transaction data, behavioural data and descriptive data, as illustrated in Figure 5.2.

Individual data (internal)

When collecting internal data, we're trying to assemble a complete view of a customer or customers. You may also be trying to understand the views of a buying unit by pooling data from different decision makers in a target account.

In terms of individual data, we're referring to name, postal code, telephone, email address, social network address etc, job information, and anything pertinent which could be used in later marketing activities.

Transaction data (company)

Transaction data would include number of products or services purchased, frequency of purchase, trends in purchase, and seasonality patterns. In the software space, you would also benefit from understanding subscription types, frequency, and breadth of subscription. This data can be found in company records, and is easier to analyse if captured via a CRM applications such as Salesforce or Microsoft Dynamix.

Behavioural data

This could be online activity specific to the account or individual: website visits, product views, online registrations or social network activity. Behavioural online data can be captured by identifying customers through cookie ID or IP address, but of course there's always the option to create a separate customer website and provide password and ID numbers; in this way, the customer activity can be more easily tracked and managed.

Behavioural data can be used to help improve content on the site, to understand which areas or pages are viewed and for how long, or just to get to grips with whether customers use the online areas.

Descriptive data

This is data that describes the individual and is used to gain a fuller perspective of the customer. Descriptive data includes age, geography, income, and preferences towards product categories. Having such data will allow you to create a persona and target them in different ways, and will also help with segmentation strategies.

Qualitative data

Qualitative data can be used to give context to a customer's potential behaviour through questionnaires. We can also understand opinions, sentiments, motivations, etc. In essence we're interested in understanding pain points, but also in capturing the positive engagements or touchpoints with the company.

Interaction data

Interaction data, sometimes called engagement data, includes clicks, downloads and browsing activities from websites and can help companies understand whether their content marketing is working and engaging

FIGURE 5.2 Types of data

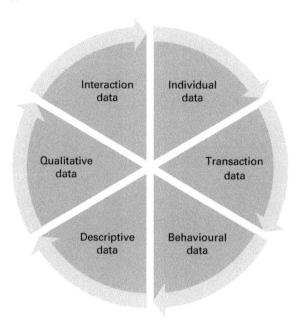

prospects. Low engagement levels may point towards poorly placed content or poor-quality content.

Within web pages, engagement data can help organizations understand which keywords or key phrases are working and help them optimize content further.

Data analytics

Data analytics comes in different forms, which can be seen on an evolving scale starting with descriptive analytics, progressing through to prescriptive analytics as per Figure 5.3.

Descriptive analytics is exactly as it sounds; it describes something which has already taken place. Diagnostic analytics dives more into the detail as to why something happened, by conducting a diagnosis through analytics.

As we move to predictive analytics, this is about forecasting something in the future based on analytics. Prescriptive analytics is about taking into consideration possible scenarios, historical and current performances to prescribe the best way forward.

FIGURE 5.3 Types of data analytics

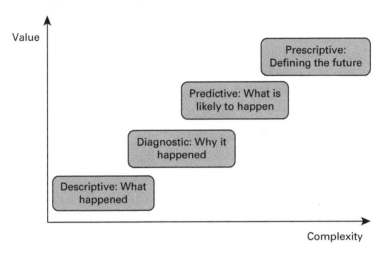

CASE STUDY
Tinuiti and data-driven marketing

One company which has experience in data and data analytics is Tinuiti. Tinuiti is North America's largest independent performance and data-driven digital marketing agency. They turned to Tableau and its product Tableau Prep to improve data management, analytics and reporting.

Through Tableau they were able to get an overview of their channel-level data in one place, as well as reducing staff time spent on working and analysing data by around 60 per cent.

Tinuiti uses Tableau to draw data from different digital channels to create customized dashboard views for its customers; in this way, customers can see the full story of their brand efforts.

As well reducing time and improving outputs for clients, Tinuiti could provide single-view dashboards for hundreds of its clients, whilst transitioning to a fully automated and scalable marketing analytics platform in less than 14 months.

EXERCISE
Put it into practice

1 Review the forms of qualitative and quantitative customer insight methods, and consider which ones you're using today.
2 Note down your main gaps today in customer insights, and from the insight methods identify which ones are most suitable for bridging those gaps.

References

Clarke, T (2019) [accessed 1 August 2019] 22+ Instagram Stats That Marketers Can't Ignore This Year, *Hootsuite* [online] https://blog.hootsuite.com/instagram-statistics/ (archived at https://perma.cc/KK78-XLHT)

West, C (2019) [accessed 09 November 2019] 17 Instagram stats marketers need to know for 2019, *Sprout Social* [online] https://sproutsocial.com/insights/instagram-stats/ (archived at https://perma.cc/5WY4-U8SG)

Further reading

Baird, F (2018) [accessed 1 August 2019] LinkedIn Analytics: The Complete Guide for Marketers, *Hootsuite* [online] https://blog.hootsuite.com/linkedin-analytics/ (archived at https://perma.cc/3B2G-HBNN)

Brence, T (2016) [accessed 1 August 2019] Customer Data Decay: Why Your Contact Data is Rotten, *Informatica* [online] https://blogs.informatica.com/2016/08/03/customer-data-decay-why-your-contact-data-is-rotten/#fbid=O4FlJ7ghyhP (archived at https://perma.cc/VK3K-59NC)

Information Commissioner's Office (2019) [accessed 1 August 2019] Alistar Green Legal Services Limited, *ICO* [online] https://ico.org.uk/action-weve-taken/enforcement/alistar-green-legal-services-limited-mpn/ (archived at https://perma.cc/3NRK-VTL8)

Spacey, J (2017) [accessed 1 August 2019] 9 Types of Marketing Data, *Simplicable* [online] https://simplicable.com/new/marketing-data (archived at https://perma.cc/R76K-JXQ9)

The early buyer journey stage

Through digital marketing approaches and technologies, B2B marketers have a greater ability than ever before to identify, target and engage customers in the early buyer journey stage. Part Two covers the main areas of marketing and marketing channels in this early stage, outlining key frameworks, methods and technologies which B2B marketers can avail themselves of.

We'll be looking at the different forms of B2B digital advertising as well as advertising targeting and retargeting. We'll also cover aspects of PR and influencer marketing, as well as the topic of content syndication.

Following that, we'll look at how search engine marketing can be applied to the early buyer journey stage and how a B2B marketer should apply SEO. Finally, we'll look at the role of the website, website design and different B2B website strategies.

06

Generating awareness

WHAT YOU WILL GAIN FROM THIS CHAPTER

After reading this chapter, you will understand:

- how to understand the right channels to use in the early buyer stage;
- the main B2B digital advertising forms;
- the different types of B2B digital ad targeting;
- how social media can be used to advertise;
- how public relations can be used to support awareness objectives.

Introduction

We saw in the previous chapter the importance of a more detailed under-standing of customers in terms of organizations as well as decision makers. This is possible through good data management, as well as through customer insights.

One of the key insights relating to customer buying behaviour from the past decade is the shift in how they research information and self-educate throughout the majority of the buyer journey without direct interaction with vendors. With this in mind, there is a need to think about all the ways to indirectly communicate, influence and help customers in the early buyer journey.

FIGURE 6.1 Indirect marketing channels

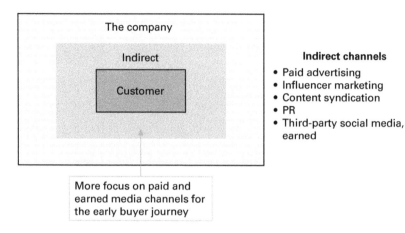

At this stage, we can use Figure 6.1 to understand where the indirect channels sit. These are channels which prospects engage with and use, and are typically not a company's owned media properties. We'll therefore look at the following marketing channels to support this goal: advertising, PR, influencer marketing and content syndication as well as social media channels.

In essence we're interested in helping prospects by providing our information or content in exactly those areas that customers are using.

Remember that customers often don't make direct contact or interact with prospective vendors early in the buyer journey. So, without directly interacting with prospects, we need to see how we influence and market to them using indirect approaches.

With digital marketing and technologies, we now have the ability to influence and shape all awareness sources. We could influence suppliers or other networks by engaging with influencers; we could also influence trends and discussions through thought leadership by posting content on professional networks.

The early buying journey stage

Defining awareness and the early buyer journey stage

As mentioned, the very first part of the buyer journey stage is need recognition. In terms of prospects recognizing a need, this can be prompted by different internal or external influences. Below are the main scenarios which highlight needs:

- Awareness influence 1: The buyer becomes aware of a need for something as a result of internal business inputs and influences, eg evolving business needs as the business grows.
- Awareness influence 2: The buyer becomes aware of a need through external business-related aspects, eg influenced by suppliers, as a result of competition.
- Awareness influence 3: The buyer becomes aware of a need or problem to solve through external market environmental influences, eg hearing about trends, or hearing about a new technology which will improve business efficiencies.
- Awareness influence 4: The buyer becomes aware of a need due to reading about something through one of their online channels.

What is not as easy for B2B marketers to define is the original source or trigger in the need recognition step of the buyer journey. In most of the above situations, these influences could be due to the buyer being on the receiving end of clever content marketing, advertising or awareness-based marketing.

So, as B2B digital marketers we're interested in what level of awareness we can create around our brand, products and services and to what extent we can influence the above scenarios.

Awareness starting points

So, one of the questions you might be asking is: where can I start identifying the best ways to generate awareness of our organization and its products and services with our target customers?

To answer this, we could use the awareness marketing mix, or 5Cs of awareness as per Figure 6.2.

The first 'C' stands for 'customer profile' and understanding our customers, assuming we've defined clearly our target customer segment. The second 'C' is the customer journey, where ideally, we try to have a view of the customer journey in the awareness stage.

The third 'C is communicated messages: which messages resonate with the customer, and what we can deliver in terms of messages which either answer any potential challenges or concerns or simply catch their attention.

The fourth 'C' – channel mix – refers to marketing communication channels which could be used to generate awareness in the B2B space and are

FIGURE 6.2 The 5Cs of the awareness marketing mix

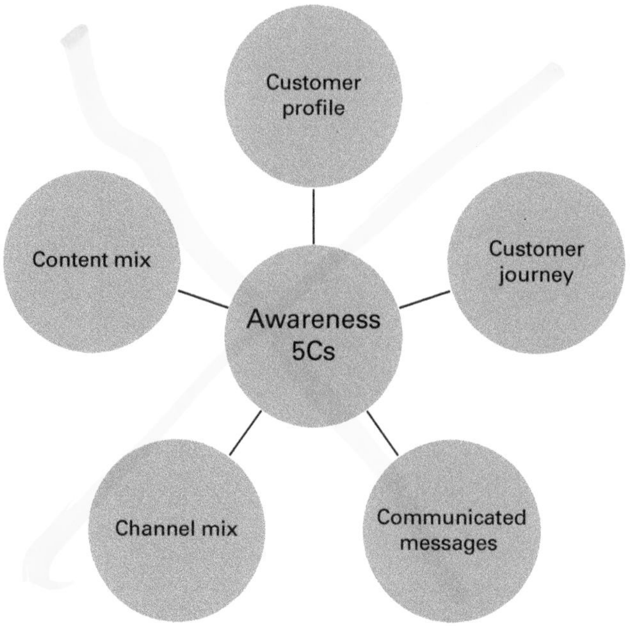

mapped to the early buyer journey. Digital awareness channels include the range of digital advertising, including advertising targeting and retargeting, SEO, online PR, content syndication, and influencer marketing.

As you go deeper in understanding how to select channels, you could look at whether to use outbound and inbound channels or a mix of them. In terms of outbound and inbound, outbound awareness channels include direct mail and outbound emails. Inbound awareness channels can include mediums such as blogging, social media and SEO.

Finally, the fifth 'C' is about getting the content mix right. This involves selecting the appropriate content formats for this stage of the buyer journey – for example, certain content formats such as video and banner advertising would be more suitable, whilst others such as SlideShare would work less well.

B2B digital advertising

Digital advertising has become a more powerful tool than ever for B2B marketing due to the way it allows you to understand, respond to and target prospects.

There are a number of differences compared to traditional advertising. Although in both you pay for space, in digital advertising there are a number of other factors which can be controlled and managed, such as where the advert is displayed, how it is displayed and who should see the advert. Unlike with traditional advertising, the advantage with digital advertising is that you are able to track performance in terms of clicks, impressions and many other metrics.

B2B display advertising

Display advertising means advertising on websites and social media, and usually comes in the forms of banners, although other formats such as video, audio and images can be used. They are generally not native adverts – they are very visibly adverts, rather than appearing aligned to the context, tone and format of the page

The role of display advertising is to deliver content and messages to prospects, and is not something invested in on its own, but should be part of a suite of advertising.

Display adverts come in a huge variety of forms, and there is really no law on what works. Display adverts in B2B become interesting, as through digital technologies and analytics it's possible to know in real time which products and services prospects are interested in. It therefore also allows B2B marketers to focus in on products and services and key needs met through them, and to respond to online behaviours quickly.

To talk about how this could work in practice, let's take a purchasing manager who regularly visits purchasing community websites or resources focused on improving purchasing department efficiencies. With the needs of this group being quite specific, one option would be to target those sites or online communities with display ads. The conversion rates would likely be a lot higher than generic ads to a generic business target.

In this way, it would be possible to understand the direct impact of display advertising.

Advertising targeting

Another way to think about display advertising is that it allows a better focus of advertising. For instance, understanding where the competition is displaying their ads can inform your strategy, assuming they're doing all the right things.

Under display advertising targeting we can consider five key aspects or dimensions as per the display pentagon in Figure 6.3. We can use display advertising contextually; that is, in relation to what prospects are reading or viewing, or by theme where we display adverts relating to the topic or topics being presented. We can also conduct display advertising according to prospects' needs – by understanding the needs of customers, we can advertise in those spaces where those aspects are talked about, or retarget customers who have looked those types of key phrases.

We could also look at particular interests or topics of interest for the prospects and display adverts aligned to such interests, and finally we can advertise according to the location of prospects.

Of the display advertising technologies, one of the most well-known is the Google Display Network (GDN), which can be used to target display ads in a variety of ways. When using GDN, in terms of getting the most out of your budget there is a difference between automatic placements, where you release the power to Google as to where to display ads, and managed placements, where you choose the sites, videos and apps for your ads to appear on.

Alternatives to GDN are Choozle DSP, DBM, Mediamath, and Trade Desk.

FIGURE 6.3 Advertising targeting types

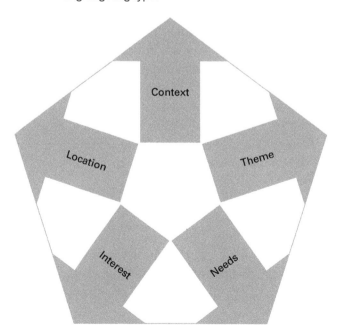

B2B native advertising

Another way to advertise is through native advertising, so called as the content or information advertised appears 'native' to the page and doesn't stick out as an obvious advert. It comes in different scales of implementation: in its purest form, it matches the style, font and presentation of the editorial content on the page. Often, it is difficult to see that it is advertising, apart from a small piece of text next to it which may say 'sponsored by'. There are other forms which are native in terms of the theme or content, as well as font, but are more visible.

Native advertising is not advertising in the traditional sense. Print advertorials are a form of native advertising, which sit alongside the main text. The digital equivalents are usually short pieces of text or a few paragraphs, with a link to a page where you can read more about the topic in question.

Forms of native advertising include paid social where the ads look like the other posts on the same page. LinkedIn sponsored ads or Twitter ads are forms of native advertising.

Native advertising works because when it is done well, it is informative, entertaining and strongly targeted, and isn't interruptive in nature.

SELECTING NATIVE ADVERTISING PLATFORMS

There are different B2B platforms which can be used to conduct native advertising. One starting point to select the right channel is to understand whether the intended platform has the right design, tone, message for you and is used by your target customers.

For example, one could use LinkedIn or Facebook and use native ads, though native advertising on LinkedIn is regarded as 277 per cent more effective than Facebook or Twitter (Boyce, 2014). Saying that, watch out for relevancy, as the use of LinkedIn vs Facebook for B2B depends on your industry. For example, if you're a gym equipment manufacturer, than Facebook ads or Instagram ads could be more effective due to the topic and platform.

Also consider the content you're creating and whether this is relevant; irrelevant content posted as native adverts will only lead to suboptimal results. Also note that native ads generate 18 per cent higher intent to purchase and a significant increase in targeted brand exposure (Boyce, 2015).

B2B mobile advertising

B2B mobile advertising has become increasingly used and adopted by B2B marketers. Smartphones are being used more and more, mobile applications and the technologies have matured and mobile advertising has become more sophisticated to suit.

One point mentioned in the first chapter is the mobility of the workforce, the fragmentation of workdays and remote working, which have meant that accessing customers at definable times has become more difficult. This is where mobile advertising can help circumvent these challenges: the smartphone is the one device we have with us almost all time.

There are a number of advantages of B2B mobile advertising, the first being immediacy. You can engage people quickly if the right prospects are targeted with the right message. It provides the ability to reach an audience which other media may not be able to reach, and there are also typically higher engagement rates with mobile advertising; open rates on SMS are much higher than on emails.

Among the different types of mobile advertising, mobile video advertising can be particularly powerful in engaging prospects. Mobile video ad spending in B2B has grown 111 per cent in the last five years (Cohen, 2018). Videos can deliver much richer experiences, and the use of video allows users to more easily digest content. Mobile video ads can be run as standalone or as part of other videos, eg running at the end and start of YouTube videos.

Mobile advertising also comes in the form of gamified mobile advertising, using game concepts and mechanics to engage users and encourage a higher response. The final form I'll mention here is native mobile advertising, similar to what has been mentioned before, but targeting mobile devices or smartphones.

B2B paid search advertising

As with SEO, one of the main success factors behind paid search is identifying the right keywords and phrases.

Other key success factors in paid search are based on the following:

- in-depth knowledge of the audience;
- adverts including key concerns, pain points and challenges;
- identifying top interests/passions;
- ensuring there is a link between paid search advertising and destinations for the paid search traffic.

In this way it is important to ensure landing pages or pages for destination traffic are relevant in tone and content to the paid search advertisements. As B2B marketing is very much rooted in the early stage of the buyer journey, these landing pages for search-based traffic need to be awareness-based content and not focused on lead-based calls to action. Pages should engage, educate and help prospects.

PRACTICAL TIP

Keywords – who selects and bids on them

Within your company take a look at who selects the keywords and key phrases, and who decides on search bidding. Look at their experience and background, thinking of those making decisions on search terms; this should typically be someone who has an understanding of what the right keywords and key phrases are, using insights around the customer and their journey.

Where the bidding on search terms is outsourced to agencies or separate central marketing teams, those agencies or teams need to be receiving the right briefs about keywords and terms. If they aren't privy to the specific terms and phrases on which B2B campaign marketers are focusing, they could be missing the opportunity to bid on long-tail keywords, and as a result wasting budget.

Types of advertisement targeting

We now know the main types of digital advertising. The next stage is to understand how to effectively implement these. One way is through advertising targeting (or ad targeting for short) which means focusing efforts on specific audiences or prospective buyers.

Let's look at some forms of ad targeting for B2B marketing.

Search engine-based

This is a form of targeting where online advertisements are placed on web pages as a result of search queries. Search engine marketing uses search engines to target different audiences, where adverts are displayed based on high user intent. This is a form of targeting based on keywords and key phrases relating to specific stages in the buyer journey.

The search network approach can be useful if you're using product or services-based search as a basis to reach customers.

Context-based targeting/content targeting

Contextual targeting is when brands place ads in a specific area based on the relevant content already displayed. This targeting method can work across channels. Native advertising is a form of contextual advertising, where sponsored ads are designed to look like the native content on a website.

Here's how it works: a crawler scans the web and categorizes pages based on context and content. As a user visits a page, the ad server is able to display relevant ads matching for keywords and content.

Contextual targeting is also used to determine the main subject, or theme, of a website, and place thematically relevant ads on the page.

Geographical and location-based targeting

Geographical targeting involves targeting users based on location or geography. Geographical targeting can be useful in different situations; for example, where you want to display ads to customers who are attending a trade event where you have a stand.

You can also use geo-targeting if you're wanting to focus your marketing efforts by region.

Behavioural targeting

Behavioural targeting takes into account the activities of users: if a customer is frequently looking for a notebook, the targeting system could pick this up and start promoting notebook offers.

When a customer views a website, analytics data such as pages per visit, amount of time on site, links clicked on and searches they make are all captured. The most engaged customers can then be served ads relating to their website behaviours.

Account-based advertising

Account-based advertising works in a similar way to geo-targeting but uses IP addresses. Typically an organization will be using an IP address across all its employees, which means you can target all employees at once.

As you can target and adapt messages by account, this method is interesting for B2B marketers as it can also be tied into your overall account-based marketing strategies.

PRACTICAL TIP
Ad targeting KPIs

Selecting B2B audience targeting platforms goes a long way towards supporting the success of advertising targeting. Some considerations are:

- Data quality: ensuring the platform you're selecting has a good set of data. For example, if you need to target specialists within an industry, check if the advertising platform has the ability to target such specialists.

- Data accuracy: having complete and specific data. Is the data up to date and is it complete?

- Integration: you'll want to be sure that your B2B audience targeting tool is compatible with your ad network of choice.

PRACTICAL TIP
Setting up ad targeting activities

Depending on which type of ad targeting you opt for, you can set up ad targeting in different ways.

Contextual or content targeting can be carried out using GDN. You could also use LinkedIn and Facebook. Search engine-based ad targeting can be implemented using the search engine's own applications such as Google, Bing or Yahoo!.

Geo-targeting can be carried out using social media platforms' geographical functions built into their promotional or advertising offerings; it can also be carried out using GDN. One could use Workstream or Google AdWords to do keyword targeting, and behavioural targeting can be implemented through social networks such as Twitter or Personyze.

All of these are summarized in Table 6.1 below.

TABLE 6.1 Ad targeting and applications

Targeting type	Technologies
Contextual or content targeting	GDN, LinkedIn, Facebook
Search-based targeting	Google, Bing, Yahoo!
Geo-targeting	GDN, LinkedIn, Facebook
Behavioural targeting	Twitter

B2B social media advertising

Many social media platforms have matured in the past 10 years, to the extent that they are end-to-end marketing platforms in themselves, encompassing a wide portfolio of advertising options and functionality to support generating awareness for a brand.

In Chapter 18 we'll look at how some of the platforms have developed and some of the aspects you should be considering for your awareness strategies. The main advertising platforms for B2B include Twitter, LinkedIn, Instagram, Facebook and YouTube.

Selecting advertising channels

So how do we go about selecting the right approach to advertise or to generate awareness?

We understand that the main forms of digital advertising are display, native, social media, mobile and search. If we start to break down the advertising forms, some of these are more push-based (or more outbound) ads such as display, whereas others are more pull-based (or more inbound) such as search advertising or even native, where the adverts and content are influenced by input from the prospect – either in terms of the search term used or by the type of content they are reading.

We should also consider that the advertising forms are not mutually exclusive, and one prospect may interact with both push-based and pull-based advertising in the early buyer stage.

As we start to summarize, the key considerations are as follows:

1 buyer persona relevance: using those channels or media which are more relevant to the buyer persona;

2 resonance: this might be where a buyer persona uses multiple forms of advertising, and therefore we're interested in selecting channels based on the interaction and engagement rates of adverts;

3 cost: as advertising is all paid, this is more about looking at cost in absolute terms across channels and per advertising channel;

4 goal: this will depend on the goal of the original advertising campaign, eg to reach, to reach specific prospects or to educate.

Ad retargeting

Retargeting is the process of targeting online advertising to prospects who visited your website or are in your database due to previous online actions. Although very much born in B2C around ecommerce, remarketing can be applied well to B2B.

Retargeting is fairly cost-effective as it means engaging potential customers who have already engaged with your own website or other media content.

There are five types of retargeting, as follows.

Search retargeting

Search retargeting comes in two forms. The first is based on the intent of the user and the keywords captured, and the categories which are used in the background to help support the retargeting strategy. The second form of search retargeting is based on search terms used on third-party sites.

Pixel-based retargeting

Pixel-based retargeting is sometimes called cookie-based retargeting. The general process of how it works is that someone visits your website and is tagged with a retargeting cookie. They'll then start to see your ads on different sites, and as they click on your ad they come back to your site.

With retargeting you're trying to get that second chance of drawing them back to you or reminding them about you as an organization.

List-based retargeting

List-based retargeting uses email contact lists that you upload of prospective or current customers. Lists are uploaded to a platform, and then those platforms identify people with that email address and show ads to them. LinkedIn and Facebook offer list-based targeting.

Static and dynamic ad retargeting

Static retargeting creates a number of formats related to a marketing programme. The idea is that you set criteria for the ads people should see, based on the web pages they visit. Dynamic ad retargeting is more personalized to content that is viewed; eg where a prospect views product A, they then receive ads based on product A.

Platforms to use

Retargeting is possible using specific retargeting software such as AdRoll, but can also be carried out through using social media network platforms such as Twitter, LinkedIn and Facebook. Google also offers a retargeting function through their GDN/AdWords application.

B2B content syndication channels

Content syndication channels are another way to reach prospects without direct interaction. Content syndication is the act of re-distributing content on third-party sites, where the third-party sites are the channels. Almost any form of content can be and is syndicated. Content forms include articles, blogs, recordings, reports, case studies and many more.

The goal of content syndication is to reach a larger group of prospective customers. The third-party channels have a wider reach to new customers, and sometimes have an established relationship with who you want to reach.

Content syndication's main benefit is the ability to reach prospects through specific channels or platforms, through engaging platforms and partners who syndicate the content. This can also reinforce the credibility of the content. Other associated benefits include improved reach, improved exposure and ultimately an increase in quality traffic to the website.

Ways to syndicate content

There are different ways to syndicate content. Selection of the content syndication route will depend on your goals. Where those goals involve the building of brand awareness, the content will need to educate customers, and will be very specific to that audience.

If, however, the goal is to increase visitors to your website, you may want to select third-party sites with a larger audience, and the content that is syndicated may feature more link building.

CASE STUDY
Techtarget

TechTarget has a membership of 19 million globally and amongst many other things they offer IT vendors the opportunity to syndicate their content on the TechTarget site. For members, the benefit is reaching and acquiring prospects using the TechTarget channel, as well as potentially generating additional traffic and interest to the IT vendors' owned media properties.

TechTarget benefits from offering a wider variety of content whilst monetizing their online real estate.

PR and online PR

PR is about building relations, which is the largely the same for B2B and B2C marketing. However, there are a number of other roles for B2B PR; these include content creation, messaging and positioning, reputation management, supporting product/service launches, market research, story-telling, social media, and thought leadership. Some of these latter aspects differ very much between B2B and B2C PR.

PR has gone through a transition over the past 10 years to involve new approaches such as storytelling, blogging, social-based PR and sustainability initiatives.

Creating content through PR

Content creation is becoming an integral part of PR, from displaying your expertise on your own blog to creating guest posts for trade publications. B2B PR agencies are seeing a growing need for content creation in order to support their PR strategy.

PR agencies or departments can support B2B marketers greatly in finding new content creation opportunities, whether this is setting up a round table, identifying themes and writers, setting a PR event or identifying new topics for a storytelling initiative.

Thought leadership

Thought leadership is very much an area of B2B marketing, and involves becoming a trusted go-to authority on topics. Successfully establishing thought leadership involves ensuring articles are placed correctly offline and online, promoting to the right audience, arranging speaking engagements, and monitoring the quality of the content.

Understanding perception

PR can help businesses and their marketing departments by monitoring trends and keeping an eye on customer sentiment through industry blogs, social media, newsletters, search engines and news feeds.

PRACTICAL TIP
PR research

Why not get your PR agency or go-to person to conduct some initial research to help you with your marketing? Some of the questions could be:

- What social networks do my prospects use?
- What trade shows do they frequent?
- Which trade publications do they read?
- What influencers are most likely to reach my prospects?
- What blogs, news media sites, and other websites do prospects frequent?
- What groups, networks and forums do they use?

Influencer marketing

Fierce competition in the B2B digital marketing domain has led to a drastic increase in the cost of paid advertising. Consequently, many B2B marketers are looking to influencer marketing to enrich their brand image and generate leads.

Influencer marketing identifies individuals who have influence over potential buyers and orients marketing activities around them and their platforms in order to leverage their influence.

The idea of using influencers to market a product or service is not new. Most consumer commercials include influencers (professional athletes, movie stars and so on), though most B2B marketing budgets are not sufficient to cover the costs of such influencers. Fortunately, these media personalities may not be the most suitable to influence business customers in their buying decisions or process. In the B2B space there are influencers with a smaller reach, but a significant influence over a very specific set of target customers.

Most B2B purchases are based on word-of-mouth recommendations. Research reveals that a whopping 91 per cent of B2B purchases are influenced by genuine recommendations and referrals (Ferguson, 2019).

Influencer marketing programmes have been known to generate 11 times higher ROI than other forms of marketing (Grin, 2018).

For B2B marketing, benefits also include:

- reaching customers that might not have been found otherwise;
- increased exposure;
- improved reach.

Types of B2B influencers

An influencer is a person who is well connected, and who is looked to for advice, direction, knowledge and opinions. Their recommendations are trusted by their audience, and therefore can impact the awareness of a brand or product.

There are five types of influencers that business buyers may be impacted by:

- peers who are regarded as leaders in their field;
- market analysts for a subject area or market;
- magazine writers or journalists;
- specialists in a field who are regarded as experts by customers;
- bloggers in a particular subject field.

THOUGHT LEADERSHIP AND INFLUENCERS

Research has shown that almost 100 per cent of B2B companies are interested in more content from industry thought leaders (Masek-Kelly, 2018). Other research shows that industry experts are the main source convincing prospects to purchase from B2B organizations. So, having a thought leadership programme which involves industry experts is probably a great next move. Thought leadership can help in a number of ways, including building brand equity and invoking trust.

Part of the thought leadership programme should include providing timely, quality content on a regular basis. Thought leadership content can also involve research which is unique and original, providing statistics about business experiences from surveys or research.

Aside from building relationships through thought leadership content, social media can be used to retain customers to build communities.

How to get started on social media

The first step in influencer marketing is to identify the influencers for your top target customers. You can do this by following some of your typical customers and seeing which influencers they follow, share and like in terms of content. You can also conduct a short poll or survey, and use this as part of your buyer persona.

Once influencers have been identified, the next stage is engagement. This could involve following influencers, sharing their content, posting content to them, or engaging them directly and inviting them to be part of your marketing activities.

Aside from the contact approach through social media, one could also use dedicated influencing digital technologies such as Socialbakers, Sideqik, Cision and Traackr.

CASE STUDY
Enterprise Holdings and Reuters: Content hub

Enterprise Holdings – through its integrated global network of independent regional subsidiaries and franchises – operates the Enterprise Rent-A-Car, National Car Rental and Alamo Rent A Car brands at more than 10,000 fully staffed neighbourhood and airport locations in more than 95 countries.

For the purpose of this case study, we'll be concentrating on the Enterprise and National brands, and their focus on serving business rental customers.

Recently Enterprise Holdings collaborated with international news organization Reuters. This was a logical partnership as Enterprise's B2B audience, which includes procurement/mobility managers and C-suite executives, are frequent users of Reuters and its content. As a result of this partnership, Enterprise Holdings was able to showcase its messages to a key audience through Reuters Plus, the branded content studio of Reuters.

The focus of the initiative was to create a content hub which would be housed on the Reuters Plus platform. This hub would house videos to enable Enterprise to reach new audiences, increasing awareness and consideration for the Enterprise and National car rental brands. These videos would reach prospects, who are business rental decision makers, in the early phase of their buyer journey. The content hub not only generated exposure, but also allowed Enterprise Holdings to view engagement of prospects through such metrics as dwell time and page views.

Through the partnership with Reuters, three main videos were created with a pan-European focus and promoted in the countries where Enterprise has wholly owned operations – the United Kingdom, Ireland, Germany, France and Spain. Reuters promoted the video content through LinkedIn, Twitter and GDN. The three main themes delivered through the video content were global mobility, technology/innovation and customer service, with each video running for three minutes.

The success of the programme was measured by impressions and clicks. The campaign guaranteed at least 750K impressions and overdelivered in this metric. The target figure for clicks was 6–8K; however, more than 10K clicks were achieved while the content hub was actively being promoted from 27 November to 31 December 2018.

The activity via Twitter was of particular interest – where clickthrough rates are typically between 1.5 to 2 per cent, the average Twitter clickthrough rate for the Enterprise/National content was 3.84 per cent, and more than 9K overall clicks came through to the content hub via that channel.

Interesting to note is that for prospects in Spain, the time spent on the content hub was one of the highest, driving nearly 3K unique users to their website. France also was particularly high at just over 1,500 unique users of the video content.

The video content is still being hosted online and continues to be used by the sales team from Enterprise Holdings to engage prospects. Enterprise was also able to leverage the content through their own LinkedIn channels, and encouraged employees to share via their personal social pages to further increase the exposure and impact of the videos that were developed.

EXERCISE
Put it into practice

1 Review the different forms of advertising targeting. Which ones do you think would be most suitable for your company to use, and why?
2 Influencer marketing is gaining in importance in B2B marketing to reach and generate awareness with customers. Which influencers are you using today? If none, which influencers do you think would be the best to use, and why?

References

Boyce, K (2014) [accessed 1 August 2019] Your Go-To Guide To Getting Ahead With B2B Native Advertising, *B2B Marketing* [online] www.b2bmarketing.net/en-gb/resources/blog/your-go-guide-getting-ahead-b2b-native-advertising (archived at https://perma.cc/L767-XXHM)

Boyce, K (2015) [accessed 1 August 2019] Digital Ad Decisions: Native Content Advertising Vs Paid Social Media, *B2B Marketing* [online] www.b2bmarketing.net/en-gb/resources/blog/digital-ad-decisions-native-content-advertising-vs-paid-social-media (archived at https://perma.cc/79LA-UGSG)

Cohen, T (2018) [accessed 10 November 2019] 4 Ways B-to-B Marketers Should Be Using Mobile Video, *AdWeek* [online] www.adweek.com/digital/4-ways-B2B-marketers-should-be-using-mobile-video/ (archived at https://perma.cc/CF6P-BWRD)

Ferguson, T (2019) [accessed 10 November 2019] The Ultimate Guide to Creating a Winning B2B Influencer Marketing Strategy, *Spiralytics* [online] https://blog.spiralytics.com/winning-B2B-influencer-marketing-strategy (archived at https://perma.cc/F63T-DK79)

Grin (2018) [accessed 10 November 2019] 15 B2B Influencer Marketing Case Studies, *Grin* [online] https://grin.co/blog/15-great-examples-of-B2B-influencer-marketing-that-prove-it-works/ (archived at https://perma.cc/JZ3H-FMYD)

Masek-Kelly, E (2018) [accessed 10 November 2019] How to Use Social Media to Build Thought Leadership, *Social Media Today* [online] www.socialmediatoday.com/news/how-to-use-social-media-to-build-thought-leadership/542035/ (archived at https://perma.cc/9W9Q-NBM6)

Further reading

Ference, A (2017) [accessed 1 August 2019] How to Get Started with B2B Native Advertising, *Outbrain* [online] www.outbrain.com/blog/B2B-native-advertising/ (archived at https://perma.cc/8BZS-9UXE)

Gallant, J (2019) [accessed 1 August 2019] 48 Eye-Opening LinkedIn Statistics For B2B Marketers In 2019, *Foundation Inc* [online] https://foundationinc.co/lab/B2B-marketing-linkedin-stats/ (archived at https://perma.cc/V2FD-896V)

Nguyen, A (2015) [accessed 1 August 2019] The Complete Display Ads Overview For B2B Marketers, *Bizible* [online] www.bizible.com/blog/complete-display-ads-overview-for-B2B-marketers (archived at https://perma.cc/DEE7-TLVK)

Sterling, G (2017) [accessed 1 August 2019] 57% of traffic now from smartphones and tablets, *Searchengineland* [online] https://searchengineland.com/report-57-percent-traffic-now-smartphones-tablets-281150 (archived at https://perma.cc/AJ4D-R3B8)

Vivolo, J (2015) [accessed 1 August 2019] Why Mobile Advertising Is Critical for B2B Marketers, *KoMarketing* [online] https://komarketing.com/blog/mobile-advertising-critical-B2B-marketers/ (archived at https://perma.cc/JEL8-JHDG)

Vivolo, J (2018) [accessed 1 August 2019] What B2B advertisers need to know about GDN, *KoMarketing* [online] https://komarketing.com/blog/what-B2B-advertisers-need-to-know-about-google-display-network/ (archived at https://perma.cc/76ZX-QCCX)

07

B2B SEO and search strategies

WHAT YOU WILL GAIN FROM THIS CHAPTER

After reading this chapter, you will understand:

- B2B search engine marketing;
- keywords and key phrases;
- link building and link-building strategies;
- how to map keywords to the buyer journey;
- tools and technologies for search engine marketing;
- the main B2B SEM strategies.

Introduction

Defining B2B SEO and search

The official umbrella term relating to search engine optimization (SEO) and paid search is Search Engine Marketing (SEM). Essentially there are three core pillars to SEM, and they operate a little differently: paid search (or PPC advertising), on-page SEO and off-page SEO.

Paid search is often called pay-per-click advertising and was explored in the previous chapter. It is a form of advertising which is based on keywords and key phrases used within advertising campaign content. The focus of this chapter will be more on on-page and off-page SEO, and overall B2B search engine marketing.

SEO is about optimizing your website and activities outside your website to support the search activities of prospects and customers. As we'll see later in this chapter, one common thing underpins all areas of search engine marketing – understanding keywords.

Search and the relationship to the buyer journey

There are a lot of statistics to highlight that in the first stage of a buyer journey, a customer will conduct research. In these initial stages use of a search engine (s) may be one of the first steps. Pardot reports that 72 per cent of buyers turn to Google when researching products and solutions (Salesforce, n. d.).

Paid search and off-page search play a big role in this early stage. However, that's not to say that some elements of search or SEO are still not valuable in the mid-buyer journey stage or even in the late buying stage.

The role of search engine marketing in B2B

Search engine marketing has many roles in B2B. It can:

- increase visibility of products and services;
- generate awareness through PPC advertising and/or SEO;
- help create more authentic and relevant content;
- be used to understand customer intent by identifying keywords and phrases according to buyer journey stages and then using it as a guide.

B2B search engine marketing

B2B search engine marketing differs from that for B2C in the following ways:

- B2B typically involves selling more complex solutions and services than in B2C, and potentially the keywords are more specialized;
- B2B SEO is about serving multiple decision makers and not one buyer. Hence, understanding the target audience and their keyword preferences is key, as these might differ between different decision makers at the same target customer account.
- SEO in B2B needs to answer both tactical and technical questions as well as higher-level business-related questions.

Key differences in B2B search engine marketing lie in the goals of campaigns, with decision making processes in B2B typically taking much longer than in B2C marketing.

SEO activities can be a more interesting area to invest in in B2B, as the impact of SEO not only takes time to build, it doesn't halt immediately if SEO investments are cut or reduced. For example, if you stop bidding on keywords related to PPC advertising, then typically you would see an immediate drop-off in traffic related to PPC ads and keyword traffic; this is not usually the case with SEO.

B2B SEO

In B2B marketing, if your SEO focus is primarily about ranking on a Google page, then you're probably approaching things in the wrong way. Ranking tends to be the result of a good SEO strategy, but shouldn't be the starting point. Instead SEO is about authentic and relevant content which engages customers and attracts them to you. It's about bringing them to your website and providing them with the right answers.

By focusing on relevant content, keywords and overall navigation, all of which supports a great customer experience, you'll likely feature highly in ranking for more meaningful search queries and terms.

When people talk about SEO and websites, it can be confusing as some of the discussions overlap. However, there are key differences between overall website management and on-page SEO.

B2B off-page SEO

Off-page SEO means everything you're doing outside your website to drive traffic back to your site. Many factors contribute to successful off-page SEO; this includes link building, social media SEO-based strategy, and blogging.

When creating off-page SEO activities, social media can be a good starting point. Likes, followers and shares on Twitter, LinkedIn or Instagram can start to build awareness and credibility of the brand.

A company could set up their own blog, publish content there, and share it using social media channels. They could also place blog posts in third-party spaces with links back to the page. B2B marketers that use blogs receive 67 per cent more leads than those that do not (Sukhraj, 2019). Furthermore, blogs are proven to increase visits to your website, and get more pages indexed by search engines.

B2B on-page SEO

On-page SEO is about ensuring your website is optimized for those off-page search or SEO activities. It is about optimizing the site and individual pages to support search queries.

On-page SEO can be further divided into technical and non-technical aspects. Non-technical aspects include content on the page, use of keywords, or a keyword and key phrase mix whereas technical on-page SEO relates more to tagging and scannability.

Technical on-page SEO involves more behind-the-scenes activities. Tagging refers to labelling the different aspects on a webpage including in the title, description and heading. Title tags or 'meta' title tags help search engines in understanding what your page is about. The meta title tag essentially names your website or website page and provides that first impression people have of your page. Get it wrong, and this will impact potential customers clicking through to your page.

'Meta' description tags are key, as Google uses this information as part of the search algorithm; they convey what users will find on the page. That is to say, search engines read meta descriptions to determine the page's topic. Each page of your website should have relevant and searchable tags.

In terms of scannability, it's important to remember that users spend a short amount of time trying to find information before they land on what they're looking for. Headings and subheadings facilitate easier scanning and make the web page feel cleaner.

PRACTICAL TIP
B2B SEO and thought leadership

Because B2B searchers aren't likely to convert on their first visit, B2B SEO tends to be more about establishing the brand in the searcher's memory than getting them to make a purchase.

Another factor to consider is the visibility of SEO content, which can be boosted through thought leadership content. Use of subject matter experts can go a long way to improve findability and optimize the search process.

Keywords and key phrases

As mentioned, one of the common issues you need to understand across paid search and SEO is keywords and key phrases. Of particular interest for B2B marketers are ranking keywords which convert, rather than just the ranking of keywords themselves. By 'convert' in B2B, we're referring to prospects or customers performing an activity based on content or keywords.

Integrating keywords and key phrases into content

Once you've defined the keywords and key phrases for your specific target customer segment, you can look to include them in content. However, watch out for 'keyword stuffing' where web pages become overcrowded with keywords which dilute the sense of what you're trying to communicate.

Keyword stuffing will reduce the authenticity of the message and will only put customers off. It is also worth noting that keyword stuffing is not customer friendly and as a result Google has introduced updates to punish such practices.

The percentage of keywords or key phrases within content is known as keyword density. It is calculated as the number of times a keyword or key phrase appears on a page divided by the total number of words on that page. In B2B marketing, keyword density levels can be subjective; in essence, it comes down to authenticity of content and how it reads. The general consensus is to keep keyword density below 5 per cent, ideally around 2–3 per cent, though some articles might be fine with 10 per cent of the same keyword content.

Search categories

If you cast your thoughts to previous searches you've conducted, it's likely that the types of searches will have been different. For example, these searches could have been based on different motives or intent. In a similar manner, your B2B prospects will be searching with different intentions depending on what they're looking for, and according to their position in the buyer journey.

For example, customers can conduct brand-based searches where the specific brand or product name is used, competitor brand searches as they look into the different alternatives, category searches to understand the overall categories, or need-based searches rather than looking for a specific product.

If prospects are already searching the branded terms of a particular company, they'll probably be in the consideration stage.

The long tail of search in B2B

The long tail describes the relationship between the cost or competition for certain search terms against the frequency with which they are used. In Figure 7.1, there are three main sections to the shape of the curve: the fat head, the chunky middle and the long tail.

Fat head keywords are those with a high volume of traffic. This where you'll find the most popular keywords, which are paid for most often. The chunky middle and the long tail of the curve are where there are respectively less bidding and less volume in traffic.

Why pick keywords which generate less traffic?

Although there is a higher volume of traffic and you'll find more popular keywords in the fat head part of the curve, these may not be the best keywords to use for your organization. In particular, in B2B where industries cover specialist areas, there will be keywords or phrases that may be more particular and specific to your products and services.

As an example if your business is in the production and selling of notebooks, you might want to use 'notebook' which is probably a very common keyword with high bidding – ie, a fat head keyword. Alternatively,

FIGURE 7.1 The long tail

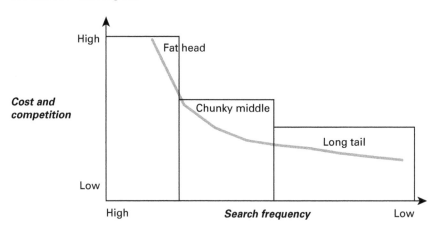

you could think about your focus customers and how they use notebooks more specifically, and generate keywords such as 'mobile workforce', 'mobile productivity' or 'mobile solutions', which might fall into the chunky middle or long-tail sections.

These long-tail keywords are interesting as they may say more about your product and services whilst at the same time resonating with your target audience.

'Target' is the key word to think of here, as you could generate volumes of traffic for popular keywords, but there are two things to consider. Firstly, you're fighting for airtime in a more crowded area, and secondly, you might be attracting prospects in the form of traffic which is not your target audience.

Finding long-tail keywords

We've covered how chunky middle keywords could be more interesting than fat head keywords and long-tail even better than that. But how do we identify long-tail keywords?

Here are a few ways to come up with long-tail keywords (summarized also in Figure 7.2):

- Using a detailed buyer persona: Assuming you have a detailed buyer persona, you could use this as a tool. What did they say as their major pain points and challenges, and what did they look for when searching for solutions? What did they like about other vendors or your company when searching? What keywords or key phrases were captured specifically?

- Identify intent: As mentioned previously, understanding what drives buyer intent will also help you identify key words and key phrases. It helps to clarify where to focus your SEO strategy, and especially the part of the buyer journey.

- Technology/software: Using various tools which can help provide similar words and phrases might also be a good start. Google Suggest, Similarweb, Google Trends and Keywordtool.io can help with the initial steps in looking for similar words or phrases.

- Forums: Look at the online and offline forums that your audience use to understand questions, phrases and terms they use.

- Social media: What are target customers liking and what comments are they making on social media?

- Surveys: Do a poll or survey with customers who are already buying from you to understand more about their concerns and challenges.

FIGURE 7.2 Finding long-tail keywords

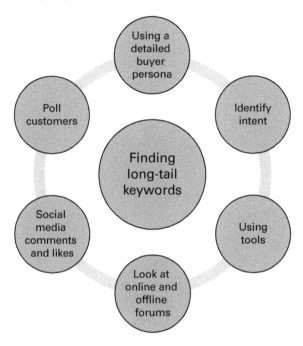

Keyword and competitor research

Researching competitor keywords is a very important part of search engine marketing, as it can help to shape the strategy for B2B.

Keyword research should be encompassing the entire website and not just the homepage. By looking at relevant keywords to use across different pages of your website, you can increase the possibility of ranking for different keywords in search engines.

Audience and keyword research

In selecting keywords you may need to think of general needs of different segments as multiple customers will land there. However, there may be particular audiences you're more interested in engaging. For these, it is a good idea to provide the ability to go to different parts of your website and tailor keywords for these pages accordingly.

Keywords and the buyer journey

Once keywords are identified for buyers, they need to be applied to your company's content. Keyword mapping is a key part of on-page SEO: it is the process of assigning relevant keywords to different pages on a company's website based on keyword research.

One way is to think about customers' intents at different stages of the buyer journey. Here is where PPC advertising and SEO tends to differ: PPC advertising is typically used in the early stage of the buyer journey, whereas SEO can be applied at all stages.

We can divide up intent according to what the customer is looking for. In a B2B context, the three stages of buyer journey can be broken and applied as follows:

- Early-stage buyer queries are focused on information, as the customer is seeking answers regarding their need or requirement.

- Mid-stage buyer queries are more for navigational purposes, ie where the prospect is looking for things more specifically to their queries. These queries can become brand related and vendor specific according to their product or service.

- Late-stage buyer journey queries are often purchase-based, sometimes called transactional queries. Prospective buyers are searching for specific products and information related to making the actual purchase.

We can see examples of generic keywords in Figure 7.3 according to the different query stages. These are not actual keywords, but descriptors of the types of keywords one could expect customers to use at different stages.

FIGURE 7.3 Keyword mapping

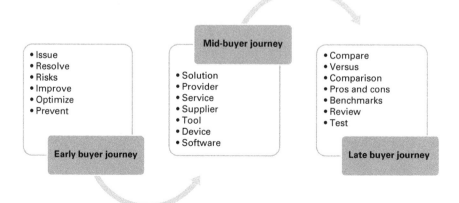

High intent and low intent

High intent keywords are those related to the late-stage buyer journey and purchase queries. Low intent keywords are based on early- and mid-stage buyer queries; that is, information and navigational queries.

Link building

In conversations about SEO you'll often hear the term 'link building'. Link building involves generating links from another website to yours. There are three main different types of link building – outreach, manual and content-based (sometimes called automatic or inbound link building).

Link building in B2B involves attracting the attention of a target audience or a link 'facilitator'. Facilitators include thought leaders, owners of websites and editors of online magazines.

The link-building process

As per Figure 7.4, the process for link building is as follows:

1 selecting the page on your website you want other websites to link to;

2 identifying the websites or types of websites that you want links from;

3 defining a link-building contact strategy for those websites – eg attracting them, directly engaging as per the strategies below;

4 implementing the contact strategy.

Link-building strategies

In B2B there are a number of strategies you can employ to improve your company's link building.

LINK THE EXPERTS

This is where you engage experts in your field or industry who are relevant to your customers and prospects. Bloggers need good relevant and unique content to draw in prospects – it should be a mutually beneficial relationship. One way to think about this is that you want to create a content distribution network or traffic attraction network by engaging bloggers.

FIGURE 7.4 The link-building process

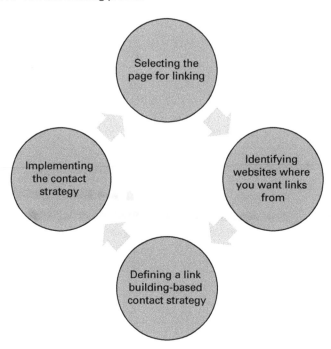

Experts who have their own blogs are the ones you want to engage to link back to your page or content. This can be done by directly contacting or engaging with them, or by providing and sharing content that links to their post so they can choose whether to link back to your site.

CUSTOMER AND PARTNER ACKNOWLEDGEMENT

Actively understanding or observing what content your customers or business partners are creating and engaging with is another great way to approach link building. By drawing positive attention to them, there's a greater likelihood they'll respond: they may read and share more of what you're doing or will develop closer relationships.

CLEANING UP LINKS

Check for non-working links which could be impacting traffic quality. You can use tools to capture 404 errors and replace these with the correct link or set up a redirect.

Tools for search engine marketing

There are a number of tools and technologies to consider for B2B search engine marketing; we've mentioned some of these already in this chapter. For B2B marketers wanting to invest further time in keyword planning, tools worth looking into include Google's own Keyword Planner, which is part of Google Ads. Other keyword research tools include Wordtracker and Keyword Discovery.

Übersuggest is another keyword search tool which is useful if you have a limited budget. You can input a popular keyword phrase, and the tool will provide you with additional long-tail variations that have been used in searches before, breaking them down alphabetically. Übersuggest is also particularly helpful for gathering ideas for industries about which you know little.

Soovle supports your research efforts by highlighting common queries built on your initial seed words, extracting search data from the four major search engines.

Moz's Link Explorer allows organizations to evaluate link profiles to look for optimization opportunities, whereas Screaming Frog determines the overall health of your site.

B2B SEM strategies

We can summarize the different B2B search engine marketing strategies according to Figure 7.5. The key B2B areas are off-page link-based strategies, on-site technical optimization, and keyword-based strategies.

In terms of off-page-based strategies, these include content development for SEO and using techniques and technologies for better sharing of SEO content. There is also link analysis, as well as the link-building strategies we've mentioned earlier in this chapter. Finally, related to content sharing is audience targeting, which is about ensuring link building, blogs, articles and social bookmarking are oriented to audience segments.

By on-site optimization we are referring to content management and refresh. As can be seen from the Frovi case study in the next chapter and information in this chapter, having compelling, relevant and up-to-date content on your website supporting audience search activities can be powerful.

The third set of strategies are around keywords, and are broken into two core areas: keyword analysis and long-tail keywords. Keyword analysis is about identifying the intent behind keywords to better understand customer motives and stage of the buyer journey. Long-tail keyword strategies include how to identify as well as use long-tail keywords.

FIGURE 7.5 Search strategies

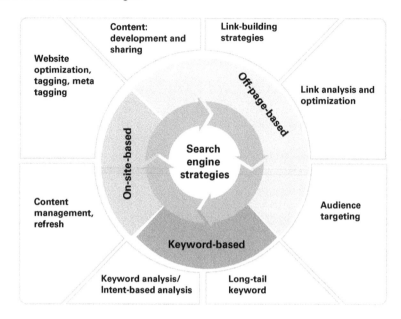

CASE STUDY
John Deere

In 1985, John Deere started publishing a magazine for farmers called *The Furrow*. The company published the magazine in the hopes of becoming a trusted resource for their customers, so they have always been at the forefront of content and content engagement. However, around 2003 their SEO wasn't performing as strongly as they would have liked.

They engaged an agency, KoMarketing, to help understand where the areas for improvement were for them in terms of search performance. They identified, for example, that as they were using dynamic and foreign URLs, rather than static ones, the dealer pages couldn't be crawled or indexed by search engines. Other aspects related to insufficient backlinking and low ROI from PPC campaigns.

Through working with KoMarketing they were able to address the above areas and more, improving indexing, rewriting URLs, improving backlinks, updating content and so on. The results was a quadrupling of search engine traffic, a jump of page indexing from a few hundred pages to as much as 60,000, and a dramatic improvement in their PPC campaign performance (Yeung, n. d.).

EXERCISE

Put it into practice

1 Create an overview of keywords by early and mid-buyer journey stages according to a customer segment or buyer persona.

2 Review current keywords used by your buyer persona or segment to create a list of long-tail keywords.

3 For a recent marketing campaign, review the links used in off-page SEO content. Do they point to relevant pages on your website?

References

Salesforce (n. d.) Understanding the buyer's journey, *Pardot* [online] www.pardot.com/buyer-journey/ (archived at https://perma.cc/AYQ6-JBUZ)

Sukhraj, R (2017) [accessed 1 August 2019] 28 Little-Known Blogging Statistics to Help Shape Your Strategy in 2019, *Impact BND* [online] www.impactbnd.com/blog/blogging-statistics-to-boost-your-strategy (archived at https://perma.cc/X2A8-WJWW)

Yeung, J (n. d.) [accessed 30 November 2019] John Deere: Integrated SEO & PPC Management, *KoMarketing* [online] https://komarketing.com/success-stories/machinefinder-success-story/ (archived at https://perma.cc/YN7R-Z322)

Further reading

Summers, J (2016) [accessed 1 August 2019] B2B marketers that blog receive 67% more leads than those that do not, *The Skills Farm* [online] www.theskillsfarm.co.uk/B2B-marketers-that-blog-receive-67-more-leads-than-those-that-do-not/ (archived at https://perma.cc/9EAP-MLV4)

08

B2B websites and website strategies

WHAT YOU WILL GAIN FROM THIS CHAPTER

After reading this chapter, you will understand:

- website roles and goals;
- considerations in B2B website design;
- evaluating websites;
- managing bounce rate;
- how to use heatmapping;
- how to improve website navigation;
- different B2B website strategies.

Introduction

The role of the website

A website can perform multiple possible roles for B2B marketers. It can act as a company brochure, particularly for products or services, as a content hub, a data hub, a relationship building interface, and a storefront for your business. Your company website allows visitors to understand you as a business, to get to know you and also wander around your business without actually getting in touch directly.

From your website, prospective customers will make assumptions about you and will develop a perception of your brand.

We understand customers use prospective vendors' websites as part of their research when researching products and solutions. If you factor early on within a prospect's research phase, then it is highly likely that they'll check out your website and other of your online properties. If they are a prospective customer and initiating a search, you'll want to make sure both your homepage and landing pages are helping customers and potentially answering their initial needs and queries.

In this sense, the role of the website is to engage customers early on and make a good first impression, similar to your first meeting with prospective customers.

Your website as a hub

Sometimes you'll hear about websites being the 'hub' or main interface with all other channels, which would be referred to as the 'spokes'. Hub-and-spoke thinking is a way to capture traffic and interest from other channels and direct them to the company website.

This is demonstrated in Figure 8.1.

FIGURE 8.1 The hub and spoke model

Website goals

It's important to set goals to ensure websites are effective. These goals can be included in Google Analytics, which help in turn in proving whether digital marketing activities are providing return. They also help maintain focus by aligning website activities and measures to marketing goals.

Goals for your website might be to increase sales, improve engagement, capture leads or become a thought leader, and for each one of these goals different website metrics/KPIs could be used.

For example, activities for better customer engagement could be reducing the bounce rate by 10 per cent, improving time on site, improving page view number, and so on.

When to use the website

We learned when looking at customer journey mapping in Chapter 3 that customers will go through a sequence of touchpoints, and by understanding the typical sequence it will be possible to see where and when to include the website as a step or touchpoint within the customer journey.

By understanding this in the awareness phase, we avoid sending customers to the wrong parts of the website at the wrong time. We can do this by incorporating the right website links in content placed outside of our website, to web pages which house relevant content for that early buyer journey phase.

Designing a website for B2B

Effective B2B website design is not just about visuals and great images, but about structure, navigation and layout, your SEO strategy, and the general logic behind the website.

Qualities of a well-designed website

Effective websites should support different stages of the customer journey. They not only generate leads for your business, but also serve in the stages leading up to that and ideally after a lead has been converted to a sale. Once visitors arrive, the website should either help visitors on that page or provide options for the visitor to receive their needed information through easy-to-follow paths as quickly as possible.

TABLE 8.1 Website design factors

Website design area	Detail	Rating [1 = OK, 5 = excellent]
Engaging and interactive	Keyword buttons or links, calls to action	
Informative and relevant text included	Maintaining keyword density to a reasonable level	
Structure	Logical website hierarchy and logical pathing based on micro journeys	
Visual elements	Use of visuals, illustrations, embedded video	
Supporting lead generation	Lead capture and nurture mechanisms included	
Optimized for interacting with other marketing channels	On-page optimized for SEO, search, optimized for mobile, and is responsive	

In terms of generating leads, well-designed websites should capture and nurture leads in an appropriately engaging manner. In being able to capture leads and nurture them, websites need to be aligned to other activities outside the site, dealing with different traffic streams relating to different stages of the buyer journey.

Some of the key aspects of a good B2B website design are summarized in Table 8.1. Though this table is not exhaustive, it outlines some of the top-level aspects according to areas of text, structure, non-text, lead generation and SEO optimization. One could take the main areas in the table and rate the website design on a scale of 1–5, where 1 is poor an 5 is excellent. For example under 'information and relevant text' one could use keyword density as a way to rate; where keyword density exceeds 5 per cent, this is poor, whereas 3 per cent or less is excellent.

In addition to the above checklist, one could make parts of the website personal. This may include explaining what the company is about, its principles and how it operates. These aspects help to engender trust. Well-designed websites aren't cluttered: they don't fill every possible white space with text and information. This can be overwhelming and can drive visitors away.

Sometimes long, scrolling webpages can be really compelling, and can avoid the need to move around too many pages. Of course, the content across the long scroll needs to make sense. Finally, make sure to include good visuals and update where necessary; having a regular fresh look for the website can make a difference.

Responsive design

A responsive website automatically changes its presentation according to the devices you're viewing it on, eg tablet, smartphone or desktop. Responsive doesn't just mean that your mobile or tablet 'can' view it; it's about offering the right user experience, which sometimes means a completely different visual layout.

This includes using easy-to-read buttons or doing away with dropdown menus, which are often difficult to use on smartphone devices. Typical views on a mobile device are buttons which are in the style of a hamburger, ie three large buttons stacked on top of one another.

Finally, web pages need to load in an acceptably short amount of time. According to one survey, 73 per cent of mobile users said they've encountered websites too slow to load (Lopez, 2018).

Calls to action

With calls to action (CTAs), we're essentially trying to shift the customer from one stage in their journey to the next stage, or one step within a stage to the next. Rather than trying to make customers get in touch or make a purchase, CTAs get them thinking about the next steps and how we can get them there.

Examples of CTAs are invitations to sign up for a mailout, join a webinar, attend an event or register to receive a free gift.

Final considerations in B2B website design

As with most things in marketing, your website should be designed around two core areas:

1 Your goals for the website.
2 The customers you're thinking of serving with the website. In B2B we typically have two main types of customer – those who are interested in the technical details of products or services, and those who are interested in the business aspects, such as how your business creates value and supports customers with achieving goals or dealing with pain points.

Website conversion in B2B

A B2B website allows your business to understand and analyse customer trends and develop techniques, tactics or strategies to convert new visitors into customers. The idea is that more conversions will translate into more sales.

Whereas B2C conversion is usually about how many visitors convert to a sale, this cannot be the same in B2B for a number of reasons. The main one is that B2B for the most part is less commercial, is less transactional and the buyer journeys are much longer. Therefore, when we talk about website conversion in B2B, we refer to capturing any specific personal contact information. This could be information provided via a chat box, in a web form, a prospect providing an email address or phone number, or a customer making a call.

The formula we could use for website conversion rate is: the number of leads from the website, divided by the number of unique website visitors.

Evaluating B2B websites

Apart from generating the desired amount of leads, there are a number of other ways you can check whether your website is effective. You can see if individual pages are effectively engaging customers, or if visitors actually found the information they were searching for. For the website overall, you can see if the navigation is working, or analyse loading speed and responsiveness.

Let's break down the effectiveness of B2B websites into two areas – quantitative, and qualitative.

Quantitative evaluation of websites

A number of technologies are available which can be used to evaluate quantitative aspects of the website. A number of elements are evaluated, but the key categories are navigability and performance.

Navigability refers to the ability to move between pages or to move from the homepage to other areas. We're also referring to the ability to find information on the page or across the website. Performance refers to the general speed of the website, and the page load speed. Of course, there are other website performance KPIs such as bounce rate, page viewing time, pages per visit, and so on.

Website analytics as part of quantitative evaluation

One great thing about your website is that you get free access to Google Analytics. As a company, this tool will help you in a number of ways. Google Analytics provides a lot of great detail including bounce rate, pages per session and average session duration.

Pages per session can indicate customer engagement. For example, a customer viewing eight pages of your website is absolutely more engaged and interested in your company, products or services than those that view only two pages.

Time on site is another factor indicating engagement; more than two minutes is regarded as good, though standards for time on site do vary by industry.

ALTERNATIVES TO GOOGLE ANALYTICS

We've mentioned Google Analytics as a key tool, but there are many alternatives you could use. You could use Leadfeeder or Kissmetrics, which focuses on detailed visitor behaviour to help you better understand your customers and leads. Other possibilities include Foxmetrics, ZAP, Open Web Analytics and Adobe Analytics.

Qualitative evaluation of websites

Websites can also be evaluated qualitatively by looking at content, and there are quantitative metrics which can give more qualitative clues such as content engagement, bounce rates, page viewing time and heatmaps (see later in this chapter).

Bounce rate, although a quantitative measure, can indicate qualitative aspects – eg a high bounce rate may indicate poor quality or irrelevant content. If viewing time is low, this can indicate that there isn't enough compelling content for viewers to engage.

Managing bounce rates

Bounce rate is a term for reviewing web traffic, and refers to the percentage of visitors who come to a site or page and then leave immediately rather than going to view other pages within the same site. Bounce rates can be categorized as good, bad or excellent, and can differ greatly depending on the industry.

There are essentially two components that determine the bounce rate: the quality of traffic which is coming to the website, and the quality of the web page.

Bounce rates above 70 per cent are regarded as very high, and reflect that the traffic is poor quality, or the website is of poor quality or doesn't have enough content to engage. Bounce rates between 40 and 70 per cent are good to average, and bounce rates below 40 per cent are excellent and reflect good quality of traffic, and/or good website content quality or relevance (Peyton, n. d.).

How to reduce bounce rates

You can focus strategies for reducing bounce rates according to the components mentioned above: quality of traffic, and quality of content.

Ways to improve quality of traffic include:

- targeting audiences more specifically according to specific criteria: here the different awareness generation-based strategies can be employed from Chapter 6, as well as the search engine marketing approaches from Chapter 7;
- better audience segmentation and tailoring your marketing content streams to these, eg to define themes and content;
- audience research: this can add more detail to the buyer persona, which helps with content development.

Ways to improve website quality include:

- Headlines: check and fine-tune headlines and sub-headlines on the website, as this will help with search-based activities.
- Navigation paths: often prospects are looking for additional specific but different information to what you're providing on the page they landed on, so they will need to be signposted to further relevant information. Check different paths on the website to ensure user information needs are supported.

- Relevant content: improve relevance of content according to your main customer segments, in terms of themes, messages and key phrases.
- Website design: without getting into subjective comments on style, there are general design aspects which impact website experience. For example, overcrowded pages with pop-up windows are generally viewed negatively.

Website navigation

Navigation on a website is facilitated through various links, such as with a website navigation menu/bar or those on pages. This navigation is particularly important considering some prospects will arrive on your homepage if they've not been directed through SEO content and links to another part of the site.

The navigability of websites is something which can either win over your prospects or lose them. Recently I was asked to review a B2B website, and in going through various links on pages I noticed that on every page there was only one main link which took me to a page asking me for my details so I could be contacted. This page was inescapable, and I was not able to simply explore and read up on information. I wasn't given any freedom to search the product catalogue or understand the propositions of the company. This was of course both frustrating and off-putting.

You need to cater for different user needs and offer different paths. Try to think how you support the micro journeys of your customers and prospects, as an immediate purchase is not always the first thing on their mind.

Where to start – the hierarchy

Creating a website hierarchy as in Figure 8.2 can help you visualize and understand a number of aspects. Firstly, one can start to understand how many levels are in the website by looking at the top and bottom of the hierarchy. If it is believed that some of the searched topics at the bottom of the hierarchy are very commonly searched items, then you may want to think about removing some layers, reviewing shortcuts or changing the website structure overall.

The hierarchy view can also tell us how many clicks it takes to get to something. From our previous chapters and understanding of the micro journey, you may want to play out this micro journey to see how long it takes customers to find information based on them arriving at the homepage. Once you've understood the clicks needed to get from the homepage

FIGURE 8.2 The website hierarchy

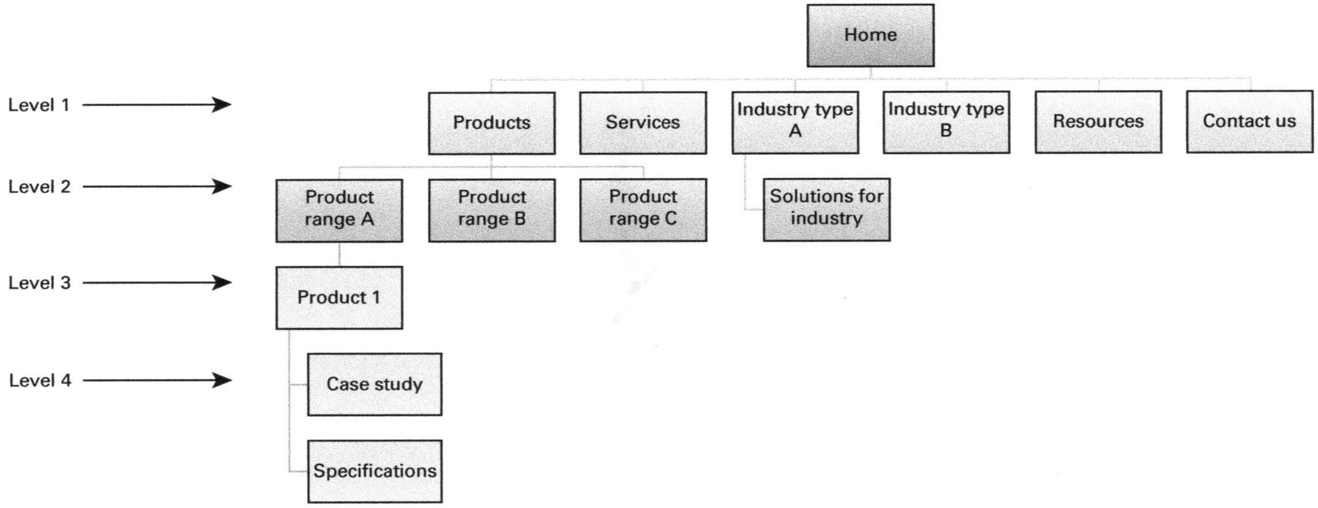

Level 1 →

Level 2 →

Level 3 →

Level 4 →

to some common topics, you can review whether this is acceptable: more than one or two clicks may mean reviewing how to reduce this to make the prospect's navigation through the website easier.

Many companies today endeavour to get customers to where they want within one or two clicks, either by having a slick homepage and navigation bar or by managing traffic and sending them to the correct pages on their website. Many also include dropdown menus, which are a great way to get the balance between shorter navigation bars and supporting the multiple paths and options customers need.

PRACTICAL TIP

Enhancing navigation through keyworded buttons

Having content relevant to your customer or industry is important – so rather than having the standard nav bar which all companies use, you might want to include specific prospect keywords or terms within the navigation buttons.

Heatmaps

One way to evaluate website experiences from the point of view of the customer is through website heatmaps. Heatmaps give us a visual view as to which areas of the website are being clicked on or viewed and, which aren't. You'll typically see red areas, orange areas and blue areas.

Whilst the usual scenario is that the majority of the website is likely to be blue, understanding the ratio is not the point of the exercise. The key to heatmaps is to understand whether key words, phrases and links to capture interest were actually clicked on or viewed, and where this hasn't happened.

Imagine you've designed a new page around some key words to help a small business understand their financing options. You've provided around five key phrases related to their pain points which also include a link to other pages. Your heatmap then shows that only two of those are red and have been clicked on. This can help understanding in two ways; either the other three key phrases are not of interest or we're not describing the pain point the right way, or the traffic we're sending to that page is only interested in those two things.

So, heatmaps are not only about getting the design right, but about keywords and phrases, and can identify if marketing activities which drive traffic are reaching the right prospects.

Analytics tools go a long way in providing metrics such as which pages users visit. However, they lack detail in terms of how users engage on the page. Heatmaps provide context and therefore a more complete understanding.

Types of heatmaps include:

- Mouse-movement heatmaps: these show where visitors look most by tracking their clicking, pausing and scrolling.

- Scroll heatmaps: these identify patterns of scrolling, picking up things like how far people scroll and when they abandon action. Scroll heatmaps can also pick up the percentage of people who scroll down to any point on the page.

- Click heatmaps: these identify where visitors click or don't click. Through click patterns, website owners can better understand users' intent.

B2B website strategies

We've already covered a number of areas which support website strategies. In terms of B2B, this can be broken down into five main areas as follows.

Personalization

This might mean leveraging dynamic content to align to a personalization strategy as well as designing a website around different user profiles. On the extreme side, this could include personalized URL addresses to support campaigns.

Thought leadership

A thought leadership website strategy might include developing areas of the website to house articles, videos, static or dynamic banners, reports and so on. The difference between this and the content hub strategy below is that the thought leadership strategy is designed to demonstrate expertise in a given area.

FIGURE 8.3 Website strategies

Content hub	Lead capture	Thought leadership	Engagement improvement	Personalization
• Content suite	• Lead capture mechanics • Gated content • Identifying prospects at right stage	• Articles, blogs • Refreshed content • Links to webinars • Compelling reports to offer	• Content refresh • Content audit • Retargeting	• Dynamic content

Lead capture

The strategy would be to design and update landing pages according to campaigns or marketing strategies, with a strategy to optimize lead capture. This might involve reviewing questions or content on the landing page, as well as contact detail capture mechanisms.

Optimizing engagement

Engagement optimization is focusing on improving the website itself and improving engagement metrics; it may also involve better engaging customers. Part of the strategy might involve a content review, audit or content refresh, and the strategy might include regular content refreshes. Other strategies might be to offer more downloadable material or to incorporate interactive elements such as chat, or more possibilities for customers to leave details and be contacted.

Content hub

In this strategy, the website or an area of the website is designed as the main hub for all content. This is more than having a PR library of assets, as it is designed to support different segments with information they would need across different stages of the journey.

Other website technologies

As you want to ensure your website is operating at its maximum level, you'll need to keep an eye on the latest technologies and to understand which ones to adopt. A summary of these is as follows.

A/B testing

A/B testing is the process of showing two different versions of the same webpage to various groups of website visitors. 'A' and 'B' are the two versions being compared, differing in just one aspect, while all other aspects of the page remain consistent. This allows organizations to understand the impact of changing the specific element in question.

Typically, headers or sub-headings are tested, but other aspects may be images, copy text, paragraph text, testimonials, call to action text, button style or placement, and links. A/B testing applications such as Optimizely allow you to test out multiple elements on your web pages simultaneously.

Landing page management

Landing page technologies are great for testing and managing landing pages. Examples of these technologies include Unbounce.

Google Accelerated Mobile Pages (AMP)

Google AMP is an open-source initiative which enables websites to load faster. According to research, 50 per cent of website visitors expect pages to load in two seconds or less (Grimms, 2019). This might be the reason for high bounce rates for some companies.

CASE STUDY
Frovi

Frovi is a family-owned British company specializing in innovative furniture designs; their focus is to create distinctive furniture in-house for agile working and social spaces within corporate environments.

Frovi is a great example of a company that has turned their focus to providing a website which truly engages its customers, before, during and after website interaction. On average they receive website visitor traffic of around 4k to 5k per month – but that's not the amazing thing about this company. Despite their high traffic, they are able to keep their bounce rate to around 2.5 to 4 per cent.

So, what's their secret? Frovi didn't always have such a low bounce rate; only last November their bounce rate was around 30 per cent (which is still, by the way, an excellent bounce rate). Good bounce rates are regarded to be around the 50 per cent or below mark, although rates vary by industry.

To understand the quality or source of Frovi's website traffic, around 70 per cent of this comes from organic search, with the rest mostly coming from directly referred traffic. There are some smaller amounts from referrals and social media. Looking at these figures, there's nothing which would indicate that the low bounce rates lie in the quality of their traffic.

When we dig a little deeper, we can start to understand a little more. Frovi place particular emphasis on the freshness of their content on their website and home, always looking to have the latest designs and fresh content rolled in on a monthly basis. Last November they decided to overhaul their content on their website. One could argue that their industry requires Frovi to have the latest design and content because that's what they sell. However, the same could be said for many B2B companies today which have nowhere near the bounce rates Frovi are able to command.

Additionally, as well as having clear governance around content updates, Frovi recently launched a new campaign which focused on how Frovi develop and create in-house designs; this was also launched late last year. They created a new blog which includes regular monthly or even weekly stories about the business. Frovi also carried out an SEO keyword review to ensure the keyword authenticity of their content was improved.

Finally Frovi's established dealers have long been using their dealer catalogue, which provides a logical, friendly and easy way to understand Frovi's latest offerings as well as review and purchase them. Recently Frovi reviewed their website to ensure this emulated the easy-to-use nature of their catalogue, mirroring its structure in terms of themes and flow.

This has meant that dealers already know how to use the website, and how to find information based on the catalogue that they have become accustomed to.

EXERCISE
Put it into practice

1   How does your company website support your marketing objectives or goals?

2   Considering some of the key customer journey or requirements as per Chapter 3, how does your website support and facilitate customers in those customer journeys?

3   Create a small dashboard which includes the key metrics against which you could measure your company's website effectiveness.

References

Grimms, K, (2019) [accessed 30 November 2019] How to Optimise Website Load Speed to Less Than 2 Seconds, *Einstein Marketer* [online] www.einsteinmarketer. com/website-speed-optimisation/ (archived at https://perma.cc/Q2L2-Y32X)

Lopez, A (2018) [accessed 1 August 2019] You definitely want to optimize your website's loading speed. Here's how, *FreeCodeCamp* [online] www.freecodecamp. org/news/website-loading-speed-optimization-in-2018-bananas-e66cc85df8dd/ (archived at https://perma.cc/G9EM-HQS6)

Peyton, J (n. d.) [accessed on 24 January 2020] What's the Average Bounce Rate for a Website? *RocketFuel* [online] www.gorocketfuel.com/the-rocket-blog/whats-the-average-bounce-rate-in-google-analytics/ (archived at https://perma.cc/5VFG-ZRQT)

Further reading

Khandelwal, A (2019) [accessed 1 August 2019] Heatmaps – The Hot Diagnostic Tool for B2B Marketers! *VWO* [online] https://vwo.com/blog/heatmaps-the-hot-diagnostic-tool-for-b2b-marketers (archived at https://perma.cc/U3ST-KFMM)

Vizulis, A (2016) [accessed 1 August 2019] How to Find Your Industry Bounce Rate Benchmark, *21handshake* [online] https://21handshake.com/how-to-find-your-industry-bounce-rate-benchmark/ (archived at https://perma.cc/B3RB-SVD2)

Digital for lead generation and lead nurturing

In Part Three we move from the early buyer stage into the mid- to late buyer journey stage, and cover the topics of lead generation and lead nurturing. This includes the different stages of lead generation, from lead capture through to handover.

In the lead nurturing chapter, you'll read about different approaches to lead nurturing in terms of channels, technologies and strategies.

09

B2B digital marketing for lead generation

WHAT YOU WILL GAIN FROM THIS CHAPTER

After reading this chapter, you will understand:

- how to capture leads;
- whether to gate content;
- how social media, websites and social media are used to generate leads;
- lead handover;
- technologies for tracking leads.

Introduction

Leads and lead generation

A lead is a person or organization that expresses an interest in your company's products, services or solution. By this definition, a lead is typically captured after a person or organization becomes aware of your products or services, so we typically refer to lead generation in the consideration stage of the buyer journey.

Awareness-based activities, therefore, usually take place in the pre-lead capture stage.

What is lead generation?

The goal of lead generation is to encourage a prospect to provide their contact information to create a richer form of follow-up engagement. Lead generation as an area encompasses lead capture, qualification, lead nurture and lead closure: each one of these parts of lead generation can be very different in their implementation.

Lead generation typically follows the process shown in Figure 9.1. It starts with an initial inquiry, from which the lead goes through a lead nurture stage until it is ready to be handed to sales in the 'lead handover' stage. Once handed over to sales, the lead is typically then further qualified and categorized as an opportunity and is further nurtured through sales (and marketing-supported) activities until the lead can be closed.

You'll notice various terms in Figure 9.1. A marketing qualified lead (MQL) is a prospect (lead) that has indicated interest in the organization, its products and/or services. It has been qualified as a lead to include in the lead nurture stream or marketing campaign; essentially, these leads have the potential to become customers.

A sale-ready or accepted lead is a lead which has been nurtured and checked, usually by an organization's marketing department, and subsequently accepted by sales. As a result there should be several details available for sales to further progress with. Once the sales department have qualified the lead, ie vetted it, and the lead is deemed to be valid as a potential sale for the business, it is then put into the sales process.

The role of digital in lead generation

When we think of the steps within lead generation, digital is playing an increasingly important role in terms of the techniques and technology that can capture, qualify, nurture and even close leads.

FIGURE 9.1 The lead-generation process

One development is better use of SEO and integration in the lead generation mix. Intelligent email segmentation is also evolving as a trend, as email is still regarded as an effective marketing channel for lead nurture. Additionally, increased personalization and account-based marketing are also influencing lead generation.

Lead capture

Lead capture is when we learn something about the prospect which we can use later to engage them, nurture their interest and develop it into something even more tangible.

Lead capture usually occurs where the prospect provides some details in exchange for something, eg compelling content or more information about an organization and its products and services.

This stage is important in terms of getting timings and the method right. There are various methods available to B2B marketers for lead capture. For example:

- Inviting prospects to leave details: this is probably the most customer-friendly manner as you leave it to them to provide their details. This can be done by offering a space on your website where they can leave their information.
- Offering presentations in exchange for contact details.
- Offering reports in exchange for contact details.
- Implementing live or automated chat features where more information is gathered about the prospect to help them in their buying journey.
- Gamified content and interaction: offering some form of game or context to engage. This is not just a B2C technique, but can be effective in B2B. It also makes the interaction a fun, engaging activity where those participating will tend to be in more of a mood to share information.

Auto-capturing of leads is also another way that technologies can be used: this may be through sign-up forms, phone calls, referrals sites, social media, PPC ads or landing pages that capture information about the prospect. Companies like LeadSquared or MyMedLeads offer this option to provide a tailored approach to capturing leads.

Gated content

The decision to gate content has been debated a lot amongst B2B marketers, though it should probably be less about 'whether' to gate content, and more about 'when' to gate it. Before we go any further, let's define 'gated content'; this is content which is provided based on users submitting their contact details. For some prospects this is seen as a nuisance, as they must fill in multiple fields to access the content they want.

So why do we gate content? Gating content is an easy way to capture customer details, and allow vendors to re-engage customers in the next stage in their buying journey. One could also argue that gating content enables B2B marketers to understand the level of interest from customers, and use this as an indicator of the stage the customer is at in the buying process.

We might have heard or read statements that gating content won't work for more digital-savvy customers. However, in a recent poll I conducted with Millennial B2B customers, I asked the question as to whether gated content was accepted by them or not. The response from almost all was that if those users had previously engaged or used content from a potential vendor, they would be willing to subsequently provide a few contact details, ie open to gated content.

From this, I would gather that it is the timing of the gated content that is more important, rather than whether to gate the content or not.

Getting the timing right

There are a few options to use to get the timing right for gating content:

- Type of content: Ideally, content should be gated in the consideration stage, as typically in the awareness stage customers are not ready to engage with vendors. In the awareness stage, prospects are understanding possible routes to satisfying business needs and educating themselves through exploring information. Hence, the gating of awareness-based content would be more of a nuisance and potentially be off-putting.
- Type of digital traffic: One way to identify customers is first by the type of traffic coming to your website. Typically traffic which is based on PPC advertising should not be gated, as this is primarily awareness-based traffic.
- Owned media properties: When visitors engage with your 'owned' media properties such as your website, social media accounts or blogs, they

could be in the consideration stage – so links provided on social media could feature gated content.

- Type of content: Understanding differences in content according to stage in the buyer journey can be incredibly useful. If a customer engages with purely educational, early-stage content, you should avoid gating it.

- Campaign traffic: Website traffic which is based on campaign themes or messages could have some form of gated content applied, as these visitors are more aware of the brand and products or services.

- Compelling long-form content: You might consider only gating unique, long-form content which has a degree of exclusivity to it. Customers who have downloaded this type of content understand it is of a certain value, are willing to take the time to read it in full, and therefore are willing to provide their details.

- Content sequencing: Another approach is to ensure consideration content only follows previous content – ie there is a logical order for the content to be digested, eg in parts or with other description or labels which highlight the logical order in which it should be consumed. See Figure 9.2.

Social media and lead generation

As recently as 10 years ago, social media wasn't thought of as a possible or effective source for lead generation. In B2B people tended to use social media to capture attention or to convey messages to the market. It was very much used to build awareness around a company, or to target customers in the early stage of the buyer journey.

Today the data shows us that social media is an important channel used to generate leads. In 2017, it was reported that 80 per cent of B2B social

FIGURE 9.2 When to gate content

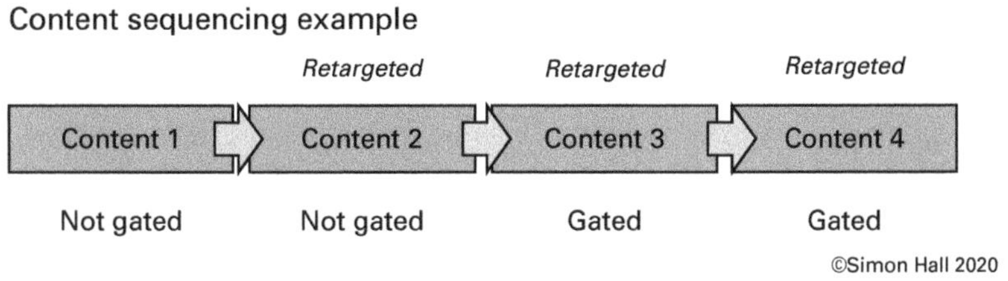

Content sequencing example

| Content 1 | Content 2 | Content 3 | Content 4 |
| Not gated | Not gated | Gated | Gated |

©Simon Hall 2020

media leads stem from LinkedIn, and that 94 per cent of B2B marketers use LinkedIn for content distribution (Rynne, 2017).

Getting started

For B2B businesses there are now a full range of different social media properties which can be used across the different customer journey stages, both before and after purchase. So how does one go about using social media and its channels for lead generation?

First, get to know your customers in terms of what they use social media for. What are their goals for using social media, and do these goals differ between the early stage and mid stage of the buyer journey? Do they use different social media channels, or use the same social media channel in different ways within the lead nurture stage? Possible social media channels which could be used in B2B marketing include LinkedIn, Facebook, Twitter, YouTube and Vimeo, although there are many, many more. For more information on dedicated online social media business communities, see Chapter 18.

Understanding the role social media plays within the customer journey and how prospects use it together with other channels is also a good starting point. If social media is used together with a website landing page, then an organization should understand how to facilitate links between social media areas and website landing pages.

Capturing leads on social media

Let's go back to the definition of lead generation or capture: where someone expresses an interest in your products, services or company. By expressing an interest and capturing that interest, we can start to look at the following possibilities in using social media.

Webinars in B2B marketing can be effective in resolving or addressing questions early in the buying process. The webinar content itself can be scoped to cover key pain points or questions and offer up time for a two-way discussion. Social media can then be used to promote the webinars or to later share as a webcast on Vimeo or YouTube.

As seen in Chapter 7, social media has several advertising targeting options and some of these can be used to capture interest and leads. Through targeting prospects with relevant information, the chances of response or engagement can be increased.

Including links in social media posts to longer-form content or to downloadable content which is gated can be an effective way to capture leads, assuming the timing is right. Obviously we need to understand where the prospect is in their customer journey, and for this we can use the customer journey map discussed earlier in the book.

Conducting social media-based polls or surveys can engage customers not only through the way the poll or survey is posed but also by providing results back to customers. Once the report has been created, prospective customers can return to leave contact information if they want to receive the full details.

Engaging in social selling can support sales through distributed content and information. This also helps sales with a softer touch in nurturing and educating prospects.

Know your audience and their social platforms

Different audiences will use different social platforms and use the same social platform in different ways. For B2B businesses, there are now a full range of different social media properties which can be used across the different customer journey stages both before and after purchase.

The typical social platforms used in B2B marketing are LinkedIn, Twitter, YouTube, Facebook and Instagram; there are of course many more, but these are the main ones.

Another consideration is to segment social media channels according to goals. For example, LinkedIn could be used to highlight business solutions, network with people and engage and target different decision makers, whereas Facebook might be used to tell engaging stories, highlight themes or talk about CSR initiatives. Twitter might be used to hook people and provide links to other social media properties.

Social media communities

When creating your lead generation programmes be aware that in order to engage prospects you will need to understand where your prospects talk to other people, and what business communities relate to your industry or to the role of your target prospect.

Some of these business communities reside on the social media networking sites themselves, although many business communities have also been created in separate online spaces. Examples include Spiceworks for IT decision makers or IT departments. Solaborate is a network dedicated to technology professionals, while ProductHunt is a social network which helps businesses share new products. Procurious is a network dedicated to those in the supply chain or procurement space.

One way to engage these might be to partner with the network platform providers or identify ways to engage members through sharing of content by or to members of such communities.

Websites and lead generation

Websites are critical in the area of lead generation. Capturing a lead on your website means you can do something with it, whether that is responding, retargeting or other activities which allow you to nurture leads.

Consider different landing page options. Where will the customer land independently, or where will your marketing lead them? There are four landing page options:

- the lead capture landing page is simply there to capture customer details, usually in return for some sort of content;
- the product detail landing page provides more details on the product or service;
- clickthrough landing pages are used more in the B2B commercial space to lead the customer to purchase;
- the lead nurture landing page is about continuing to nurture the prospect rather than capture their details immediately at that point.

Email and lead generation

Email for most B2B companies plays an increasingly important role. As we come into the lead generation space and mid-buyer journey to late buyer journey, there are several considerations for this. These can be broken down into four core areas, as follows.

Email lists and data

In producing email lists it's crucial to think about how to segment them. Unsegmented email lists and blanket emails sent without any tailoring of messages risk suboptimal responses. By dividing email lists into smaller segments, we can align the segmentation to the marketing segmentation or other segmentation criteria.

Segmenting lists allows for personalization of the email and so improves email response rates.

Email triggers

Automated emails can be sent based on an event or a customer action. Email triggers can help to build relationships with customers or prospects: as in most cases they are seen as a response to a user's action, they are typically very timely and relevant to user activity.

Trigger emails can help move users through steps in a buying process or in their journey to become better customers. Email triggers can be created using either general marketing automation technology such as SendGrid, or specific email automation software.

B2B email triggers include the following:

- **welcome emails** for new customers;
- **reactivation emails** which aim to reengage customers and bring them back to purchasing, usually for customers who haven't purchased anything for a specific period of time;
- **onboarding emails**: these emails remind recipients to carry out an action such as providing more details or setting up their account;
- **recurring triggers**: these might be related to renewing a licence or where a customer purchases something regularly;
- **event reminders**: in B2B these might be related to the end of the fiscal year or a warranty expiry;
- **milestones**: when a customer reaches a milestone with your company or achieves a spend threshold, sometimes called spend threshold email triggers;
- **transaction emails** which are typically related to the action itself, such as confirming receipt of an order or confirming delivery.

Timing

Understanding the best time to send emails is the key to maximize the possibility of them being opened or clicked on. The best timing for an email is based on understanding the buyer persona really well and usually looks at a typical day in the life of the customer.

For example, the busiest period for business email activity occurs between 8am and 9am, with the second busiest period occurring after lunch. However, if you look at the construction industry the best email period might be on a Friday evening or just before Sunday evening; according to a recent discussion I had with someone from the construction industry, Saturday morning or Sunday night is when contractors summarize the status of construction projects.

Privacy

With GDPR in effect since 25 May 2018, there are more concerns around sending emails to prospects and even to customers. In lead capture, make sure to get permission to send future email communications.

Also consider whether the customer has a legitimate interest in reading the information you're sending – for example, if it helps them comply with a legal obligation. A final consideration is that all emails should contain a very easy option to unsubscribe.

Webinars

I've mentioned webinars previously in this chapter within social media, but they can be good standalone channels as well. Webinars can target new audiences whilst allowing vendors to explain complex offerings or use rich content and high-quality visuals to communicate. They can establish trust and provide opportunities for audiences to engage, ask questions and clarify any issues they may have.

Webinars can help also build rapport and, therefore, support the progression to the next stage in the lead generation phase, whether that is purchase or further discussion.

For those audiences who attend webinars, the great news is that they are already more engaged. They've made a commitment of 30 minutes or more to a topic, and are therefore likely to be ready to take action.

Audiences are often more willing to share details in exchange for the compelling content in a webinar – they see the value you are providing, and will likely want more.

PRACTICAL TIP

Maximizing webinars for lead generation

To get the most out of webinars, organizations can use the webinar itself as content to further engage either the same prospects who attended, or new prospects. To add value to the webinar content itself, it could be further edited to include any comments, questions asked and answered and to include links to additional content as well as highlight key takeaways. It can then be provided publicly as slidedeck content, either in a easily accessible online site or via a social media site eg SlideShare.

Organizations can use webinars and the content to further nurture prospects this way and also by providing additional content related to the webinar. See Figure 9.3, which highlights potential follow-up nurture flows.

FIGURE 9.3 Webinar and lead nurturing

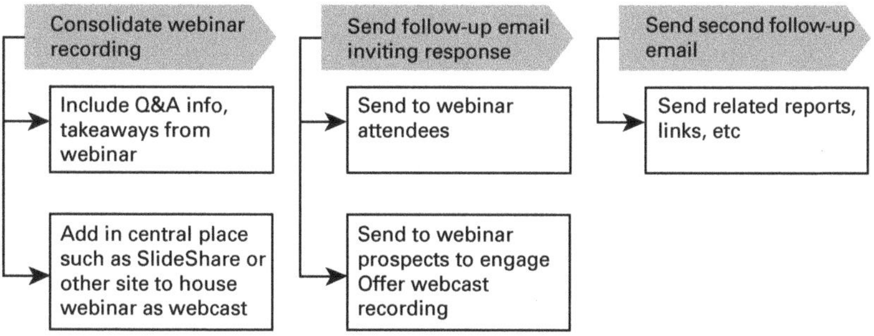

Defining the lead generation mix

So how do you go about defining the right mix to generate leads? As we've seen in earlier chapters, customers don't use one channel or a single piece of content, but will use and consume multiple channels and content, sometimes within minutes or even seconds.

One way to approach this question is to understand the effectiveness and cost of each channel, where effectiveness is defined as the ability to achieve the specific goal, and cost includes time as well as money. Let's assume the goal is to reach the right audience and thus be able to capture some details. Figure 9.4 shows where channels may be plotted to reach this.

The lead generation channels which are least costly and most effective are the ones we want to run with first, followed by less effective, less costly.

FIGURE 9.4 Lead generation effectiveness and cost matrix

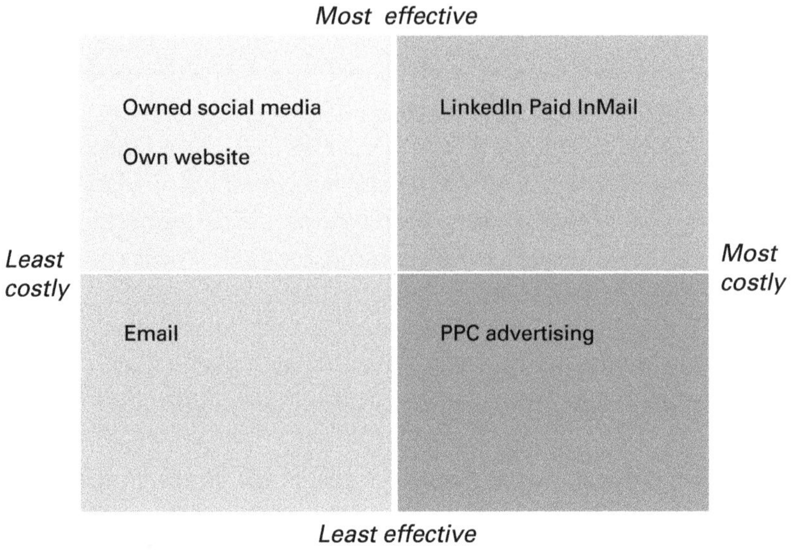

Most effective

Owned social media

Own website

LinkedIn Paid InMail

Least costly

Most costly

Email

PPC advertising

Least effective

Another way to select lead generation channels is to think of a paid, earned and owned combination. Owned and earned are a priority, with paid media depending on budget.

The final factor in selecting lead generation channels is time. Lead generation often has a short-term focus so it's important to think about tactics which accelerate the lead capture, nurture and close stages, rather than focus on awareness pre-lead capture. With that in mind, you'll want to target prospects who are already aware of your company, but haven't purchased products and services.

Lead handover

In the B2B space it's clear that there has to come a point when the lead is passed from marketing to sales, called the lead handover stage. However, this is often the cause of much tension between marketing and sales teams. The main success factor in lead conversion is in the handover process to sales.

There are a number of things to consider here in defining the success of the lead handover:

- the quality of the lead when it is handed over;
- when exactly the lead is passed on to sales;
- how the lead is handed over;
- the information provided in the handover;
- to whom the lead is handed over.

Ensuring the quality of lead is about nurturing it to a certain level before it is passed on to sales. Handing over poor-quality leads which were not previously agreed between sales and marketing just results in poor lead qualification and follow-up, and creates friction between the two departments.

Sometimes it can be the case that even if the lead is handed over, marketing agrees to provide sales with necessary content or other tools and tactics to support them in continuing to nurture through to lead close.

When the lead is handed over depends on the timing of the lead and the readiness of the customer, as well as the stage in the buyer journey they're at.

The way in which the lead is handed over can be very manual, via business cards or Excel lists, or through use of tools such as CRM systems. Once the lead is handed over there usually needs to be some communication, whether manual or automatic, to highlight to the salespeople the lead is ready for them to follow up with.

The information provided in the handover should relate to the quality of the lead, but also give more context about it. If the company has multiple marketing campaigns across different products, there should be information relating to the type of lead, their interest and anything which can help sales in the follow-up process.

Finally, who the lead is handed over to can make a difference – not only making sure the right salesperson is sent the lead, but the right sales type. For example, if you have a pure greenfield customer, make sure to hand over to a salesperson who has the experience to follow up acquisition customers. The type of salesperson and their background can make a difference in terms of how they typically are used to selling.

When handing over leads it is worthwhile flagging the temperature of the lead through some form of scoring mechanism. Some marketing automation platforms support a points system to highlight the temperature of the lead; other ways can be to talk about number of pieces of content or emails they have clicked on or engaged with. These scoring systems can go a long way towards clearly determining when and when not to hand over a lead.

Technologies for tracking leads

One great benefit of digital is the ability to track and understand where leads are in their journey. Some of the aspects we're interested in are the number of content pieces consumed or items downloaded, to get a view on whether a lead is just considering or evaluating in depth. (In the purchase stage this includes whether they're about to purchase or intending to purchase products and services.)

Digital technologies can help us with such things by providing data such as most viewed pages, what is downloaded, where traffic is coming from and the number of pieces of content viewed.

Most viewed pages

This shows what a lead has engaged with on your site. If a particular lead is viewing a page a number of times, it may mean you want to provide further information. It might be that the pages are viewed often as the customers is looking for answers to questions.

Download activities

Download activities shows which leads are more engaged. Download activities can be tracked through applications such as MonsterInsights, which acts as a plugin to Google Analytics.

Traffic

We can also understand lead generation temperature or intent from the source of the traffic. Depending on whether the traffic is from SEO, branded traffic activities or advertising campaigns, the lead may very well be at different stages of their journey, and you should be adapting reengagement and lead nurture approach accordingly.

Content number and type

The number of pieces of content viewed will give us an indication of where the lead is in the buyer journey. These can be tracked through marketing automation platforms. Finally, through the type of content download and the type of web pages viewed, we can also get a good idea of the user intent.

CASE STUDY
Calla: Capturing interest and leads through social media

Calla is a company which produces body-worn camera technology. They focus on key sectors such as education, healthcare and care homes.

Calla as part of their marketing efforts focus on key decision makers in these sectors, which can of course include the users themselves. The commonality of these audiences is that all involve front-facing staff who must deal with, in some circumstances, very difficult customers. Calla's cameras help to deter aggression and act as an independent source of evidence to support both sides in any disputes over how a situation was handled.

As the Calla technology is quite new, they turned to social media amongst other channels to reach new audiences as well as to specifically target decision makers. The main channels used were Facebook, followed by LinkedIn and Twitter.

As part of their targeting activities, Calla encountered various learnings in targeting. For example, nurses on social media don't always register with their profession, or, if they do, they don't always use consistent titles, so the targeting needed to include a loose descriptions as well as multiple titles such as Director of Nursing Service, Hospital Administrator, Hospital Manager and Nurse Manager.

On the other hand, narrowing down the criteria too much in terms of job title can mean that the size of target groups becomes too limiting, so additional criteria needed to be used such as interests. In addition to targeting based on interest and title, Calla employ retargeting on Twitter, AdWords and LinkedIn.

Calla employed actions along the way to improve ad performance. They run ad sets across gender and age group cohorts to see which target set performs better. To keep track, these audiences are labelled and saved. Ad sets performance can be tracked using Facebook and Google Analytics.

For one of Calla's recent campaigns, they used Facebook for an ad campaign focused on lead generation. The background was that Facebook lead ads provide quick and justifiable returns, with an attached cost per acquisition (CPA). The CPA and quality of leads tended to vary across audiences and geographies. There have been several successes for Calla using Facebook ads, particularly in Spain, with CPAs 20 or more times lower than in the UK. Success was even more intense in Madrid.

Aside from the cost and targeting effectiveness, Facebook has appeared to be a good platform and an economic option for testing ad copy, statements and images.

Some final learnings have been the result of great targeting methods as well as a more refined segmentation. The result was more lead form completion. Calla have seen a reach of over 130,000 people from the Facebook ads in Europe, and around 2,000 links clicked on their ads. One potential reason for the good click rate is that forms are completed natively on the Facebook platform which has reduced the clicks on Calla's website landing pages, but facilitated details being more easily captured, rather than sending customers to another online page to fill out a form.

EXERCISE
Put it into practice

1 Review the different options you have in place for capturing leads. Are there any missed opportunities in capturing leads in terms of marketing channels or ways of capturing leads?

2 Review the five elements for lead handover. Is your current lead handover process well defined, or does it need further refinement? If so, in which areas?

References

Rynne, A (2017) [accessed 26 January 2020] 10 Surprising Stats You Didn't Know about Marketing on LinkedIn [Infographic], *LinkedIn Business* [online] 1 Feb, https://business.linkedin.com/marketing-solutions/blog/linkedin-b2b-marketing/2017/10-surprising-stats-you-didnt-know-about-marketing-on-linkedin (archived at https://perma.cc/Q9N9-S9EU)

Further reading

Clarke, M (n. d.) [accessed 1 August 2019] 7 ways to use social media for B2B lead generation, *OurSocialTimes* [online] https://oursocialtimes.com/7-ways-to-use-social-media-for-B2B-lead-generation/ (archived at https://perma.cc/DA4Q-CU84)

Hutchinson, A (2017) [accessed 1 August 2019] The Case for B2B Marketing on LinkedIn, *Social Media Today* [online] www.socialmediatoday.com/social-business/case-B2B-marketing-linkedin-infographic-1 (archived at https://perma.cc/9FXX-VUZY)

Inco (2017) [accessed 1 August 2019] Improving the lead handover process, *Inco* [online] www.inco-marketing.com/blog/mql-to-sql-improving-the-lead-handover-process (archived at https://perma.cc/7N4P-EFYH)

Miller, J (2017) [accessed 1 August 2019] Our pick of the most important B2B digital marketing statistics for 2017, *LinkedIn* [online] https://business.linkedin.com/en-uk/marketing-solutions/blog/posts/B2B-Marketing/2017/Our-pick-of-the-most-important-B2B-digital-marketing-statistics-for-2017 (archived at https://perma.cc/AX4R-XL6L)

Sweet, K (2018) [accessed 1 August 2019] 5 ways B2B SAAS companies can use triggered emails, *Evergage* [online] www.evergage.com/blog/5-ways-B2B-saas-companies-can-use-triggered-emails/ (archived at https://perma.cc/26YM-CJ39)

10

B2B digital and lead nurturing

WHAT YOU WILL GAIN FROM THIS CHAPTER

After reading this chapter, you will understand:

- types of lead nurture strategies;
- how to use email, social media and your website for lead nurturing;
- lead recycling;
- key technologies to use for lead nurture;
- lead nurture plans and templates.

Introduction

Digital and lead nurturing

With the lengthening sales cycle and changing customer behaviours, organizations need to look after prospective customers' needs and questions over a longer period of time. As a consequence, sales and marketing have a more challenging task in keeping prospects warm across these longer periods.

This chapter looks at all the possible areas and techniques which organizations can use to support this challenging task.

Lead nurturing defined

Lead nurturing is defined as anything which is done to progress prospective customers in their buyer journey. Lead nurturing usually takes place after a lead has been captured, and spans from that point through to the purchase stage.

Typically, we talk about lead nurturing within the pre-purchase stages for prospects but this could also apply to existing customers post-purchase as they buy additional products and services. Lead nurturing involves multiple marketing channels and encompasses the use of content or other information types to support customers.

Through lead nurturing, the potential supplier is looking to create a relationship with prospective customers.

Importance of lead nurturing

Lead nurturing is particularly important in the B2B relationship as the time between lead capture and purchase can be lengthy. On average this period for B2B companies is around 12–18 months. The challenge for the organization therefore is to keep customers interested in the organization's products.

For B2B marketers, it is important to understand roughly the length of this lead nurture period, as it will help with the lead nurturing planning later on. Lead nurturing is about improving the possibility of conversion, as the warmer the lead is, or the more interested the prospective customer is, the higher the chance they will move to purchase.

The statistics behind lead nurture demonstrate the importance as well as the benefits of this. According the Annuitas Group, nurtured leads make 47 per cent larger purchases than non-nurtured leads (Lovell, 2016).

The sales cycle and lead nurturing

The sales cycle used to start with sales accepting the lead (creating a SAL: sales accepted lead). The final stage of the sales cycle involves closing the deal. As shown in Figure 10.1, this sales cycle has changed, and is probably better understood as the 'lead nurturing period' due to two factors.

The first is that the handover to sales for some industries and customers is happening much later as customers themselves prefer not to enter a sales conversation so early.

The second reason is the increasing demands on sales from customers before purchase as they explore, learn and review their prospective purchase decisions. Sales have a bigger challenge than before as they not only need to use softer sales skills by offering information and facilitating conversations, but also need to understand how to distribute content, usually with support from marketing.

FIGURE 10.1 Where the sales cycle fits

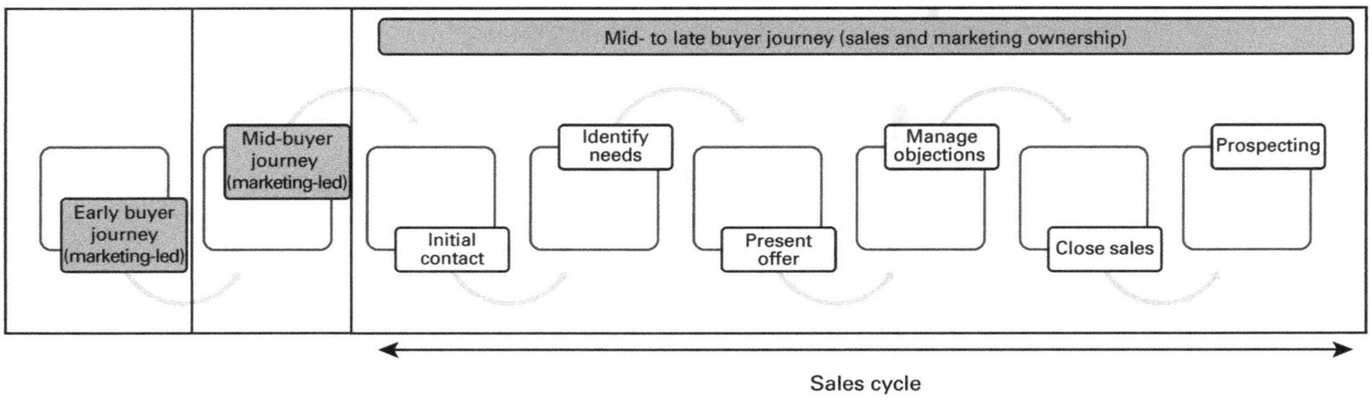

Early buyer journey (marketing-led)

Mid-buyer journey (marketing-led)

Mid- to late buyer journey (sales and marketing ownership)

Initial contact

Identify needs

Present offer

Manage objections

Close sales

Prospecting

Sales cycle

Facilitating lead nurturing

As we saw earlier in the book, different customer segments have different buyer personas and different paths in their journeys. With the current digital environment offering a matrix of possibilities in terms of channels and content for customers to progress in their buyer journeys, lead nurturing in turn also needs to be more sophisticated.

Figure 10.2 shows different visuals in terms of how lead nurturing can be facilitated or optimized based on a better understanding of the customer and the customer journey. Three options are illustrated: add another touch-point, remove a touchpoint or provide an alternative paths.

Aside from these options, lead nurturing can be improved through better integration of content and channels through integrating links or social media widgets.

Lead handover and sales readiness of leads

I'm often asked about when a lead is ready to hand to sales. This of course will depend on how organizations structure themselves around lead generation and nurturing, but a good approach is to use the BANT label to highlight a high-quality lead:

- **Budget** doesn't necessarily mean that a prospect divulges all information regarding budget and flexibility, but organizations can get an idea by understanding the type and number of product and service they are interested in. Through scale and type, organizations can then do the simple maths in calculating their budget.

- **Authority** refers to whether the contact has decision authority for the purchase. If not, organizations should look to finding the person who does.

- **Need** is about identifying the prospect's needs more precisely.

- **Time or timing** is about identifying when exactly the products or services are required by the prospect. If the purchase is needed immediately, marketing would need to hand over much faster to sales; where the purchase may be made one year later, marketing may need to further nurture the lead before passing on.

FIGURE 10.2 Lead nurturing options

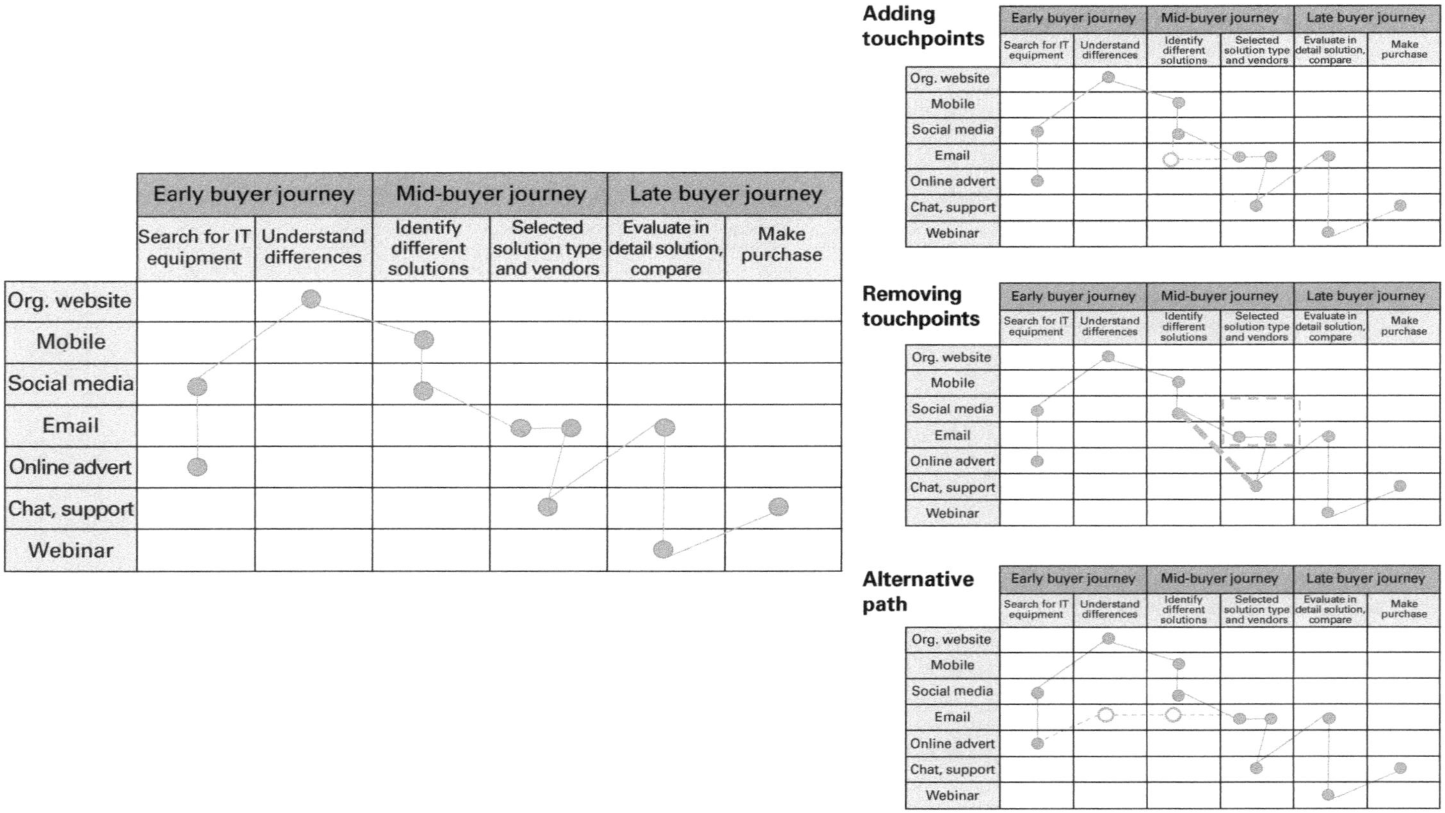

Types of lead nurture strategies

Figure 10.3 demonstrates some key strategies that you may want to consider for your lead nurturing.

Inbound lead nurturing

Inbound lead nurturing, sometimes known as incoming lead generation, is when traffic or leads come to your website, ideally due to some well-thought-out customer journey mapping and associated marketing activities.

The success of inbound lead nurturing hinges not only on capturing interest or a lead from owned company digital properties, eg website or social media, but in successfully taking a lead through the subsequent steps.

The advantage of nurturing an inbound lead is that they're already thinking of and approaching you, so there is some intent in their decisions, whether it is about exploring your site, researching a specific area, or

FIGURE 10.3 Lead nurturing strategies

interacting with you as a company. The challenge for B2B marketers is understanding this, and doing the right and appropriate level of lead nurturing.

GETTING PERMISSION

With inbound leads, one of the areas you'll need to check is whether you have permission to conduct lead nurturing. Make sure to ask permission once customers are at the point of engaging you, which may be related to preferences in terms of the information the prospect is interested in receiving. Permissions should also comply with GDPR and e-privacy laws.

LEAD SCORING

One of the initial goals with incoming leads is to understand their stage and intent in the buyer journey. This is a form of lead scoring, marking them correctly for the next stage. Scoring typically uses a point scale; as you can see from Figure 10.4, leads have different points assigned to them based on their activity, with higher points for engaging with mid-level content or responding to emails.

As they move through the journey, the greater the total number of points a prospect has, the warmer or hotter the lead is. Points can also be assigned based on demographics or firmographics, with those accounts or stakeholders fitting more closely the criteria of the perfect stakeholder or organizations being awarded higher scores.

Most marketing automation technologies already provide support for lead scoring, in the form of suggestions or guidance in setting up manual scoring systems, or both.

FIGURE 10.4 Lead scoring

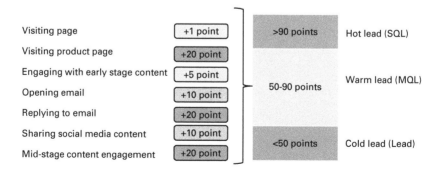

Drip nurturing

Drip nurturing is when marketing communicates with customers, usually using email, at regular frequent intervals, regardless of the buyer behaviour relating to the content communications.

Drip nurturing is a basic form of nurturing (some would argue that it is actually not nurturing), so why do companies still conduct it? It may potentially be due to a lack of understanding of customer journey or a lack of being able to target and identify pools of customers to properly nurture. It may also be that there simply aren't the resources to use other forms of lead nurturing – remember, email nurturing is basically free.

Drip nurturing doesn't account for email behaviour, and follow-up emails are not based on behaviours such as what has been opened or clicked through. As a result, there is often less than optimal performance and this practice may result in a proportion of recipients being put off the company.

Post-sales nurture

Post-sales nurture campaigns focus on helping customers with additional needs, and helping them progress through their post-purchase customer journeys (this will be discussed further in Chapters 16 and 17). Post-purchase nurturing can come in many forms, including nurturing by identifying possible next purchases, nurturing by cross-selling, and nurturing to improve loyalty.

Post-purchase nurturing can also be broken down into micro-nurturing, where specific steps or moments are nurtured. This may be helping customers to deploy their purchased product or services, or explaining how to engage with the company if they need to make further purchases or to ask a question.

To support your nurturing of these leads, you could identify touchpoint emails which allow customers to understand more about the product or service they purchased, or offer complementary products or services through suggestions which support the cross-sell or upsell.

Account-based lead nurturing

Account-based lead nurturing is where lead nurturing techniques are used across an account. This can be thought of as part of account-based marketing. Account-based nurture covers a broad area and includes nurturing techniques to develop interest and move the prospective customer to the next stage in the buying process or improve the relationship between organization and vendor.

Account-based nurturing can occur where there has been interest from an organization, from one or two decision makers. The difference between general lead nurturing and account-based nurturing is that potentially several people within an organization are engaged, targeted, nurtured as opposed to one decision maker.

Email lead nurturing

Arguably one of the most commonly known and used forms of lead nurturing is email nurturing, especially as email marketing can help you qualify those leads in the first place.

Recent research has shown that email marketing and nurturing, when done well, is remarkably effective: for every $1 spent, email marketing yields $44 ROI, and companies that excel at lead nurturing generate 50 per cent more sales-ready leads at a 33 per cent lower cost (Miller, 2018).

Understanding email behaviours

There are a number of recognized behaviours and actions related to email marketing including open rate, clickthrough rate, landing page hits, bounce rate and delivery rate.

Open rate refers to which emails have been opened. Clickthrough rate shows that recipients have both opened an email and clicked on something within it, and therefore indicates further interest.

Delivery rate identifies how many emails got delivered based on your email list, and bounce rate refers to the percentage of email addresses in your subscriber list that didn't receive your message because it was returned by a recipient mail server.

There are a number of ways to improve delivery rates, such as using fewer graphics, making it easy to unsubscribe from emails, having ongoing data cleansing activities, avoiding using attachments and personalizing emails.

Email retargeting

This is about retargeting prospects who have shown an interest in your products or services. Focusing on these customers for targeting or retargeting will improve the chances of a higher conversion for those prospects. Retargeting can be useful when you want to capture the attention of prospects who've visited your organization's website or a specific page of it, or when you want to tailor communication to prospects who have downloaded specific pieces of content.

There are two types of email retargeting – targeting an audience with display ads after they've read an email from the advertiser, and emailing a website visitor, which is achievable by matching cookies on the website to the email address of the user who just visited. The user can then receive personalized messages concerning the product or information they just viewed on your website.

PRACTICAL TIP
How to email targets correctly

There are a number of best practices in email targeting. Some of these include targeting your opt-ins correctly, and targeting or retargeting prospects relevant to actions they've taken or content they've engaged with.

You can also exclude your existing customer base or existing subscribers, and use CRM technology to improve targeting of your emails.

PERSONALIZED EMAILS

Email personalization can come in different degrees – from simply referring to the recipient by name and business role in the introduction to an email to discussing their specific needs and background.

Research has shown that personalizing your email messages boosts click-through rates by 14 per cent and conversions by 10 per cent. Meanwhile, the Direct Marketing Association found that segmented and targeted emails generate 58 per cent of all revenue (Foster, 2018).

Calls to action

Another way of improving lead nurturing impact is through the use of calls to action (CTAs). A CTA is an image or line of text that prompts your visitors, leads and customers to take action, such as highlighting a video product demonstration which prospects can watch.

Nurture emails are most successful with some form of CTA. Embedding a CTA button or message can push progress compared to just sending informative emails without any next steps.

Social media marketing and lead nurturing

Social listening

Social listening is about listening to online conversations between customers and potential buyers, with the purpose of gaining better insights about them. It's possible to monitor what customers are saying by:

1 using Google Alerts to receive an alert every time your brand, industry or competitors are mentioned;

2 using social media management tools which track posts;

3 tracking hashtags and keywords, especially through Twitter.

By picking up mentions and capturing insights through social listening, you can support the nurturing process by proactively supplying answers to commonly asked questions, for example.

Nurturing across social media channels

One thing to think about is the diversification of social media channels in the B2B space in the past decade. Through the customer journey and deepened insights, organizations should understand how to nurture leads not only within the channel, but across channels and different areas of social media. For example, some customers may be using Twitter, LinkedIn and Instagram simultaneously, whereas others are heavy users of one social media channel.

The customer journey should also give us an indication of when particular social media channels are used and in what sequence this may occur.

Sharing relevant content on social

Content can be distributed directly or via sales, and can be scheduled. We can identify relevant content to share through an understanding of the buyer persona, as well as understand when and which platforms they use, their key interests, pain points and keywords used.

For example, if we know that certain buyers have an interest in particular themes but wish to digest these themes in the mid-buyer phase of the buyer journey in infographic, video and SlideShare formats, we now have sufficient and specific enough detail to work with and can ensure we have this ready to share on social media.

Promote gated content

Gated content on social media can capture more details about a prospect, which subsequently help to tailor messages and content to them and in turn improve response rates. Although there are disadvantages for gated content, the quality of captured leads can be better assessed as people leave details behind.

Website and lead nurturing

Your organization's website plays a crucial role in lead nurturing as it is the one main area where you can collect and analyse data to understand prospects. There are a few things to consider regarding the website's place within the lead nurturing process.

As websites can be the destination for a lot of prospects from social media, other online sites, emails, and other sources, the destination of a link to a company website should be related to the type of content most relevant to the customer or prospect. Is it more about educating the prospect, or to help them explore options or to support final decisions in the purchase process?

Websites therefore act as the hub for all other channels to not only capture leads, but also provide information to other areas. Websites can also help customers through dynamic content; in the education phase, customers can be provided with content according to the search term by which they arrived at your website.

Finally, as websites can house different types of landing pages, whether hosting information, capturing contact details or acting as a nurture page, you should consider which is the most relevant for your prospective customer.

PRACTICAL TIP
Using your website to help prospects

Websites can help with queries by having pages with embedded videos, or by having automated chatbots which answer questions in real time and can direct queries accordingly.

FAQ web pages are also good to include for more general and common queries. Dropdown help menus are also useful, as they offer common paths for customer queries.

Lead recycling

Lead recycling is about including leads from previous marketing programmes or activities in your current lead nurture initiatives. These leads which have fallen out of the lead nurture process are regarded as leaked, and these would be good to put back into a lead nurture programme of their own. We can call this 'lead recycling'.

What are leaked leads and why do they exist?

So what are leaked leads? Essentially these are leads that didn't get followed up, weren't passed on or were not ready to be nurtured. This can happen for different reasons: incorrect assignment of leads to salespeople, salespeople being absent or leaving the company, salespeople not trained in follow-up or lead qualification issues.

Other background reasons are due to sales bandwidth in managing leads. It may be that some salespeople received a disproportionately high amount of leads, and needed to focus their attention on the most likely to purchase, meaning some wouldn't have been nurtured fully.

Why recycle?

Even if these leads weren't passed on or if nothing happened with them, this does not mean they are not viable.

In the B2B space some companies operate in very tightly defined industries where there are relatively few opportunities per given company or territory, so there isn't the luxury to not re-engage prospective customers. Other leads are recycled because they are not yet 'warm' and need further nurturing.

How to manage leaked leads

The first step is to categorize leaked leads and score them; how warm were they, what level of content were they engaging with, and which areas of the business were they interested in. Once categorized, ensure you have different re-nurture streams based on any different needs and lead 'temperatures'.

Considering they are being recycled, it is important to manage these leads more closely and track and monitor their progress. Establish clear rules on lead temperature and use technology to track this. You might employ trigger-based nurturing and dynamic content to move them through their customer cycle until it's time to hand over.

Where the lead leakage was due to a sales issue, then make sure to assign leads more carefully and plan for the correct follow-up.

Technologies for lead nurturing

In terms of technologies, marketing automation and/or CRM are probably the core tools needed for lead nurturing. Most companies' first starting point is having a CRM system in place which can be used to track leads in terms of follow-up and progression.

However, CRM systems are usually less equipped to automate, manage, and monitor digital nurturing of leads. This is where marketing automation technology comes in.

Marketing automation

Through marketing automation platforms, one can score leads in different ways. Each company can have different approaches to scoring leads due to different industries, different target segments and different products and services.

In lead scoring you will assign attributes to the lead, usually scoring based on a point range of 0 to 100. Marketing automation can track and assign scores to your leads, according to the criteria that best suits your strategy.

IP look-up and reverse IP

You could also use advanced IP look-up technologies such as GatorLeads. Tracking IP addresses can improve and enhance your website analysis, boost marketing campaign success and benefit lead generation for sales success.

Google Analytics uses IP tracking to provide details about the audience visiting the website in question, including geo-location, and to identify organizations which visit your website. Open Web Analytics includes advanced website metrics and uses IP tracking to better understand the most visited locations. Some companies do this to match IP addresses to their own database of business contacts to provide more enriched data.

Some technologies can provide names and locations of businesses visiting your website, and names and contact details for key decision makers to further support this.

Another technique is reverse IP look-up, the process of querying the domain name system (DNS) to determine the domain name matching the IP address. Here your website analytics technology might help you identify the IP address and the reverse IP look-up allows you to identify the company.

Lead nurturing planning

Steps in lead nurturing

The usual process for lead nurturing is shown in Figure 10.5. As with almost everything in marketing, it starts with defining the segment and audience. The next steps are to define the scope and steps to set up the timeline, and consider how to support the needs through a content and channel plan.

FIGURE 10.5 The lead nurture process

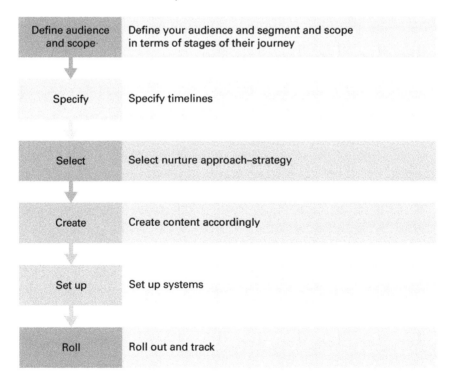

TABLE 10.1 Lead nurture plan template

	Nurture stage 1	Nurture stage 2	Nurture stage 3
	Considering options	Comparing alternatives	Purchase stage
Touchpoint and nurture activity – Channels			
Touchpoint and nurture activity – Content			

The scope of lead nurturing is usually the time from where the lead is captured through to the point of handing off to sales – this can be nine months, for example. You need to have a plan to keep the lead warm during this period. This includes properly identifying initial interest and understanding how to develop that interest into something more tangible.

For this, use the template in Table 10.1. The template is broken into different stages of the buyer journey in the mid-buyer (consider and compare alternatives) and late-buyer journey (the purchase stage). For each stage we need to think of channels being used, touchpoints and the content we'll provide in terms of content format.

Using this template, it will be possible to understand your needs in terms of content required as well as who needs to be involved. The template can also help set expectations between sales, marketing and other departments of the stages involved in nurturing a prospect.

CASE STUDY
Sage

In 2016, Sage, an accounting software company, were looking to target decision makers in three different departments, HR, Payroll and Finance, in companies with 1,000 employees or more. The campaign centred around a survey called the Big HR and Payroll Quiz.

Sage created a high-impact video to accompany the quiz, working with MOI Global. The quiz was centred around personalities, and was provided in a quick and easy format where respondents were able to discover their work style and assess skills related to key work areas. Respondents could find where they placed overall in the fields of HR and payroll professionals.

The campaign resulted in a substantial increase of 110 per cent in leads over the previous year, as well as accounting for almost a third of the marketing leads for the financial year (Edwards, 2017).

EXERCISE
Put it into practice

1   Which lead nurturing strategies do you use today?
2   To what extent are you applying email for lead nurturing?
3   Create a lead nurturing plan using the template in Table 10.1 for your next lead nurturing activity.

References

Edwards, J (2017) [accessed 24 January 2020] Awards case study: How Sage drove a 48% lead gen increase through a brand awareness digital campaign, *B2B Marketing* [online] www.b2bmarketing.net/en-gb/resources/b2b-case-studies/awards-case-study-how-sage-drove-48-lead-gen-increase-through-brand (archived at https://perma.cc/PRV4-ERUS)

Foster, R (2018) [accessed 1 February 2019] 5 Best Practices for Successful B2B Email Marketing, *business2community* [online] www.business2community.com/email-marketing/5-best-practices-for-successful-B2B-email-marketing-02091426 (archived at https://perma.cc/ZR48-9LWB)

Lovell, J (2016) [accessed 1 February 2019] Why Do Nurtured Leads Make 47% Larger Purchases?, *MD Prospects* [online] www.mdprospects.com/general/why-do-nurtured-leads-make-47-larger-purchases/ (archived at https://perma.cc/Q6B8-6Q4C)

Miller, G (2018) [accessed 1 February 2019] How to Use Email Marketing for Lead Nurturing, *Campaign Monitor* [online] www.campaignmonitor.com/blog/email-marketing/2018/10/how-to-use-email-marketing-for-lead-nurturing/ (archived at https://perma.cc/5BRG-D69K)

Further reading

Breyer, L (2016) [accessed 1 February 2019] 4 Advanced Lead Nurturing Strategies You Should be Using, *Kuno Creative* [online] www.kunocreative.com/blog/lead-nurturing-strategies (archived at https://perma.cc/G594-6TN6)

Humphrey, N (2018) [accessed 1 February 2019] Top B2B lead nurturing strategies for 2018, *Marketingland* [online] https://marketingland.com/top-B2B-lead-nurturing-strategies-2018-232854 (archived at https://perma.cc/3MYR-HG7Z)

Digital campaign management and integration

In Part Four we'll be covering key areas of digital marketing campaign management, integration, roll-out and monitoring. As you may have experienced, the challenge for digital marketing today in B2B is not just how to integrate digital with digital in the lead nurture phase, but also how to integrate digital with offline, digital with sales and digital with other departments.

Within the other areas of digital campaign management, we look at content marketing, sales and marketing alignment and measuring digital marketing.

11

B2B content marketing

WHAT YOU WILL GAIN FROM THIS CHAPTER

After reading this chapter, you will understand:

- B2B content marketing in general;
- how to align content to the customer and customer journey;
- B2B content formats;
- core content and fragmented content;
- when to update content;
- content activation and distribution;
- content amplification.

Introduction

With the rise of digital has also come the rise of content marketing, and digital technologies have made it easier to create richer and higher-quality content. Content marketing is a term which has increasingly been used in the last 10 years, although the concept has been around a lot longer than that.

This chapter looks at how to leverage content for digital marketing, and the different aspects of content marketing in a B2B context.

What is content and content marketing?

We can define 'content' as information which comes in different formats. Content marketing is the art of understanding what your customers need to know, and delivering it to them in a relevant and compelling way.

Most great content ticks the following boxes:

- it's relevant to the person and what they ask for;
- it's timely, so that content is provided at the right time in the buyer journey.
- it is compelling, ie it is unique and not something found everywhere;
- it creates a sense of urgency in that it helps customers think about the next stage in their journey.

Great content marketing in B2B is when content is used to optimize different stages of the customer journey or journeys, whether to develop brand affinity, to drive leads, to generate leads, to develop business or to nurture customers' interest through their journey.

How B2B content marketing differs from B2C content marketing

Ultimately, the user or recipient of B2B marketing is very different to that in B2C marketing. The role of the content, as a result, is different. Content in B2B has many roles, from making prospects aware of something such as a product or service through to educating them and supporting them through their evaluation of something. Content in the B2B space needs to also align more directly to the needs of the customer.

Even in in the awareness stage where you'd expect there would be similarities between B2B and B2C content, the focus is different. In B2B you'll probably hear a lot more about thought leadership content, where B2B companies are demonstrating their expertise in a particular area, something not so common in the B2C arena.

The message being delivered can also vary. Within B2B, this can be more fact-based and appeal to business concerns.

The digital channels used can also differ between B2B and B2C, as some may be more effective in reaching B2B audiences. Webinars, for example, are used a lot more in B2B marketing, whereas within B2C more traditional advertising such as TV or online TV is used.

As such, content formats also differ: advertorials, infographics, SlideShare, case studies and whitepapers are more typical of B2B marketing. The rich variety of content types may also change according to the stage of the buyer journey a customer is at.

Content and its roles

Generally content is used to inform, educate, excite and engage customers. Even in B2B, content is being used to generate excitement and to actively engage customers. Content is there to generate awareness, to resonate and initially connect with customers when used in adverts and SEO. In many situations, content can help answer customer questions related to the company or its products and services.

Content in B2B can be used to support the sales process and enable salespeople in progressing conversations with prospects with, for example, a compelling report, a piece of information or a story. It is also invaluable when supporting account managers in developing relationships and business with customers.

Content marketing checklist

Where you need to create content, it may be beneficial to develop a checklist. One way to do this is using the ROLSS framework:

- Relevant: is the content relevant to the buyer persona(s)?
- Original: is it original and new? Does it say something different and unique to your proposition?
- Locatable: can users find it? It is it placed in areas where the prospective buyer or customer are likely to look?
- Stage-specific: does it relate to a stage in the customer journey? Has the content been developed in line with the needs of that stage, and does it therefore highlight specific activities or actions?
- Shareable: can users share and use the content?

You can then go on to assessing the content using Table 11.1 below, rating each on a scale where 1 equates to 'not at all' and 5 equates to 'very much'. Eg a 5 rating under 'original' means that the content is entirely unique.

TABLE 11.1 Content marketing checklist

		Rating	Possible actions
R	Is it relevant to the buyer persona or industry they are in?		
O	Is it original and new?		
L	Can users easily find the content – is it placed in relevant areas?		
S	Is it specific to a stage in a customer buyer journey or a generic piece of content?		
S	Is it easy to share?		

Aligning content to the customer journey

We can look at aligning the content to the buyer persona with the following process.

Step 1: Start with the customer segment and buyer persona

In terms of content it is best to understand the key segments selected for targeting, as the relevant formats, types and content itself can differ. Using the customer segment, you should also create the buyer persona(s) to target.

Step 2: Deep dive into stages and touchpoints

According to the customer segment and buyer persona, now is the time to break down the stages of the customer journey into the key moments of focus and touchpoints. This stage involves two main tasks: journey/touchpoint mapping, and insight gathering.

Some of the information may be to hand already, but for gaps it's important to do the proper research to identify touchpoints and sequences.

Step 3: Touchpoint role and content alignment

The previous step is about creating a detailed journey map. This step focuses on understanding the roles of the individual touchpoints, and understanding what exactly the buyer persona wants to achieve with it. By identifying the role and purpose, you can now think about the content format as well as form an idea of the message to deliver.

To help identify touchpoint roles, consider creating a set of questions as part of a more detailed survey. Some potential questions are outlined below:

- What pain points did we answer in the awareness stage?
- What questions or information would buyers be looking for relating to their needs?
- What alternative solutions would the buyer be researching?
- How can our company's solutions be differentiated from the competition?
- How do my buyers review different alternatives to solving challenges?
- How can we nurture their interest?
- Which types of content do they respond to?

Key content formats in B2B

Figure 11.1 below shows the content formats that are often most effective for the different stages of the buyer journey.

For some content formats there has been a recent increase in their use and effectiveness. Let's take a look at the main ones.

FIGURE 11.1 Content by buyer journey stage

Stage	Awareness	Consideration	Purchase
Goal	Awareness	Build brand preference	Convert to customer
Content	ARTICLES	EXPERT GUIDES	PRODUCT COMPARISON
	INFOGRAPHICS	WEBCAST	CASE STUDIES
	THOUGHT LEADERSHIP	VIDEO	LIVE DEMO
	ANALYST REPORTS	COMPARISON	PRODUCT LITERATURE
	RESEARCH REPORTS	LIVE INTERACTIONS	ROI TOOLS
	WHITEPAPERS	WHITEPAPERS	DETAILED ASSESSMENTS
	EXPERT CONTENT	SOLUTION PAGES	SALES ENABLEMENT
	EDUCATIONAL CONTENT	EVENTS	

Blogs

One increasing phenomenon is the use of blogs in B2B, specifically in the area of lead generation. Blogs are informational pieces housed online, on blogging sites, on company websites or elsewhere.

Blogs are cost-effective pieces of content which can also build more traffic for your website. Some blogs are used to turn prospects into leads through embedded calls to action (CTAs). Blogs with integrated CTAs might include a free trial of a product or service, or some free downloadable material such as a report.

Blogs are also great ways to demonstrate thought leaderships for B2B marketing, whilst at the same covering long-tail search terms, attracting prospects in the awareness and consideration stages of the buyer journey.

Podcasts

Podcasts have had an interesting history. They are long-form audio programmes, and were originally used in the early 2000s. They were typically geared towards niche audiences in the consumer space.

More recently, with the increasing pervasiveness of smartphones and the increased use of mobile marketing, podcasts have become a very interesting content format, not only for B2C marketers but also for B2B. According to recent data from LinkedIn, over a third of users listen to podcasts (Miller, 2016).

BENEFITS OF PODCASTS

The benefit of podcasts is that they are an easy-to-consume content format, and can be listened to while doing other tasks. In fact, some B2B customers will listen to podcasts while running in the morning or while doing some other work or activity.

Podcasts for organizations also help to establish further their thought leadership as well as expand their audience.

RECORDING AND PUBLISHING PODCASTS

Podcasts can be recorded with most audio technology. For example, Audacity and Garageband are suitable for making recordings.

In terms of publishing the content, there are some interesting free options such as Podbean and Buzzsprout, though it is advisable to check the regular platform a buyer persona may use to listen to podcasts. Some B2B customers will use iTunes, others prefer Spotify.

Case studies

Case studies are a key part of your content marketing portfolio, especially for lead generation. They are probably one of the most asked-for types of content. They can attract customers because they are usually about customers. Ideally, they involve customers talking about their experience and so can provide invaluable advice to other people in the same situation.

Case studies are particularly useful for providers of more complex products or solutions as they are a great way to tell a story.

Gamifying B2B content

WHAT DO WE MEAN BY GAMIFYING B2B CONTENT?

Gamification means using gaming concepts to engage users and/or to have them respond or to carry out actions. Gamification has in the past been very much the home of B2C marketing, but it's coming into B2B marketing more and more in the pre- and post-purchase journeys.

Gamification is about providing a fun experience, using gamified concepts to entice and engage content consumers. It has been proven to result in much higher engagement levels, as well as more stickiness in customer loyalty.

Here are some ways to implement a B2B gamification content strategy:

1 define the incentive: what a B2B customer will get for participating in the game (even if you don't call it a game);

2 drive participation and enable a community approach: games require multiple participants and are based on people playing against each other;

3 define the game mechanics: will you drip-feed content, or include an unlock mechanism (eg a password or QR code)?

Core content and fragmented content

Many B2B marketers are concerned about finding budget to create all the pieces of content required. One way to deal with this challenge is not to secure more budget or create more budget, but to think of the content creation approach. An alternative to creating multiple pieces of content and subsequently stitching them together is to find a core theme and create a large piece of content around that.

This main piece of content is sometimes called core content, or 'Big Rock content' as LinkedIn calls it (Caltabiano, 2015).

Examples of core content

Core content can be a big piece of research, potentially presented as a long-form piece of over 2,000 words. It could be a compelling B2B story related to your industry or company, or a case study. These could be used later to support other pieces of content or presented as a set of customer stories which align to a theme.

You might also consider a gamified programme as your core content, which engages B2B customers and can actually generate its own content.

You'll be able to identify this core content by understanding the buyer, the industry, and what interests them.

Content fragmentation

Once this big piece of content has been created, the next step is to fragment it or 'atomize' it to support a content strategy.

Fragmenting an original base piece of content means there will be consistency in the messaging, tone and style, even as they are used and distributed separately. Also, in its core form, a large piece of content is usually not digestible; some pieces of research can encompass thousands of words, which is certainly not viable for most customers to be receiving. Therefore, making it more readable supports greater sharing and amplification.

Taking your main piece of content and breaking it up is more resource-efficient; marketers can cover more ground, but avoid having to pay for lots of separate pieces of content. Finally, as is the case with identifying the touchpoint roles, fragmentation is usually done according to content formats and the needs of the buyer persona(s).

How much content do you need?

So how much content do you really need, and how much is too much content? As discussed in Chapter 1, over the past five years there's been a steady increase from B2B marketers in the volume of content produced, as well as the budget they allocate to creating content.

One way to approach this is to first define your marketing goal or the focus for your marketing activity, as with a broader scope you'll need more content. Some of the questions which will help you define scope are:

- How many decision makers or buyer personas am I focusing the marketing activity or campaign on? Start to think about the decision-making unit for your intended customer segment. Are you focusing on one persona for a particular marketing action, or on multiple buyer personas? This will determine the type and the amount of content you will need.

- How many stages of a customer journey will be covered? Usually each stage will require slightly different content types/formats, although some formats can be used across some of the stages. For example, for generating awareness in the need recognition and need quantification stages, you might create videos, banners and infographics which can be used across both stages.

- How long is the sales cycle? Think about the length of time it takes for customers to move from the initial need recognition stage through to the purchase stage and the purchase itself. As mentioned in previous chapters, in the B2B relationship space it is quite common to hear about sales cycles lasting 12–18 months.

When to update content

Is there a 'best' time to update content? Should this be a continuous process or at intervals, and how long should those intervals be?

To answer this question, think of the following key areas:

- How targeted was the content marketing? Was it focused on a specific target segment and within that a targeted pool of customers? If the content was used previously to target specific customers, then these can be removed from the next campaign and so the content can be re-used.

- Is there a timeliness to the content – is it seasonal or does it have an expiry date? Understanding ageing of content will help address the first point; if it doesn't age, then chances are that you could use this again. In many B2B industries, the trends and themes don't change as rapidly as they do in the consumer space, which means messages and themes can span multiple quarters, even years at a time.

- Core and fragmented exposure: was the original core content given any exposure in its original form? If not, you could rework and repurpose this core content.

- Breadth in applicability: could this content also cater for a different target segment? This is similar to the first question, but here we are using the content to go after a different type of customer or segment.

Essentially, if the content is still very relevant, doesn't age and has only been used for a very targeted segment previously, then chances are it could be used again and wouldn't need to be updated.

Another angle is to understand if only some of the fragmented pieces of content have been used, and whether aspects of the core content could be repurposed in a different way.

Ageing of content and freshness of content can also be industry-specific, though there are situations where content probably needs refreshing, such as blogs and the front-page content on your website. This is where customers' interest is captured and they could be viewing these areas multiple times.

Content activation and distribution

Getting the content to audiences can be called content activation, as you're distributing, promoting and implementing it.

It's important to think about resource and budget to activate content relative to resource and budget in creating it. It's no good to have all this great content and no means or budget to actually promote it. As a lot of the focus of B2B marketers goes towards content creation, the risk is that the budget is used primarily in creation, with little left to activate it.

Budget for content activations includes promotion on different marketing channels to reach customers. These could be both digital and non-digital channels, and may involve signing up paid influencers.

One formula to potentially apply is that of sponsorships. Typically sponsorship models tell you to have a 3-5:1 ratio between sponsorship fees and sponsorship activation: for every £1 you invest, you need between 3 and 5 times that to activate sponsorship through advertisements and paid media.

This means that if you spend £100,000 on content creation you would need at least three times that to activate it, and therefore the total content marketing budget needs to be around £400k.

Paid, earned and owned

Another way to think about content activation is according to the type or category of channels and content you intend to use. Channels are typically broken into paid, earned and owned:

- paid channels are those on which advertising is paid for;
- earned channels are those where a company can contribute content or media to without payment;
- owned channels belong to the company itself.

OWNED MEDIA

These are properties owned by the company such as websites, blog, social media pages, PR sites and email newsletters. One of the drawbacks of owned media is that there may be less opportunity to reach 'new' customers if you use these alone. However, owned media does mean you have more control over its content, and it is much cheaper to run.

With the explosion of content marketing and content creation technologies in the last decade, there are more opportunities for organizations to create their own content and use own media channels. Organizations are capitalizing on becoming their own publisher, which has also meant a shift away from advertisers and PR agencies who would previously manage media and content for companies.

FIGURE 11.2 Digital paid, earned and owned

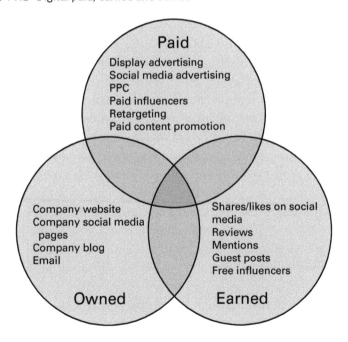

PAID MEDIA

Media you pay for includes most forms of advertising, and paid search. It can be a key part of revenue growth and of brand awareness as it allows you to reach new audiences and prospects, and can be very effective depending on the form of paid media you use.

With new forms of B2B digital marketing, there is more control over who you reach and how you target them. The obvious drawback with paid media is that it comes at a cost, both financial and in terms of time resources.

You have to research and understand which paid media to use and how to use them, as you'll want to make sure you're getting your money's worth. In the same way that the cost-effectiveness grid was used for defining the lead generation mix in Chapter 9, you could use this for any aspects of paid media or content.

Another consideration with some forms of paid media is the credibility of it. If you understand paid search and know that the shaded listings at the top of the Google search page are the ones paid for by companies, you may view these results as less credible than other parts of the page which haven't been paid for.

EARNED MEDIA

Earned media is also called free media or free distribution. The term 'earned' comes from the fact that you've earned your opportunity to appear somewhere, based on previous paid or owned media efforts.

Earned media happens when you're talked about through simple word of mouth, or when someone shares your content, likes it or comments on it on social media. It can be when a blogger spontaneously talks about you as a company or your products and/or services, without being paid a fee.

The benefit of earned media is that it comes from other people and can contribute to organic search rankings. These are regarded as more credible than if you are promoting your own company. And, of course, earned media is free.

Some of the drawbacks with earned media are the degree of control you may have; you're relying on what people say, and their credibility within the industry. Understanding how earned media works and how to monitor and understand it is key. This can be done through social media listening technologies.

Other drawbacks with earned media are the reachability of audience and the ability to target with earned media. In essence, you can't target with earned media because it is out of your hands.

In selecting your content and media, make sure to define your goals. If the goal is to generate awareness or to acquire 'new' customers then an owned media strategy may not be suitable. Similarly, if the goal is to improve retention of existing customers, then a pure paid strategy may not be right. Depending on the goal, your paid, earned and owned mix will differ.

Scheduling content

As part of the content management and creation process, you need to think about how to plan and schedule content. In scheduling content one creates a time-based view over weeks, months and quarters of when the content should be planned for, made available, and distributed.

This is done for many reasons. One is to understand if there is enough content overall for the period in question. For this reason, scheduling is worth carrying out before the content is created. It's also key for understanding if you have enough of certain types of content. For example, video content may be essential to your strategy, but you might find you don't have enough for the given period.

Additionally, by scheduling content one can show if one theme is enough for the period or if the period needs to be broken out into sub-themes which support the overall message of the campaign. Finally, content schedules can be used to plan with other departments, eg sales, or with external companies such as PR agencies and media agencies.

Publishing and distributing timings can be considered on smaller scales such as during the day or week, or more broadly over weeks, months or quarters. For some types of content getting the time down to a few hours is important. For most B2B audiences the peak times for receiving emails are during the morning or after lunch.

Scheduling on a broader scale may be required to hit the right month or period, eg to catch the end of the fiscal year. Schedules for certain social media like Twitter may mean that there needs to be multiple posts of the same content over time, potentially with different captions accompanying them to ensure maximum exposure.

Technologies which can be used to schedule include dedicated content management platforms such as Kapost and Percolate, or general scheduling platforms such as Monday.com, which also provides content-planning templates.

Content amplification

A further strategy to maximize the content you've created is to have a plan for amplifying the content. Content amplification may also be called earned media, although amplification is broader than that; it's probably the earned media of the earned media.

Content amplification looks at the collective strength of anyone who can promote and share your content. When mastered and done well you can grow your content's reach beyond its organic potential and drive more leads for your business.

As shown in Figure 11.3, amplification can be managed across three core areas:

1 your employees;

2 your customers;

3 your partners.

Employee amplification is about understanding your employees' power to share and promote your content. It involves a structured approach in terms of training, sharing, tracking and empowering employees from different departments; it is not just about sales advocacy. Amplification can also involve non-digital methods so that your employees are consistently messaging and describing your activities both offline and online.

Customer amplification means identifying customers who are real advocates of your company. They may even be strategic partners, so more engaged than your typical customer. Partner amplification can be carried out by channel partners. Partners can also include B2B industrial associations, vertical associations and influencers.

When thinking about setting up a content amplification initiative, make sure to optimize for search to make sure your content is visible, and for sharing by including social widgets in your content.

User-generated content in B2B

User-generated content in B2B is becoming an increasing trend. It is often regarded as more credible content than company-generated content, and can be extremely powerful if you find smart ways to do it.

FIGURE 11.3 Content amplification

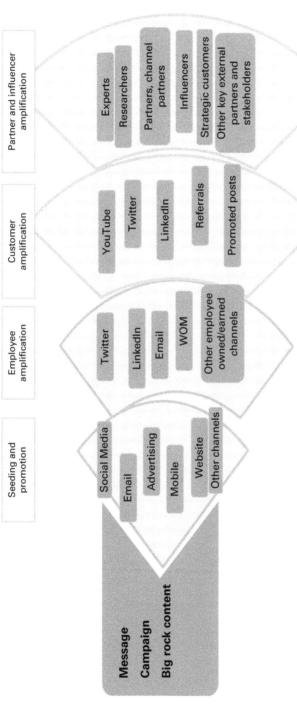

Following are some possibilities for creating user-generated content:

- **Leverage employees**: Train, support and encourage employees to create their own content. The idea here is that within companies there will be different content sources and levels of expertise, so tapping into this resource can help complement B2B marketers' activities.

- **Survey customers**: Using polls and surveys to understand customers' views on a particular theme can be interesting. The resulting survey and summary of results can serve as compelling content for potential customers.

- **Create customer video testimonials**: Usually, a company will identify customers for creating testimonials and short case studies, but with the UGC approach companies can facilitate customers providing them independently. It could be through a Twitter handle, or through a central web page where customers can upload testimonials. Such testimonials can then be used as content to engage prospects.

- **Use guest bloggers**: Companies can invite bloggers to submit articles, and link these guest blog pieces to particular topics.

- **Bring journalists and customers together**: By bringing journalists and customers together at a venue or area to allow them to engage and explore topics, both groups can subsequently create content that you can use. One example is a PR-based panel or meeting, allowing different business partners and customers to talk about a topic while journalists write up an article

B2B content marketing strategies: a summary

As we come to the end of this chapter, we can start to see different strategies forming relating to B2B content marketing. Below is a summary of these, and some additional ones for you to consider:

- **content amplification**: using employees, partners and customers to further distribute content;

- **streamlining content**: managing content more carefully according to customer journeys; not over-creating content but finding the right amount of content and budget to support content creation goals;

- **user-generated content strategies**: providing opportunities for your own networks to create their own content and testimonials;

- **mapping content:** better mapping content to the customer journey;
- **content distribution strategies:** strategies to leverage earned, owned or paid can be employed depending on the goals;
- **content syndication:** another strategy we explored in Chapter 6, this is about leveraging third-party platforms as partners to distribute content.

CASE STUDY
ADP

In 2015, ADP, a leading technology company offering business processing services like payroll and human resource management, launched a new content marketing campaign to target and engage their audiences. The idea of the campaign was to generate demand for their ADP Workforce Now product.

The campaign, titled 'Take the HCM Challenge', used multiple content pieces ranging from infographics to whitepapers, cookbooks and a diagnostic assessment tool. The results from the campaign were impressive, with $3.7m in business won and a $23 million pipeline generated over three quarters.

In addition, the ROI for the campaign was estimated at around 900 per cent (Cothran, 2015).

EXERCISE
Put it into practice

1 Apply the ROLSS content checklist to your most recent content. How does it fare against the different criteria?

2 Look at one of the areas of your customer journey, and map content to the different customers' needs for each of the touchpoints.

3 For your next marketing campaign think of possible candidates for core content. What could they be?

4 Review the frequency of content updates for a particular customer segment or theme. Understand whether there is a need for updating as much content the next time around, or whether existing raw content (in its original form) can be repurposed instead.

References

Caltabiano, G (2015) [accessed 1 August 2019] "Big Rock" content in a nutshell, *LinkedIn* [online] www.linkedin.com/pulse/big-rock-marketing-content-nutshell-giuseppe-caltabiano (archived at https://perma.cc/XXC8-B742)

Cothran, K (2015) [accessed 30 November 2019] Content Marketing Campaign of the Week: ADP, *ASPE Training* [online] https://aspetraining.com/resources/blog/content-marketing-campaign-of-week-adp (archived at https://perma.cc/6X2P-EVJ2)

Miller, J (2016) [accessed 30 November 2019] Who listens to podcasts – and why they matter to marketers, *LinkedIn* [online] https://business.linkedin.com/en-uk/marketing-solutions/blog/posts/B2B-Marketing/2016/Who-listens-to-podcasts-and-why-they-matter-to-marketers (archived at https://perma.cc/MHY4-LT2G)

Further reading

CMI (2018) [accessed 1 August 2019] 2018 Benchmarks, Budgets, and Trends – North America, CMI Marketing Profs and Brightcove, *Content Marketing Institute* [online] https://contentmarketinginstitute.com/wp-content/uploads/2017/09/2018_B2B_Research_FINAL.pdf (archived at https://perma.cc/PKY2-5B57)

LinkedIn (2016) [accessed 1 August 2019] Sophisticated Guide to Content Marketing, *LinkedIn* [online] https://business.linkedin.com/content/dam/business/marketing-solutions/global/en_US/campaigns/pdfs/LNK_LMS_SophisticatedGuideToContentMarketing.pdf (archived at https://perma.cc/YWM7-SVLT)

12

B2B digital marketing campaign planning

WHAT YOU WILL GAIN FROM THIS CHAPTER

After reading this chapter, you will understand:

- digital campaigns;
- the digital marketing campaign process;
- methods for selecting digital channels;
- resource definition for campaigns;
- how to set budgets;
- how to track campaigns.

Introduction

We've covered a number of aspects of customer journeys and how marketing fits into different stages, from awareness-based marketing in the early buyer journey to lead generation and lead nurturing in the mid- to late buyer journey.

This chapter looks at how to bring this all together, and plan campaigns which encompass different goals and stages of the buyer journey.

Digital marketing campaigns

What is a digital marketing campaign?

A campaign is an organized set of actions to promote and sell a product or service. In that sense, a digital marketing campaign is an organized set of activities comprising mainly digital marketing and digital technologies to promote an organization, product or service.

Campaigns can come in different forms and have specific goals – to capture attention, generate leads or reinforce customer loyalty – but the overall purpose of campaigns is largely consistent. They deliver messages, tell stories, and engage customers.

The campaign framework

To help us understand the campaign plan elements, let's refer to Figure 12.1 which sets out eight elements to consider, including goals, target segment, account and persona, budget setting, and campaign tracking.

Having these elements correctly investigated and managed are keys to digital marketing campaign success.

Another aspect linked to the goal and the target customer group is the bigger themes which will resonate (these may be referred to as buyer triggers).

FIGURE 12.1 The campaign process

Buyer triggers shift customers from whatever position they are in to a state of needing to purchase something more urgently. In campaigns, these typically centre on stories which highlight benefits, potential pain points and problem resolution – real benefits which can help customers.

An example of a buyer trigger could be new or changed legislation which influences customers to purchase something.

Goal and objective definition

Goal definition requires some thinking. The key question to ask is: what exactly are we trying to achieve? Does the organization need to generate awareness around a new product or service, does it need to change perception, or is the focus just to generate leads?

Once you've defined your goals, you need to then be a lot more specific as to the objective of the campaign. Well-written objectives should follow the SMART criteria – they should be specific, measurable, achievable, realistic and time-bound.

Examples of poorly defined objectives would be 'to generate more website traffic' or 'to reach more people with emails'. Alternatively, specific campaign objectives might look something like this:

- Acquire 20,000 visitors, 500 leads and 12 customers within the next 12 months from our inbound marketing efforts, in order to achieve our revenue goal of $600,000.

- Generate two customers from our current client list using email marketing in the next six months.

- Rank #1 for the keyword term 'B2B consultant', with the estimate that this will generate 300 visitors to our website per month.

As we look at the goal and objectives, think about the stages and scope of the campaign. Does the campaign cross multiple stages of the buyer journey, or will it just focus on one stage?

The target customer

The next logical step is to define the target customer. This clarifies the 'main' focus of the campaign: it doesn't mean excluding other customers if you can attract them, but focusing a campaign can line up messages, channels, content and formats much better.

Below are some key questions to think about:

- Who is our target market? Different segments might need different content; if we're considering more than one segment, are we building various content streams into the campaign?
- Are we focusing on accounts or account level by looking at multiple decision makers within an account?
- What is the buyer persona or customer profile we're thinking of?
- Do we have behavioural information?
- Are we targeting completely new customers, or existing ones?
- Are we targeting customers who know of us already?

This area of targeting can typically be determined by following a process starting with segmenting, then account definition and then the buyer persona(s).

Segmentation

When defining the main segment to use for the campaign, think about what the basis for segmentation is. Is could be geographic region, size of company or growth stage of the company (such as start-up, growing or consolidation).

The best way to define a good segment follows the ADAM criteria (adapted from Iannuzzi, 2014):

- Accessible: can the segment be effectively reached?
- Differentiated: will different digital marketing mixes in terms of content, communication channels etc be needed for different segments?
- Actionable: are the segments profitable enough to serve?
- Measurable: can we measure progress against segment marketing activities?

Accounts

Once the segment is defined, the next stage is to think of the type of organizations or accounts to focus on. This might be defined in the segmentation task above; however, usually segmentation is a bit broader.

Look at the type of industry sector and the size of company in terms of buying potential or buying power. Consider existing customers as well and include share of wallet as a criterion. As mentioned previously, share of wallet shows how much of a customer's potential spend in a given period they are spending on our products and service.

Buyer persona

In terms of target audience, this would be the buyer persona or buyer personas we're focusing on as covered in previous chapters.

Reaching audiences

Now that goals and target customers are defined, it's time to choose the ideal marketing channel mix.

Applying what was covered in the previous chapter, consider the pros and cons of the mix between paid, earned and owned media. Remember that during the mid- to late buying cycle you will be able to use more owned media channels as the customer is engaging with vendor media channels, eg your website and social media pages.

There are other methods for channel selection which can be used as alternatives or to complement the paid, earned and owned approach. These are:

- a baseline approach using ongoing analytics;
- an experimentation approach;
- buyer persona detailed research;
- media research, usually with support from a media agency.

Baseline approach

With the baseline approach, we would take data from the previous campaign and select channels based on learnings, assuming we're capturing channel mix in terms of contribution and output.

Experimentation approach

Another way is to start to roll out the campaign in a controlled, monitored fashion and adjust or tweak the mix depending on performance and use of channels. For example, if social media is delivering some interesting quality traffic to a website landing page, then we should maybe increase social media mix relative to another channel.

The risk with this is that the channels and content might be complementing each other and supporting a customer journey. However, this approach requires minimal planning investment, it's faster to implement, and supports organizations to learn as they implement.

Buyer persona research

This involves understanding the buyer persona to a detailed level, understanding which communication channels are consumed at different stages in their customer journey and how often social media or email is used. You can then define the appropriate mix and weighting in terms of contribution per channel.

Media research

Media research is usually done with support from companies who specialize in media – this could be a media research company or media agency. Media research would usually be conducted according to customer segment, by understanding which media channels they use for a particular goal.

Additional media research can be carried out to complement the above, such as polls or surveys to understand specific aspects in terms of customer media usage. Digital and data analytics could be used additionally – for example, looking at source traffic to a website for a given campaign can help us understand mix and quality of traffic.

Establishing KPIs

This part of the process relates to the goals established in the first step. If the goal is to increase brand awareness, for example, then you need to establish corresponding KPIs such as sentiment, or press mentions.

You should also consider the scope and timing of the campaign. Shorter campaigns can have a focused set of KPIs for the time period, whereas campaigns which run over multiple quarters will need to have KPIs associated for each period.

Defining resources

In this step you should define resource requirements for making the campaign happen – that is, for creation of campaign content, and in implementing and monitoring the campaign. To define the resource mix and review resources, take a look at Figure 12.2 which shows a 4S model.

You may notice that some of these areas are dependent on each other: in order to use the technologies, staff may require specific skills.

Staff

This involves knowing what human resources are needed to create, manage and review the campaign in all its different aspects. Types of resources that are of particular interest are content creators, media specialists, data analysts, and campaign managers.

By looking at the roles required, you can start to understand whether there are colleagues already available in-house or if you need to source externally.

Skills and competencies

Alongside this you should consider which competencies are required for the campaign. These could include copywriting skills, editing skills across

FIGURE 12.2 Marketing resource definition – the 4Ss

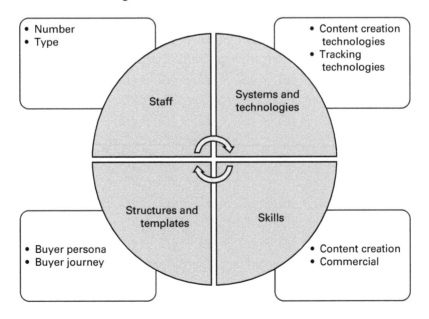

video, audio and written content, project management experience, and interpretation skills.

Systems and technologies

For campaign creation and roll-out, organizations may need various systems and technologies. These might include marketing automation technologies, CRM-based technologies, and video creating and editing tools. Applications to track the prospect across the campaign may be valuable, or website engagement, retargeting, lead scoring and management technologies.

If the focus of the campaign is around accounts, would account-based marketing technologies be required? If the campaign is dependent on social media, would you need to invest in social listening and monitoring technologies?

Structures and tools

The final resource might be templates and tools to have at hand before the campaign is developed. This might include a buyer persona or personas, the buyer journey view, content audit, customer journey map and content and channel view.

Setting the campaign budget

One way to define the campaign budget is to look at the goal or specific objectives, and then use these to shape the necessary budget.

Lead generation

If the campaign is based on generating leads, one relatively quick way is to look at current cost per lead based on previous activities. For example, if the cost per lead is $200 and the goal is to generate 100 leads, then the budget requirement is $20,000.

Awareness generation

For this you might want to look at reach. Reach information can be taken from social media-based campaigns, as platforms including Twitter and LinkedIn have calculators built into campaign tools to estimate the required budget for getting messages in front of audiences.

Content syndication platforms that are already communicating to our intended audience may be another avenue to explore, as through them it may be possible to understand budget requirements.

Desired share of voice

Understanding desired share of voice can help to determine associated budget levels. Example of companies include Nielsen Analytics, who have ways to show current SoV and associated media spend.

One could also look at return on investment-based budgets, where marketing commits to deliver a return based on committed budget or incremental budget.

Affordability

A final method could be looking at affordability – that is, what can the business afford to invest? Where budget is limited, the marketing department needs to look into more owned and earned media to implement the campaign and complement the limited paid media spend.

Campaign creation

Content creation was covered in detail in the previous chapter, but it's important to note here that creating a campaign means producing all digital assets, not just content. If the campaign runs over multiple quarters, then not all campaign-related assets will be needed out the outset.

The budget, scope and resource definition will help to guide your decision making, but the type of digital campaign will also factor. Will this be a campaign run through a social media platform or with a third party? Is the campaign going to include offline elements?

Campaign tracking

Once implemented, the campaign needs to be tracked to evaluate its progress and success. Campaigns are usually more budget-consuming than single marketing tactics or activities as they include a range of tactics. Some marketing campaigns can even last years – for example, IBM's Smarter Planet campaign spanned four years (Coolmedium, n. d.).

Hence, you need to really understand if campaigns are delivering according to objectives as they progress, and not just at the end.

The focus of the campaign will be a key factor in how things are tracked. Awareness-based campaigns may be tracked using Google Analytics and ad-tracking software, whereas broader campaigns resulting in leads may be tracked through landing pages, tagging and UTM codes.

Options for tracking campaigns

A summary of options for tracking campaigns can be found in Figure 12.3, including UTM codes, pixels, landing pages, phone tracking, ad tracking and CRM tracking. These methods aren't necessarily mutually exclusive, but can complement each other. As already mentioned, some may be more suitable than others depending on what is being tracked.

UTM CODES

UTM codes, sometimes called URL parameters, are tags which are added to the end of an URL and used typically by Google Analytics to track web browsing by cookies. UTM codes can provide insights such as where your visitors have come from, and which campaign led them to click on a link.

PIXELS

Pixels (sometimes called floodlight tags) are pieces of code placed on websites to track user behaviours. Pixels are particularly useful in specifically tracking the actions within a site, such as completion of forms. For each activity, a new pixel is generated.

FIGURE 12.3 Campaign tracking

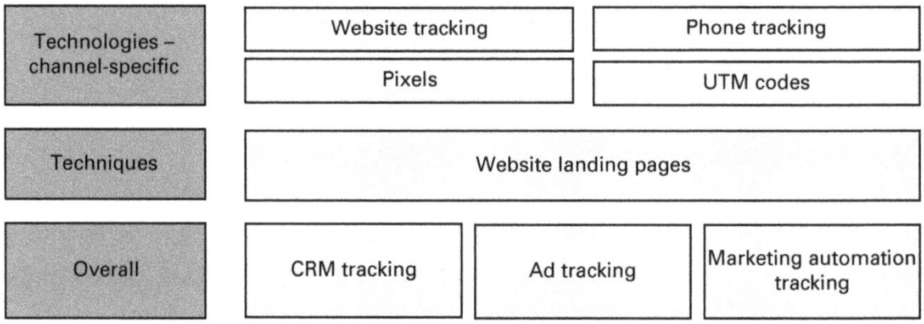

Technologies – channel-specific	Website tracking	Phone tracking
	Pixels	UTM codes
Techniques	Website landing pages	
Overall	CRM tracking	Ad tracking	Marketing automation tracking

AD TRACKING

Ad tracking can be carried out by using Google AdWords, LinkedIn campaign building and Bing Ads, among other tools. They can track conversion by covering areas such as newsletter sign-ups, downloads of apps, and other activities related to advertising.

CRM TRACKING

CRM tracking works by assigning a code to an activity such as a campaign or a webinar, or downloaded content. CRM tracking is usually used more for leads-based campaigns to monitor the progression of a lead through the buyer journey.

CRM tracking of leads might happen at the point the lead is handed over to sales, or once the campaign is started.

PHONE TRACKING

Phone tracking in B2B marketing should probably be included as part of the campaign tracking process, complementing other tracking mechanisms. Using technologies such as CallRail and Mediahawk, one can assign a phone number per marketing campaign and display this number on owned media properties.

You can then monitor the volume and effectiveness of calls to understand this aspect of the campaign's reach.

LANDING PAGES

When creating a campaign, make sure to set up 'appropriate' landing pages which align to the campaign tone and focus. Some landing pages educate, others capture the lead, while still others can be created to nurture it.

As an example, where campaigns are purely educational in nature the landing page should reflect this, with opportunities for the customer to leave details to received further information or educational content.

PRACTICAL TIP
Selecting agencies for campaigns

If you need to select agencies for your marketing campaign, you need to understand their fit for your company. Does their speciality and focus in the industry match your requirements? Do they understand B2B marketing, or do they only have a consumer marketing background?

It's important to check their digital expertise – as the digital space can change so rapidly, they should be up to date with the latest digital technologies and approaches. Sector expertise is also a factor to consider – if you operate in oil and gas, for example, do they understand marketing within that space?

You may also want to check their ability to implement results tracking for the campaign so that you can interpret and evaluate the campaign's success fully.

EXERCISE
Put it into practice

1 Reflect on a previous marketing campaign. What resources made the campaign successful? Would any different resources have meant a different level of success in the campaign creation and implementation?

2 The next time you need to create and implement a marketing campaign, apply or use an adaptation of the marketing campaign framework.

3 Using the ADAM segmentation model, how robust or strong are your segments? Do they fulfil each criteria of the ADAM framework?

References

Coolmedium (n. d.) [accessed 1 August 2019] IBM Smarter Planet, *Coolmedium* [online] www.coolmedium.com/ibm/ (archived at https://perma.cc/D7BM-8UXF)

Iannuzzi, A (2014) [accessed 1 August 2019] Marketing segmentation criteria – Five essential criteria, *LinkedIn* [online] www.linkedin.com/pulse/ 20140730082827-41390803-market-segmentation-criteria-five-essential-criteria (archived at https://perma.cc/SFS4-YUFC)

13

Digital integration marketing in B2B

WHAT YOU WILL GAIN FROM THIS CHAPTER

After reading this chapter, you will understand:

- what digital integration marketing is;
- how to integrate offline and digital;
- PR and digital integration;
- techniques and technologies for integration.

Introduction

What is digital integration marketing?

Digital integration marketing involves three key areas:

1 integration of digital marketing into offline marketing channels such as print, events, etc;

2 integration of digital marketing with other functions and departments;

3 integration of digital marketing with PR.

We'll address a fourth point – the integration between sales and marketing – in the next chapter.

Digital integration marketing is about developing a cohesive approach to the business using digital marketing and associated technologies, which results in improving the customer experience. We've already seen examples of how digital marketing can improve the lead nurture process in a previous chapter.

With recent digital technologies such as smartphones, better-quality content creation and editing software and distribution platforms, almost anyone can publish and produce different forms of content, whether text, image, or video. This ability to create more forms of content has also brought about a greater volume and fragmentation in content and, in turn, companies providing messages and marketing to customers who need to consider digital marketing integration more than ever before.

In this chapter we'll explore this growing and challenging task for B2B marketers, and how to truly integrate across these different areas.

Why integrate digitally?

The task of integrating digital with other areas, whether other forms of digital or offline channels, comes down to one main purpose: the customer. The customer now consumes content across multiple channels in short periods of time, so integrating digital across channels can provide a better and more seamless customer experience.

Another consideration is how organizational departments are adopting digital channels more widely. Customer service, for example, is overlapping more with marketing as the same channels are being used by customers to engage customer service departments, and vice versa.

Challenges in digital marketing integration

Below are some of the key challenges that you may initially come across in the task of integrating digital marketing. This chapter will give you some ideas to consider for overcoming these:

1 **What to integrate:** With multiple digital channels and multiple forms of content, the challenge is knowing which pieces of content to integrate with which channels.

2 **When to integrate:** Knowing when the right time is to integrate across channels can be difficult. Here, it's good to ask where the points are in the customer journey where digital needs to be integrated most.

3 **How to integrate:** As there are different methods for integrating, knowing the most suitable ones for your content and company is important.

4 **What not to integrate.** Other considerations are knowing whether some channels are redundant in their role in the customer journey, and so need to be removed or skipped.

5 Functional integration: Knowing how to integrate departments and functions.

Integrating digital and offline

Integrating digital with offline is based on the fact that prospects and customers don't conduct all tasks by interacting with organizations digitally. There are a number of situations where customers (and organizations) naturally still prefer to use or need to use offline channels.

That being said, there has been a huge shift of marketing channels to digital, and this move has led to benefits in terms of customers being easier to reach, target, engage, understand and generally market to. Therefore, finding a way to integrate offline activity into overall marketing, whether at content level or through each channel, can be very beneficial.

Before going further, let's quickly define what is meant by 'offline'. Offline channels include all marketing channels not leveraging the internet or online technologies. This includes printed magazines, printed brochures, catalogues, leaflets, billboards and events.

Where to start

One good starting point in the integration process is the customer journey. Most of the early B2B buying cycle channels tend to be digital so there are fewer issues in integrating digital with offline in that stage. However, as a customer moves through the other stages there are some offline touchpoints.

You should first understand which of the touchpoints in any given phase are offline, and then understand the main ones to focus on if there are multiple offline touchpoints. Creating a map similar to Figure 13.1 may help to visualize this for you:

FIGURE 13.1 Online and offline touchpoints

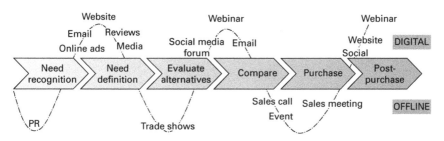

Planning for digital integration

Planning for digital marketing integration is about understanding touch-points and creating a touchpoint map. Where would customer service most commonly be used as a touchpoint? What are the offline and digital touch-points? Which sales touchpoints are common?

The planning of integration is to satisfy one main goal – to ensure and optimize the customer experience.

Considerations for digital marketing integration

- By stage, what is the touchpoint sequence today? What do customers do today to research and evaluate options in the consideration stage?
- By stage, what is the ideal touchpoint sequence?
- Identify the gaps in the current touchpoint sequence compared to the ideal version.

We've covered this part of optimizing the touchpoint sequence and touch-point map in Chapter 3. However, the idea of viewing touchpoints for improving digital integration is different in that we're also looking at customer service, PR, sales and offline marketing touchpoints. Sometimes this can be called customer experience mapping, as opposed to customer journey mapping.

Techniques and technologies for offline integration

Knowing how to integrate can be complex, and there are multiple options and possibilities available to B2B marketers. Marketing departments or companies are using some or all of the following as a way to improve inte-gration: QR codes, calls to action, URL shorteners, hashtags, Twitter addresses, personalized URLs, and search terms.

Let's look in a bit more detail at some of these techniques and technolo-gies which can enable integration between offline marketing and online, also summarized in Table 13.1.

QR codes

Visually, QR codes are square images with lots of squiggly lines. It is highly likely you're already using these if you've been taking flights recently or

TABLE 13.1 Techniques and technologies for offline integration

Offline activity	How to integrate
Phone calls (phone calls from websites, phone call tracking in general through digital technologies)	Phone call tracking technologies
Events Capturing leads at events Tracking activities at event	NFC, badge readers, hashtags, mobile apps, URL shorteners
Direct mailers Direct mailer with digital integration Capturing leads	Hashtags, URL shorteners, social media address, personalized URL
Other offline promotion Billboards, print leaflets and brochures	Hashtags, mobile URL, social media address, QR codes
Meetings Capturing contact info from meetings	Business card reader

going to the cinema, as QR codes are now being increasingly used in retail marketing and retail operations.

QR codes, whilst fairly established in B2C in various areas – at events, for example, to capture contact information and business cards – are now increasingly being used in B2B. Some examples of where QR codes can be used are in printed or any offline adverts to help redirect people to social media sites, case studies, whitepapers or any appropriate digital touchpoint.

They're also increasingly being applied to direct mailers to provide a more integrated experience for customers.

Using online calls to action in offline marketing

One way to use calls to action (CTAs) is to add them to printed materials which prompt audiences to visit your website, a social media page or a dedicated landing page. CTAs could include simple messages such as 'follow us on Twitter' or 'visit our website for more information'.

By sending audiences to online owned media areas, you can capture information more easily. Additionally, this may help direct the prospect or customers to the right channels and content, and in turn improve the nurture experience.

Hashtags

Hashtags are a type of metadata tag often used on social networks, especially on Twitter. Hashtags were introduced to LinkedIn in 2018 and operate in a similar way to Twitter, to categorize content.

Hashtags are great to use in offline content as they are easier to remember than website addresses. Tools which allow us to track hashtags include RiteTag, Hashtagify and Talkwalker.

URL shorteners

The use of URL shorteners has been a practice in online marketing for some time, but they are also becoming useful for offline marketing. URL shorteners help to condense the length of your site's URL, which allows more space for marketing messages in confined online spaces, such as on Twitter, where there are character limits.

They are also useful offline; a shortened URL can be easier to remember, therefore helping generate traffic to websites. By creating a URL tied to an offline campaign or content, companies can track those who arrive using that specific URL.

Typical URL shorteners include TinyURL, Bit.ly and is.gd. Most URL shortener technologies can also provide an overview of clicks on the shortened URL to your website. Additionally, most URL shortener technologies can also convert the URL to QR code, so you can use both techniques simultaneously.

PRACTICAL TIP

Use custom URLs to support trackability

One way to track offline traffic is to use custom URLs. Without these, a good portion of your marketing goes unmonitored and important insights or traffic are lost.

Implementing a custom URL means tying a web page or different web pages specifically to a campaign or persona. If you have more than one marketing campaign running simultaneously, you may want to run different URLs for different campaigns.

Personalized URLs for mailers

Personalized URLs are URLs created according to a persona or a type of person. They are very useful for direct mailers, as the URL can be printed on the leaflet or mailing, and with that organizations can track engagement and capture information for this segment.

Trackable phone numbers and UTMs

In addition to or instead of URLs, phone numbers can also be used on printed marketing material. The difference is that the phone number relates to a specific advert. Tracking how the phone number is used or a URL is accessed will tell us how campaigns are progressing.

Other techniques are to use UTM codes, which are simple codes attached to a URL to track source, channel, and campaign. They allow Google Analytics to analyse where searches came from.

Integrating direct mailing

Direct mail means any form of commercial information sent through the post. Direct mailer usage in the early 2010s decreased due to the advent of email marketing, but for some B2B marketers it is still regarded as an effective tool.

A recent survey of over 1,000 B2B marketers found that 57 per cent of these marketers considered direct mail marketing to be at least somewhat effective, and 22 per cent said they felt it was very effective (MRP, 2016).

With the increase in email and the shift of B2B communication moving to digital, the volume of physical post people receive has diminished dramatically in past years. By being a less-used marketing channel, direct mail has now become an interesting channel to leverage again, as it stands out more from other communication channels.

Integrating direct mail through technologies

Direct mail can allow marketers to reach, and capture attention – but it is expensive. To make this really effective and to properly integrate direct mail into an overall campaign, you could use some of the following approaches:

- Include QR codes, Twitter addresses, hashtags or all of these to offer opportunities for customers to engage further digitally.
- Offer a reason for people to engage online by showing them something compelling they'll find when they do so.
- Provide a personalized URL so that customers feel they've been given keys to an exclusive area.
- Use NFC (near field communications) technology: this can allow prospects to engage immediately with your digital content. It works by embedding a small microchip in the mailer which emits a short-range radio wave. If a customer has an NFC-capable mobile phone, the digital experience is activated by moving their phone over the mailer.

Integrating social media with direct mail

Direct mail and social media can be integrated in different ways as follows:

- You can test your direct mailer content (and any assumptions it is based on) by running it on social media first, by using social media targeting techniques to reach a group of customers aligned to the direct mail target customer sample.
- When the material is finalized and has been created, showing the direct mailer content on social media platforms will ensure it is distributed (and viewed) as widely as possible.
- Include social media icons in direct mail materials.
- Use social media data and customer insights to support the direct mail campaign.

Integrating events

The role of events

When people think of events, some people think of a consumer-oriented event or something involving an outdoor entertainment experience. In B2B marketing, events can come in literally hundreds of different flavours, to serve all the different roles of marketing and business needs. Events can be created to survey and understand customers, to increase awareness of a product or service, to engage customers, to retain customers and to nurture customers.

Of course, when we talk about events, the main part of it is physical in nature, so where does digital come in? Here are some ways where digital can be used with events.

Mobile applications

Mobile applications can be created for the event to facilitate engagement. A good example of this is where mobile applications both allow people to follow parts of the event according to themes and topic as well as engage with other attendees in sharing comments, posting images or any form of interaction.

For B2B marketing, this can also serve as a way to create user-generated content.

Video capture at the event

Previous event video content could be used as teaser videos for the up-and-coming event. Teaser content and teaser messages could also be used to generate excitement for the event as well as drive event attendance.

Another option that works just as effectively is to film content on the day of the event, and create a post-event recap video.

Collaborate with influencers

Another way to integrate digital is to use influencers or industry experts who are active on digital platforms. They of course will be active on social media, but they may have their own blog as well. Through collaborating with influencers, this can serve to amplify the event marketing.

Collaboration with influencers can come in different forms, from sharing with them the event links and Twitter handles to inviting them to physically speak and engage at events.

Using social media for events

Social media can be used at events by creating a parallel networking and engagement zone to enhance the experience. At the very basic level, this involves creating a hashtag of the event or posting about it on your owned media accounts.

FIGURE 13.2 Events and digital marketing

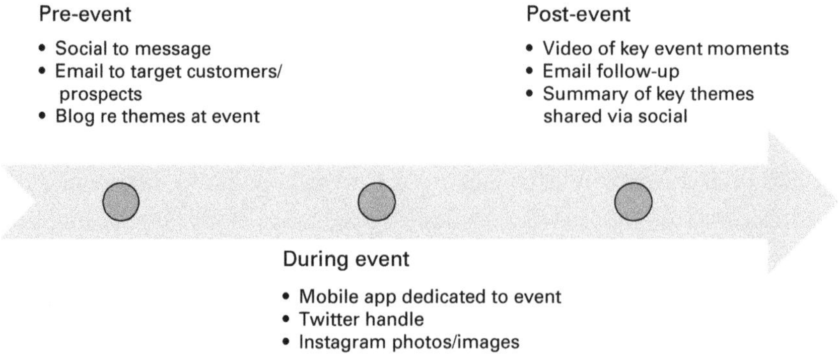

Pre-event

- Social to message
- Email to target customers/ prospects
- Blog re themes at event

Post-event

- Video of key event moments
- Email follow-up
- Summary of key themes shared via social

During event

- Mobile app dedicated to event
- Twitter handle
- Instagram photos/images

As shown in Figure 13.2, another way to think about events is the PDP digital approach: pre-event activities, during-event activities and post-event activities.

Pre-event digital marketing

Before the event, digital technologies can be used to identify the best type of customers to engage, depending on whether these are prospects or customers. Different types of targeting can be used, whether this is advertising targeting or more detailed selection based on industry and title.

Types of event digital marketing can include communications or event reminders via email. Blogs can be created according to themes at the event, and posted on corporate owned media sites or used as part of an SEO strategy to promote to prospects.

During event digital marketing

Twitter is undoubtedly one of the most suitable digital channels to use during events. This is due to the nature of short messages and text, which can be both more easily written and read on the go. Twitter can be used to provide updates and latest event highlights.

Official hashtags can be set up to engage participants to support sharing of content, answer questions and start conversations. Another favoured digital channel to use is mobile, so that delegates can be reached while at events.

Types of activities might include the use of short videos, Q&As with attendees and interviews with speakers, all of which can be used to create rich content even after the event is over.

Post-event digital marketing

After the event is finished, the knowledge that was shared and created does not have to go away. You could repurpose the content that you have in new blog posts, whitepapers, ebooks and other interactive items.

Statistics from the event could be used to create content such as an infographic to support further engagement of customers and prospects beyond the event.

PR and digital integration

It's quite normal to find PR as a function or department operating separately from marketing teams in organizations. In many companies, PR is regarded as an overall business function serving multiple departments, and as a result engagement with marketing can sometimes take a backseat in terms of priority.

The following are some reasons why PR and B2B marketing need to work closely together and act as one team:

- PR can support content marketing creation activities, helping to identify themes, activities and paths to planning and producing content;
- PR can improve earned media by ensuring messages, reputation and thought leadership contribute to the media efforts of B2B marketing;
- PR can be a big part of successful SEO strategies such as link building, through their links to influencers, industry experts, journalists and bloggers;
- PR can help identify key partners for marketing, and can also support the management of those relationships.

Earned media

As we've seen in previous chapters, earned media is a powerful tool in terms of free coverage that supports efforts to reach audiences but is also perceived by customers as extremely credible. Additionally, earned media is still considered 80 per cent more effective than owned media (Smith, 2019).

By integrating PR with other areas of marketing, the messages can operate in unison. As B2B buyers use a variety of sources to research throughout the early and mid-buyer journey, having one voice which is consistent ensures the message is not only delivered, but also remembered. Consistency also conveys trust; as prospects hear the consistent message, they will tend to believe you and believe you're knowledgeable about that topic.

How to integrate PR

Start with audience. Share and agree on audience profiles, and share buyer personas with your PR department or agency. That way they may be able to help with identifying public relations channels used by the target audiences.

Include PR as part of the content creation plans and understand where and how PR can support different areas – for example, PR may be able to support with UGC-based content activities.

Include PR colleagues as part of content distribution or amplification activities. For example, most PR departments or agencies can support influencer marketing initiatives by identifying key players or even managing the outreach and management of influencers. In terms of distribution, there are multiple earned media channels in the PR space.

Finally, embedding keywords into your press releases, press reports and any PR content means more audience reach and offers more backlink opportunities. This can help with SEO and generating website traffic.

Digital and customer service

As mentioned earlier, we're seeing customer service – which used to operate more through email and phones – increasingly adopt digital technologies and channels. It is now customary for companies to have a dedicated customer service Twitter handle, to provide a customer service company blog, and to have space on the website dedicated to customer service issues.

There are strong arguments to suggest that customer service now needs to work more closely with marketing:

1 Customer service pain points: an issue which wasn't covered in the previous marketing of a product or service can be addressed in future marketing, reducing customer service queries.

2 Managing perception issues: one bad customer experience may have brought about a wrongly formulated opinion about the company. Therefore, together with marketing, customer service can address this through correct and consistent communication.

3 Consistency: this relates especially to new offerings or areas which were captured through customer insights from marketing. Marketing, together with customer service, now need to focus on a consistent message both digitally and offline

Customer service can be further integrated into digital marketing in the following ways: relevant company website pages (such as for more complex products) can include help windows, short Q&A boxes, and chat services. Additionally, links can be provided on customer service emails or tweets directing customers to information.

Ultimately, the benefits of an integrated digital marketing and customer service strategy will result in reduced costs as well as improved loyalty.

To integrate digital with other areas, you should consider the following:

- How to integrate digital channels with other digital channels using content – can marketing content be used to provide a more seamless experience?
- How to integrate any potential offline points into the digital experience.

Aside from the customer journey, one should consider all the transition points in terms of opportunities to integrate or merge. Transition points are the points at which digital and non-digital channels should be connected.

Finally, rather than only doing this research through customer insights, it's important to do a virtual walkthrough of these touchpoints with customers to understand how things integrate; such a simulation can help to highlight any final weak points.

The digital integration process

The digital integration process can be summarized in the steps below (also see Figure 13.3):

1 Define the challenge, goal and why you're trying to solve it – eg to improve nurturing, awareness, overall customer journey or experience.

2 Identify channels relating to your goal. Understand which channels contribute to the experience or goal, and therefore which ones have the greatest impact, considering technologies.

3 Review content used. Check using existing information and your buyer personas which content is most suitable.

4 Create content accordingly and relating to the channel integration. Create content and integrate content considering the role of content and its relationship with other channels.

FIGURE 13.3 The digital integration process

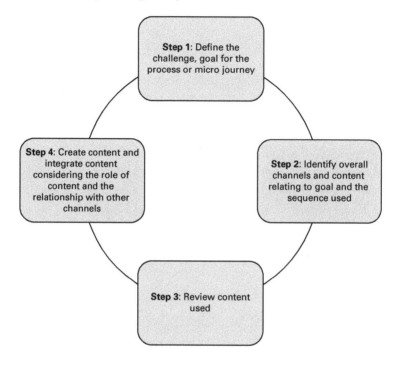

References

MRP (2016) [accessed 3 August 2019] 3 Myths About B2B Direct Mail Marketing Debunked, *MRP* [online] www.mrpfd.com/resources/3-myths-B2B-direct-mail-marketing-debunked/ (archived at https://perma.cc/54TJ-M3LE)

Smith, A (2019) [accessed 18 December 2019] A look ahead for marcomms in 2019: The technological advances that will hold the key to success, *Marketing Tech News* [online] www.marketingtechnews.net/news/2019/jan/07/look-ahead-marcomms-2019-technological-advances-will-hold-key-success/ (archived at https://perma.cc/Y9NF-HYMD)

Further reading

Alloca, L (2018) [accessed 3 August 2019] Why Integrated Marketing Needs To Be The Foundation Of Your B2B Strategy Earned Media, *Forbes* [online] www.forbes.com/sites/forbesagencycouncil/2018/01/16/why-integrated-marketing-needs-to-be-the-foundation-of-your-b2b-strategy/ (archived at https://perma.cc/483U-SYAK)

Yu, J (2015) [accessed 3 August 2019] Digital Marketing Integration: The Impact Of Cross-Channel And Content, *Marketingland* [online] https://marketingland.com/digital-marketing-integration-impact-cross-channel-content-130060 (archived at https://perma.cc/TET2-6USJ)

14

Digital marketing and sales

WHAT YOU WILL GAIN FROM THIS CHAPTER

After reading this chapter, you will understand:

- how to enable sales;
- how to empower sales;
- how to evaluate sales;
- how to consider email and track sales emails;
- social media and sales;
- account-based marketing.

Introduction

Sales and marketing engagement

In the past, sales and marketing would have been considered as completely separate roles, The divide would be that marketing typically looked after the four Ps of the marketing mix, and sales would look after selling to prospects from earlier on in the buying process through to ongoing managing of the customer relationship. As the customer would be engaged earlier in their decision-making process, sales traditionally also had greater opportunities to guide customers through their buyer journey and nurture the prospect's interest.

In the past one would also see marketing's role as more confined, even limited to marketing communication (one of the Ps of the marketing mix).

Today that has all changed, and as most B2B marketers have experienced, the role has become much broader, to the point of overlapping with sales a

FIGURE 14.1 The sales and marketing process

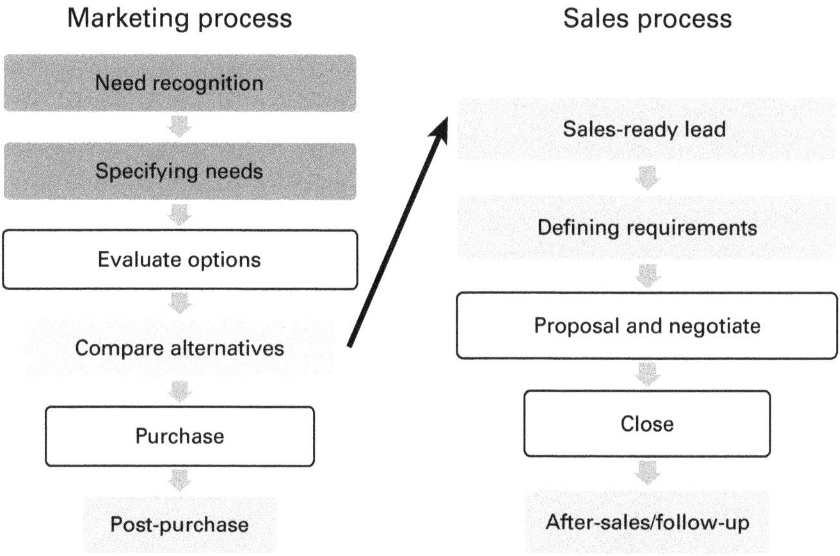

lot more. Figure 14.1 shows how the crossover between sales and marketing usually occurs somewhere in the mid-buyer journey phase, though this differs by organization and industry.

Why B2B sales and marketing need to work together

So why should B2B sales and marketing work together? In short, they need one another to do their jobs well.

Sales and marketing can help each other in different ways. Marketing have more technologies than ever before, such as digital technologies that help to identify interests and the digital behaviours of customers. Marketing can also help identify customer sentiment through online listening.

Overall, as a result of digital and digital technologies, marketers today have much greater exposure to the customer than 10–20 years ago. This exposure previously was only possible through research and conducting surveys. Now marketers can directly capture this through websites, social media channels or other digital analytics on an ongoing basis both before and after their purchase.

Customers also use more digital content and digital channels, whether they are a prospective buyer or an existing customer. This means both marketing and sales increasingly need to understand how to use digital channels, content, and technologies to improve the customer experience.

Marketing now own a lot of data relating to customers, organizations, and buyer personas because of digital technologies and applications, This has resulted in marketers becoming data experts, and they need to have capabilities not only in housing the data but in bringing the data to life through extracting and applying insights.

The sales role and remit has also changed: some salespeople are seeing their roles becoming a lot broader, and are increasingly asked to embrace a softer sales approach, involving amongst other activities the leveraging of digital social networks. As sales start to understand how to use their social networks and various other forms of digital marketing, marketing now has the possibility to use an additional digital channel with the help of sales.

Challenges for B2B sales

Modern B2B buyers are much more involved in the sales process. They drive the pace themselves through researching and evaluating options and alternatives, and they prefer to conduct a lot of this without being bothered by prospective vendors.

The increased availability of information has led to prospective customers engaging and interacting with organizations at much later stages in their buying journey. This so-called sales cycle has transformed more into a marketing and sales cycle, with marketing taking on more responsibility to identify, engage and guide prospects until they are at the point to engage B2B salespeople.

Studies show that this increase in research and planning on the buyer's side has led to the buying cycle becoming longer overall. According to Forrester Research, 74 per cent of business buyers conduct more than half of their research online before making an offline purchase (Wizdo, 2015). Additionally, sales interactions with customers come a lot later in the buyer journey, and customers expect an organization's sales team to be more prepared to know and support customers, which seem like two opposing trends.

Cold calling (where sales contact prospects out of the blue, usually by phone) is not effective any more. As we've already seen, an organization today needs to make eight to ten calls before a person on the receiving end picks up the phone. A decade ago, the number was a third of that (Clarke, 2018). With customers being armed with more information at the point of engaging salespeople, this means that sales will have to approach customers differently. They need to move away from the sales pitch, and towards understanding customers' particular questions and guiding them more to the purchase stage.

With all these aforementioned changes, sales and marketing need to work more seamlessly with each other. Together, sales and marketing will have knowledge about the market and customers; combining this information will empower and enable both departments to be more effective in their areas.

Identifying improvements in sales and marketing engagement

To improve sales and marketing engagement, a company should start by looking at whether sales and marketing are engaging the right areas, and in the right manner. Ideally, you want to rate the level and quality of interaction.

Some aspects you might want to consider in a sales and marketing audit could include the following, broken down by a sales review of marketing first:

- sharing of customer insights;
- sharing the background to marketing campaigns;
- frequency of communication;
- availability of information;
- quality of information;
- quality of leads provided;
- proper lead handover to sales with communication;
- content to nurture prospects and customers.

And then a marketing review view of sales:

- sharing of customer insights;
- sharing of information on accounts;
- follow-up on leads;
- timely feedback;
- timely requests for information;
- usage of content.

The above is just an example. One could rate these aspects on a scale of 1 to 5, where 1 is poor and 5 is excellent.

Key areas of success in sales and marketing alignment

- **Common KPIs:** Defining goals and KPIs in a language which is common to both sales and marketing means both teams can work towards a single goal and track performance. Digital-based KPIs should be communicated and explained so sales understand how this relates to their targets. Examples of KPIs could be number of sales-ready leads, number of opportunities, and pipeline and revenue associated with marketing leads.

- **Sharing technology:** One of the challenges between sales and marketing is to improve sharing of information as well as collaborating on tasks. With various digital technologies, these challenges can be greatly alleviated. Examples of applications include WeTransfer, Dropbox and Google Drive.

- **Collaboration tools:** There are also various options for 'live' collaboration, including Slack, which is a chat-style collaboration tool allowing employees to communicate and transfer files. Alternatives include Evernote, Google Hangouts and Fuze.

- **Using buyer personas:** By using and sharing buyer personas, sales can understand more context behind marketing's focused campaigns and initiatives. Inversely, marketing may be able to get some feedback and input into the buyer personas as it is updated over time.

The 3Es of digital sales and marketing

Aside from the overview above, there are probably three core areas where digital can improve the effectiveness of sales and marketing and how they work together. We can break these out into how sales are empowered, how they are enabled and how they are evaluated – we can call these the 3Es of digital sales and marketing, as seen in Figure 14.2.

Empowering sales

It's often forgotten how valuable sales specialists and their sales knowledge can be, and what an asset sales are for the business and for marketing.

To empower sales, they can be given access to owned media platforms. This means potentially providing them more opportunities to use social media to reach and engage their customers or prospects, as well as offering them the ability to write on a topic and share their knowledge.

FIGURE 14.2 The 3Es of digital sales and marketing

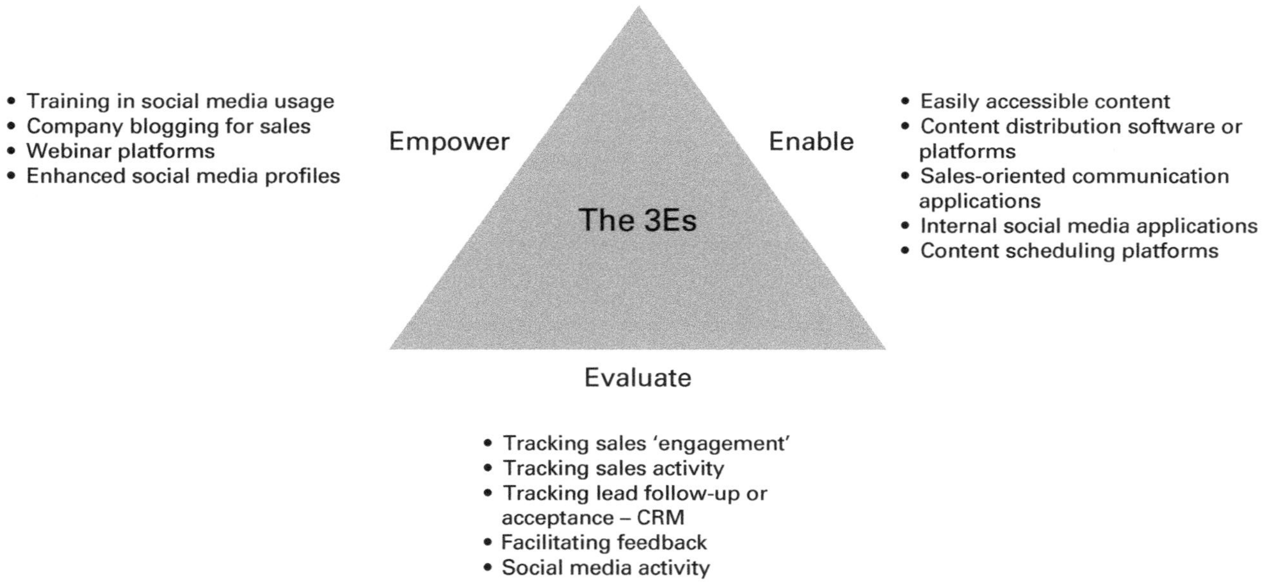

- Training in social media usage
- Company blogging for sales
- Webinar platforms
- Enhanced social media profiles

Empower

The 3Es

Enable

- Easily accessible content
- Content distribution software or platforms
- Sales-oriented communication applications
- Internal social media applications
- Content scheduling platforms

Evaluate

- Tracking sales 'engagement'
- Tracking sales activity
- Tracking lead follow-up or acceptance – CRM
- Facilitating feedback
- Social media activity

Aligned with this may be more structured or advanced social media training, covering how to use it in an ethical and proper fashion. Although social media activity should in essence be authentic, there are some dos and don'ts when using social media to represent a business.

Some salespeople have a network in the industry outside the company, and have become subject matter experts in their own right. Providing a webinar for these SMEs might be interesting in conjunction with a themed marketing campaign or activity. Some companies look to their subject matter experts in-house to create SEO content, eg short videos or articles or other forms of content to then post on platforms. This way sales can really work for you to support your search engine marketing efforts.

By distributing content through word of mouth, email and social networks, your sales team can be great amplifiers of marketing messages and content. Providing them with the right content at the right time is a key element of this, to ensure that messages are shared widely.

Enabling sales

The second E is about enabling sales. It's the process of providing information, content, and tools that help salespeople sell more effectively, helping them successfully engage buyers in the appropriate manner, and at the right time throughout the buying process. You may want to consider the following approaches:

- **Internal social media**: Updating sales with the latest information can ensure they are always kept up to date. Internal social media apps such as GaggleAMP can ensure sales receive updates in a more topical and content-friendly manner. There are other applications which support internal employee communication such as Hootsuite, Amplify and Everyone's Social, and some CRM applications have their own function for employee advocacy communication.

- **Content scheduling platform**s: Through content scheduling platforms sales can receive content according to timings. This can also support consistency of message at different periods. Research carried out by Kapost reveals that 65 per cent of sales representatives say they can't find content to send to prospects (Murphy, 2015), so focusing on this process can improve the dynamics between your sales and marketing teams.

- **Content sharing**: Having a central online space for sales reps to access content in a structured manner can help them greatly. The important thing to remember is to ensure sales know how to use online central portals. While content can be distributed through online portals, well-structured emails or social media-'friendly' emails with ready-to-tweet links, or post with links can also be used. Examples of content planning and scheduling tools include Trello, Hootsuite and, for scheduled distribution, Gaggle AMP, Circulate.it, and list.ly.

- **Assisted email**: Rather than sending automated emails on behalf of sales, provide them with email templates containing the non-personal elements. Sales can then decide when and how to send these emails, and how much personalization they add to the message. This is a form of assisted digital marketing whereby sales use digital marketing manually, but in a more suitable manner for engaging. In this way, a salesperson may decide to send an email directly before calling a customer, or even during a call.

NUDGING WITH EMAIL SIGNATURES

One way to help with communication to sales is through email signatures and associated notes. In email signatures, companies can include calls to action or reminders at the bottom of the email.

Email signature solutions serve to 'nudge' the recipient. In terms of sales enablement, these can help nudge sales regarding activities which marketing and sales collaborate on. Examples might be to remind sales of the latest content available, customer insights, a new available report or leads which need to be followed up on. One such technology is Rocketseed, which offers email signature solutions for intercompany communication, as well as supporting marketing to customers and prospects.

Customers using Rocketseed have seen a 20–30 per cent improvement in engagement, which can be powerful when engaging sales without creating friction (Hamp-Adams, 2017).

Evaluating sales

Evaluating sales is the third E relating to digital, and is about tracking how sales use and participate in digital platforms:

- **Tracking use of digital platforms**: If you've set up a content-sharing platform, then you can track sales actions on that platform. You can see when they log in, what they view, which pages they view, what they download and so on. Some content platforms include questions or short tests to ensure content is understood. Allocating a unique ID to each salesperson can also help sales leaders track their team's engagement.

- **Tracking leads and lead handover:** Digital applications such as CRM systems or marketing automation can help to track lead acceptance and lead follow-up from warm lead to lead closure. Some CRM applications allow for setting email triggers based on lack of lead follow-up – eg, if the lead is not followed up within two days then the time-triggered email is sent to the salesperson reminding them to do so.

- **Content consumption:** Evaluate which content is being downloaded. Consider including an area in your content hub for comments to allow sales to discuss whether they like the content, or feel it could be optimized in any way. One can also use content analytics to track download rates, click rates and page views. These and other metrics can also be indicators of the quality of the content.

- **Conducting a poll or survey with sales:** This can help to evaluate more qualitative aspects relating to roll-out of marketing activities and information. Some applications can also track email usage. Sidekick and Mixmax can allow you to track which email templates were used, as well as more general internal email activity. Sales email tracking software places a tiny image pixel in sent messages (not visible to the naked eye). This pixel provides information to the sender about when and where an email is opened, how many times it is opened, on what type of device, and so on.

CASE STUDY

Maersk Drilling: How digital sales enablement technology improved sales and marketing – Showpad

Maersk Drilling, a global leading offshore drilling contractor, turned to sales enablement technology in the form of Showpad to improve not only its sales and marketing operations, but to improve engagement with customers.

Key benefits and challenges addressed

Maersk Drilling's own marketing leveraged the Showpad technology to address a number of challenges. One of the main challenges was to provide content and information both online and offline for the sales organization.

The nature of sales is that they could be operating in remote locations and still need access to good quality information. Other challenges where Showpad was used included ensuring large files were available via the cloud. These files could be video files, or rich content such as interactive brochures. Such content was not only accessed by its salespeople but also by customers, which meant it needed to look professional and in keeping with a company providing high-value solutions.

The Showpad content solution which Maersk Drilling licensed acted very much like a professional content hub for all requests, internally and externally. So if salespeople needed product information, videos, etc, it was all found in one place. Of course, this required Maersk Drilling's marketing department to be regularly updating content and uploading this to the Showpad site.

How Showpad benefited marketing

Showpad not only benefited sales greatly, but supported marketing in their work, as marketing were able to understand activities of each salesperson using Showpad. They could see which content they used, and how often, which was then used to inform the content strategy and the budget decisions of the marketing division.

The detailed analytics which the Showpad platform provided also meant that marketing could have more informed conversations with salespeople regarding content usage. This technology mean that marketing didn't need to worry about sending any information over email or finding ways to provide internal communication information, and they could simply upload this content. The versatility of the Showpad platform meant any type of video or rich content such as CAD drawings could be embedded into documents or housed on the platform.

Ultimately this greater transparency and a central go-to hub for both sales and marketing meant greater alignment between sales and marketing could be achieved.

The sales process and Showpad

Showpad not only helped marketing with distributing content, but also acted as a great tool for salespeople to improve customer engagement and meetings. Through Showpad analytics, salespeople could understand when customers were viewing documentation or content, which areas they viewed, which pages, which content they were clicking on and which they weren't. This allows sales to understand the interests of their customers.

Also, Showpad would notify sales when their customers were viewing documents. One scenario which Maersk Drilling highlighted was a meeting with a customer which involved seven people. All seven decision makers were given access to Showpad. By understanding who then viewed the content, the salespeople could then understand the dynamic/level of interest in that group, and therefore which people they needed to focus on more.

Showpad indirectly helped improve the meeting dynamics and facilitated the salespeople in maximizing the output of the meeting.

As well as acting as a necessary support system for sales, implementing Showpad allowed Maersk Drilling's marketing department to better engage sales, and better support them.

Sales email tracking

Sales email management and tracking requires some different thinking compared to traditional marketing emails. Marketing emails are usually for a one-to-many situation, whereas sales communications are more personal and on a one-to-one level.

Autodiallers and lead tracking

Sales email tracking for the most part now includes autodiallers, which allow for lead management and outreach to be included into one tool.

An automatic dialler is an electronic device or piece of software that automatically dials telephone numbers. Once the call has been answered, the autodialler either plays a recorded message or connects the call to a live person.

Reporting

Sales email trackers usually report on a number of metrics by individual email, such as when the email was opened and how many times, as well as time of day the email was opened. Other, more detailed aspects can also be tracked such as content engagement (how long the recipient spent looking at attachments or slides within the email).

There are various sales tracking software options. The most popular ones are Outreach, Yesware, Sidekick and Mixmax.

CRM, and how sales and marketing leverage it

CRM is customer relationship management technology. It's often talked about in relation to sales, but can provide numerous benefits for marketing, including improving how sales and marketing cooperate.

CRM is typically the main technology used by sales, as it is used to track all aspects of the customer. However, in relation to marketing activities CRM can be used by sales to better track marketing campaign-based leads, and can be used to identify next-stage purchases.

For marketing, CRM can provide some real benefits such as improved segmentation of customers using data housed in the CRM system. It can also support data-driven marketing using insights into customer purchase behaviours, both current and past. Marketing can also use CRM to track leads uploaded based on marketing activities and campaigns.

Sales and social media

B2B sales is all about reaching prospects and building connections and relationships in order to steer them in the direction of purchasing. Here is where the use of social media becomes interesting, as social media in the hands of salespeople (obviously with some training) means sales can start to understand and gauge interest of prospects, and use appropriate methods to capture and nurture that interest.

Tools for social selling

A range of technologies, such as Upload or LinkedIn Sales Navigator, can help sales monitor prospects. LinkedIn Sales Navigator allows salespeople to import contacts and business information from a CRM account into the tool, and use it to track the account in LinkedIn and what they do.

After analysing accounts, defined territories, industries and products, the Sales Navigator tool makes recommendations for potential viable leads. Other tools which can be used to monitor accounts or prospects are account-based management software technologies, which are dedicated software used to track marketing to accounts across multiple stakeholders within target customer organizations.

Participate in groups

One great way of using social media platforms is to monitor or participate in the forums and groups where prospects or customers are active. This serves as a great source of research for sales, as customers will ask questions, gather information and inform themselves most of the time in a very public and transparent channel. Be aware that some social forums are membership-only.

Some of the most used areas for doing product research are Quora, Facebook Groups, LinkedIn Groups and subreddits for your industry, but of course there are many more, including industry-specific online forums.

Through these social media groups your sales team can understand what customers or prospects are asking, and can inform themselves better for potential meetings, or inquiries.

The Sales Enablement Maturity Model

A Sales Enablement Maturity Model is an interesting way to understand the level of sales enablement across an organization in general. Figure 14.3

FIGURE 14.3 Sales enablement maturity model

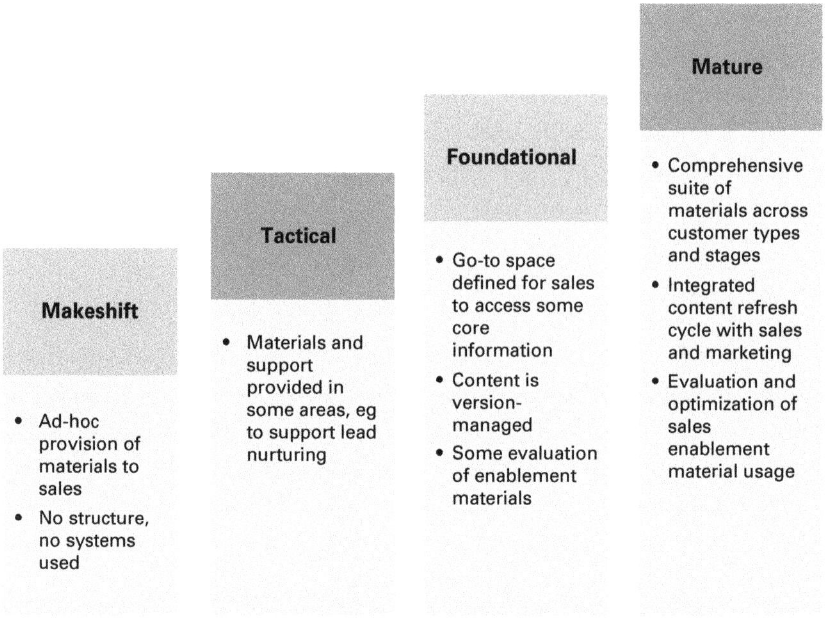

Makeshift

- Ad-hoc provision of materials to sales
- No structure, no systems used

Tactical

- Materials and support provided in some areas, eg to support lead nurturing

Foundational

- Go-to space defined for sales to access some core information
- Content is version-managed
- Some evaluation of enablement materials

Mature

- Comprehensive suite of materials across customer types and stages
- Integrated content refresh cycle with sales and marketing
- Evaluation and optimization of sales enablement material usage

shows sales enablement maturity in relation to marketing in a model I have developed. Below are the key stages in maturity:

- **Makeshift:** At this stage there might be periods where there are no materials for sales enablement. Typically, there isn't a structure for sales enablement and very little or no dedicated sales enablement content. Sales and/or marketing adapt existing materials to support sales activities in relation to marketing.

- **Tactical:** Tactical sales enablement refers to short-term tactical areas being worked on. Again, there is no established process, but budget and/ or resource is used at times to support some key sales activities.

- **Foundational:** Core sales enablement materials are provided across key areas and a system is in place to share these. Some budget is usually allocated as part of the marketing budget, and sales can access this when key information is needed.

- **Mature:** This is where there is a more sophisticated system for providing sales enablement materials for different customer types and at different stages in the customer journey. Update and feedback mechanisms are incorporated, as well as more detailed usage statistics, eg number of sales downloading materials, percentage of salespeople using material and so on.

Account-based marketing

Account-based marketing (ABM) has been around for a while, although until recently only the larger enterprise organizations were practising it. This was due to the resource-intensive, manual nature of the work. Now, though, digital technologies companies of all sizes are able to carry out this type of marketing, thanks to the creation of dedicated ABM software.

ABM is about viewing the whole customer organization as an account, rather than only dealing with a single go-to contact. It uses customer insights to improve engagement with an account and the different people within it. It is about better aligning processes and resources against specific accounts.

A big success factor for ABM is the collaboration between sales and market-ing. In fact, without this collaboration the approach doesn't really work.

The ABM process

Figure 14.4 outlines the framework of steps involved in ABM:

1 **Account analysis and identification:** The first stage is to build customer intelligence and profiles, and use existing insights from sales about current customers related to target segments. Target accounts are identified by working closely with sales, based on a combination of sales input and third-party databases. Predictive analytics may also be used to determine the specific accounts most likely to buy.

2 **Scope definition:** The scope and size of accounts are defined and account lists are created. The scope will depend on sales force size, sales objectives, and the ability for marketing to support sales with tasks such as providing content.

3 **Asset and activity preparation:** Marketing build related assets and infor-mation for account-based initiatives, such as qualification scripts, whitepapers, associated infographics or potential associated promotions. In the same way as content is created for a campaign, a suite of content is typically created for an ABM initiative.

4 **Launch ABM and roll-out:** Account data is loaded, typically, into a CRM application and the ABM activity is launched based on pre-agreed scheduled timings. Coaching or training accompanies this step to support sales in using marketing assets and tools. Sales follow up on leads which are part of the ABM stream or make outbound calls for the pre-defined set of accounts.

FIGURE 14.4 The ABM process

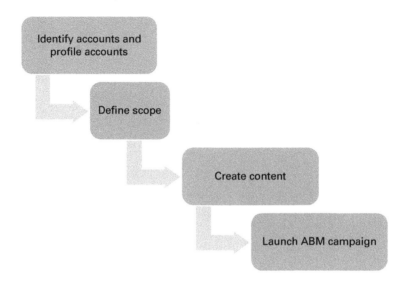

ABM key success factors

So, what constitutes successful ABM or a successful ABM strategy? Below are some observations drawn from companies who have demonstrated best practice in this space:

- **Sales inclusion:** Co-leading or involving sales in the ABM process upfront can help with improved selection of customer accounts, as well as improved focus in follow-up.
- **Insight-led:** Having some level of insight clearly helps in the identification process. Although sales involvement should help define customers, this should be focused on criteria used for selection and informed input, rather than ad-hoc input.
- **Business-focused:** Having ABM programmes aligned to the business can help have the broader business aligned to making ABM a success.
- **Programme design:** Programmes should be designed as a response to specific business challenges or needs, and thus add value. Content should be provided at different touchpoints for the intended target, both offline and online.
- **Technology-enabled:** Marketing integrating with CRM, whether through marketing automation or not, will help with reporting and tracking

performance on a regular basis. Digital applications such as IP or audience-based programmatic applications and social media applications can further complement ABM.

- **Communications:** How ABM is communicated and re-communicated to sales makes a difference. The purpose behind the activities needs to be emphasized.

Setting up ABM

ABM can be introduced using digital applications and dedicated software, including Demandbase, Engagio and Vendermore. It can also technically be managed through adapted CRM or marketing automation platforms.

You might also consider carrying out account-based advertising on social media platforms. For example, LinkedIn support advertising by account.

EXERCISE
Put it into practice

1 Review possible options for enabling sales. Which ones do you use today? Which ones would you consider in future, and why?

2 Consider some of your current marketing challenges. Do you see opportunities where sales and marketing can work better together to tackle those challenges?

3 Conduct a survey with some of your salespeople to understand their key needs and where they need support from marketing.

4 Carry out a questionnaire across sales and marketing to understand where there are gaps in alignment between the two departments.

References

Clarke, M (2018) [accessed 3 August 2019] 21 Important B2B Cold Calling Statistics, *ZoomInfo* [online] https://blog.zoominfo.com/21-statistics-to-improve-your-cold-calls/ (archived at https://perma.cc/FS2L-YUPW)

Hamp-Adams, D (2017) [accessed 3 August 2019] The Rocketseed Round-Up: News, Reviews and Some Top-Tip Must-Dos, *Rocketseed* [online] www.rocketseed.com/blog/the-rocketseed-round-up/ (archived at https://perma.cc/TMV4-28UA)

Murphy, A (2015) [accessed 3 August 2019] 10 Stats on the Business Impact of Marketing and Sales Alignment, *Kapost* [online] https://kapost.com/b/sales-marketing-alignment-stats/ (archived at https://perma.cc/T6LJ-FP6V)

Wizdo, L (2015) [accessed 3 August 2019] B2B Buyer Journey Map Basics, *Forrester* [online] https://go.forrester.com/blogs/15-05-25-B2B_buyer_journey_map_basics/ (archived at https://perma.cc/8QRG-AQ63)

Further reading

Adams, N (2018) [accessed 3 August 2019] Top 5 facts you need to know about Account-Based Marketing (ABM), *NapierB2B* [online] www.napierB2B.com/2018/11/top-5-facts-you-need-to-know-about-account-based-marketing-abm/ (archived at https://perma.cc/9VQ3-KYKH)

Bookbinder, S (2018) [accessed 3 August 2019] 9 Social Selling Stats to Motivate Your Sales Approach, *Impact BND* [online] www.impactbnd.com/blog/social-selling-stats (archived at https://perma.cc/HTA7-GT94)

Fagan, B (2017) [accessed 3 August 2019] 10 ways sales and marketing should be working together, *PandaDoc* [online] https://blog.pandadoc.com/10-ways-sales-marketing-working-together/ (archived at https://perma.cc/CYZ8-NP58)

Geraghjty, S (2014) [accessed 3 August 2019] 7 Secrets to Prospecting Using Social Networks, *TalkDesk* [online] www.talkdesk.com/blog/7-secrets-to-prospecting-using-social-networks/ (archived at https://perma.cc/N9XB-PWAN)

Holzman, S (2019) [accessed 3 August 2019] How to Make a Sales Team More Productive: A Guide for Marketers, *ZoomInfo* [online] https://blog.zoominfo.com/marketing-sales-productivity/ (archived at https://perma.cc/UB23-MRCA)

Jones, A (2015) [accessed 3 August 2019] Study: 78% of Salespeople Using Social Media Outsell Their Peers, *Social HP* [online] www.socialhp.com/blog/study-78-of-salespeople-using-social-media-outsell-their-peers/(archived at https://perma.cc/3WPN-CKHX)

Malone, E (2018) [accessed 3 August 2019] A guide to Account-Based Marketing (ABM), *oe-gen* [online] https://oegen.co.uk/2018/a-guide-to-account-based-marketing-abm/ (archived at https://perma.cc/9M75-N7PN)

15

Measuring digital marketing

WHAT YOU WILL GAIN FROM THIS CHAPTER

After reading this chapter, you will understand:

- how to measure marketing effectiveness;
- how to measure different stages of the customer journey pre- and post-purchase;
- absolute marketing metrics;
- attribution modelling;
- how to communicate metrics.

Introduction

Measuring the effectiveness of digital marketing

Measuring the effectiveness of digital marketing shouldn't be a difficult task. After all, there are lots of possibilities when it comes to finding and accessing data. However, with the volumes of marketing data in various forms at our fingertips, the challenge is in understanding which data to select, how to analyse and how to interpret it.

As it suggests, marketing effectiveness is a measure of how effective a digital marketer's activities are in meeting their intended goals. It is also related to the return on marketing investment.

When considering measuring marketing's effectiveness or value, you need to think about what you mean by 'effective'. Are you measuring the effectiveness in relation to improving engagement, increasing retention, generating awareness, shaping the buyer journey, or something else?

Measuring the value or contribution of marketing tends to be easier for those activities producing leads or more closely linked to generating opportunity and revenue, as they can be more easily translated into quantitative value. Measuring activities related to generating awareness or improving consideration tends to be more challenging, so it's important to think more carefully about what the value is, and what 'effectiveness' means in consideration-based or awareness-based marketing.

Creating a digital measurement framework

Marketing impact matrix

Throughout this chapter I'll discuss various measurement approaches. The first is the impact matrix as seen in Figure 15.1. It shows marketing effectiveness in terms of impact and cost in a visual form, identifies the association of greatest influence on value and provides a measure of current performance.

FIGURE 15.1 Impact matrix

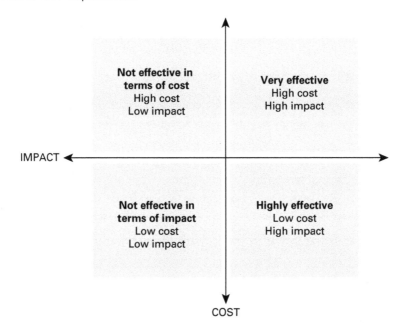

For example, where an activity requires a high amount of effort or cost and has a high impact, then it is probably effective. The high-impact activity which costs less might be more effective.

As you can see from the matrix there are four areas by which to assess digital marketing:

1 **Low impact, low cost:** These are marketing activities which are easy to deliver or distribute and don't require a lot of resources to make happen. Examples could be email-based campaigns, presentations or use of resources at hand such as owned media channels.

2 **Low impact, high cost:** These could be initiatives which can draw on resources not at hand, so require investment in people and/or technology, and don't yet demonstrate full impact in the short term. These could be activities or campaigns involving a lot of content, where the impact is reviewed in the short term, but the full impact and benefits of the content are yet to be seen in the long term.

3 **High impact, low cost:** These are the programmes that don't cost much but have a great impact. In terms of marketing activities, they may be initiatives rolled out through partners, where the partner also invests both human and financial resources, thus contributing to delivering and implementing the marketing activities. Other examples could be where the marketing is based on existing in-house systems, technologies, people or knowledge, where relatively little marketing budget is invested, but the impact is high. Employee advocacy programmes for promoting the brand or products through social media can fit within the high impact, low cost area

4 **High impact, high cost:** Activities based on paid media such as advertising or other paid marketing efforts usually fit within this space. The cost is high, but the impact is also correspondingly high.

Process and outcome

Another way to approach measurement is to think of evaluation in terms of process and outcome metrics.

Before looking at this, it's crucial to define the scope of what you're measuring. For example, are you measuring reach, awareness, consideration, retention or purchase/acquisition? By defining the scope in different ways, you'll be drawing on different process and outcome metrics.

Process and outcome metrics applied to the early buyer journey

In measuring awareness-based (or early buyer journey) activities, some metrics don't convey the impact or result of what these activities deliver. We can call these process metrics or even vanity metrics. Examples of these could be impressions – these describe how your marketing activities are progressing, but don't show the final result.

Process-based evaluation and metrics are about measuring ongoing elements of the marketing activities, usually including qualitative and quantitative data collection.

Metrics which demonstrate the result and outcome of the activity in the early buyer journey might be share of voice and change in awareness or perception. Outcome evaluation identifies the final results or effects of a marketing activity or programme, and can measure attitude and changes in behaviours.

Building on the process and outcome metric thinking and the buying journey pre- and post-purchase, you can now create a digital measurement framework as shown in Figure 15.2.

There are two main parts to this: measures based on customer lifecycle or journey from early buying stages through to retention, and metrics which

FIGURE 15.2 Digital marketing measurement framework

	Early buying cycle	Mid-buying cycle	Late buying cycle	Post-purchase
Process metrics	Impressions, Website traffic, Social awareness	Content engagement rate, Email open rate, Website engagement metrics, Social media engagement metrics	Content engagement rate, Email open rate	Content engagement rate, Email open rate, CTR
Outcome metrics	Brand uplift, Share of voice, Reach	Consideration uplift, MRL to SRL conversion, Lead quality metrics	Consideration uplift, MRL to SRL conversion	Repeat purchase rate, CRR – Customer retention rate

are process- and outcome-based. (Post-purchase is summarized here as one stage, but can be further broken down into other stages, as we'll see in the following sections.)

To measure the customer journey you could look at different stages separately, or at the journey overall. With an overall approach for the pre-purchase customer journey, the outcome would be the customers acquired or leads converted. The process metrics and outcome metrics can also be split by buyer stage in terms of early buying stage, mid-buying cycle and late buying cycle.

Measuring the early buying stage

As mentioned, we can use a number of metrics to measure the early buying stage, such as website referral, share of voice, impressions, brand lift, reach, brand metrics and engagement rate.

PRACTICAL TIP
'Where are the leads' questions

It's quite common to hear about B2B marketers implementing a focused awareness activity, and then asking 'Where are the leads?' or 'How many leads did it generate?'.

One way to avoid this is to highlight in advance the length of the awareness-based initiatives according to the length of the buying cycle for prospects. For example, if the buying cycle is over one year and the awareness initiative lasts two quarters, then everyone should be clear that there won't be leads from this initiative. Therefore, it's important to clearly set expectations upfront in terms of process and outcome metrics.

Additionally, most businesses will want to know what happens with the prospects exposed to the awareness campaign 'after' it has ended. It is prudent to create a follow-up step to your awareness campaign, explaining how and when those prospects will be further nurtured.

Website traffic

By analysing your website traffic, you can start to draw on some valuable insights into the early stage buyer journey. Google Analytics breaks down sources of traffic, as seen in Table 15.1.

TABLE 15.1 Google Analytics sources of traffic

Traffic source in GA	What it means
Organic search	Visits from organic search results from search engines
Direct	Visits from a visitor typing your exact URL; this traffic knows you
Social	Visits from social networking platforms
Referral	Visits from links clicked on other websites; this could be where your SEO link-building strategy impacts
Email	Visits from links clicked in emails
Display	Visits from display advertising like remarketing or banner ads
Paid search	Visits from search PPC campaigns
Other	Visits that cannot be tracked by Google and are most likely spam

You can also view changes in direct traffic to give you an indication of whether any invested activities are paying off.

It's best to note here that website traffic will relate to those prospects who take the step to come to your website and check your organization in their awareness stage. There will still be a portion of customers who don't do this, so you'll need to look at other metrics to complement any website traffic information.

Macro and micro conversions

In B2B marketing, views of conversions can vary, particularly for macro conversion because the sales cycle and lead nurture process are much longer than in B2C. We can view B2B macro conversions as those that result in capturing contact information relating to the prospect. For B2B companies operating a more transactional ecommerce model, these macro conversions could relate to capturing an opportunity or warmer lead, or even closing a sale.

Micro conversions are small actions which may not result in the final conversion, and so align to process metrics, while macro conversions align with outcome. Typical micro conversions could be viewing an article on the site or signing up to a newsletter.

Impressions

Another interesting metric is impressions. An impression is when an advertisement or any other form of digital media renders on a user's screen.

Impressions are generally measured using the CPM or cost per mille (thousand) metric. Impressions come in two forms: viewable and served. The viewable impression is a measure of ad viewability. According to the Interactive Advertising Bureau (IAB), if a ad appears at least 50 per cent on a screen for more than one second, this constitutes a viewable impression (IAB, 2014). Served impressions are based on served or sent ads, meaning that the advert was sent to a online publisher.

As impressions refer to the number of times your content is displayed, no matter if it was clicked or not, only using impressions as a metric can be limited. They are not action-based and are merely defined by a user potentially seeing the advertisement. A viewer doesn't have to engage with the post in order for it to count as an impression.

In summary, your 'impressions' can be quite impressive, but it doesn't mean your advert or piece of content was engaged with or clicked on. However, it can tell you when most of your followers were online, and therefore when the best time to post is.

Share of voice

Share of voice (SOV) is quite a popular metric for measuring brand awareness. It's the percentage of coverage and conversations about your brand, and can be measured as follows:

- Take the total number of mentions (yours plus your competitors) over the specified time frame, and divide it by 100.
- Separate out your brand's total number of mentions and divide it by the number calculated in the previous step.

Share of voice can be measured for SEO, PPC and social media, as well as advertising, but remember that SOV only measures the amount of coverage, not the quality of coverage.

Measuring SOV for social media can be done manually, in conjunction with a mention monitoring tool. For all platforms that you promote content through, track the number of mentions made of your brand over a specified time frame. The same can be done for competitors.

There are a number of tools that can help with the process, including Cision and TrendKite.

Reach

Reach is the total number of people who see your content. Reach is also a measure on social media and describes the number of people who could be exposed to your social posts and mentions. The number of people reached is always much larger than the number who engage. A benchmark goal is to see 2 per cent to 5 per cent engagement, based on your overall reach.

A more valuable and specific metric is unique reach, which measures the total number of people who have been shown an ad. These metrics go beyond cookie measurements and help you understand how many times people have been shown an ad across different devices, formats and networks. You can measure reach via Google AdWords or with social media.

Brand metrics

Brand lift refers to an increase in interactions with a brand as a result of an advertising campaign. Brand lift can be measured through survey and polls, but various digital platforms can also measure brand lift. For example, measuring brand lift on YouTube ads means calculating how much impact the ads have on perceptions and behaviours of customers.

Brand lift gives companies insights into brand awareness, ad recall, consideration, favourability and purchase intent as measured by organic search activity.

Brand lift can be one figure as an aggregate number based on a poll or survey, or can be broken down into key elements such as SOV gain and top of mind awareness (TOMA). TOMA refers to a brand or specific product being first in customers' minds when thinking of a particular industry or category.

Engagement rate

Engagement rate is the number of interactions that require an action (like a click, share, like, or repost), over the total amount of messaging. A post's engagement rate is a good indicator of how the content is resonating with people; on social media, this can be measured through comments, likes, shares and other interaction with the post.

Measuring the mid-buying journey

As discussed in previous chapters, mid-journey is usually defined as the stage(s) after initial need recognition and need quantification (the awareness stage), and could finish when a lead is ready to hand over to sales, ideally as a sales-ready lead. The definition of when the mid-buying journey ends varies by industry, company and ties to the activities surrounding lead capture and lead nurture.

In some industries where the buyer journey can last years, this mid-buyer journey becomes more important, as lead nurturing plays a bigger role.

The mid-buyer journey is important to measure so that you can understand how leads are progressing, as well as the extent and level of a prospect's interest. By measuring the mid-buyer journey better, there is an increased chance of improving the responses, marketing to and finally converting the lead.

Exploring the mid-buyer journey metrics

By defining the start of the mid-buying journey as when a lead is captured, and the end as the point when we hand over leads to sales, some of the process metrics we could use here are repeat visits from customers, most forms of email-based metrics, engagement rates according to identified traffic, clickthroughs, and website engagement behaviours.

Outcome metrics could include consideration uplift, number of converted sales-ready leads, and marketing to sales-ready lead conversion.

You could also use the following metrics to measure success:

- percentage of highly qualified leads vs total leads based on lead score;
- number of sales-qualified leads (SQL);
- conversion rate of marketing-qualified leads (MQL) to SQL;
- email clickthrough rate (CTR) and open rate;
- lead nurturing CTR and open rate;
- returning direct visitors;
- retargeting lists.

Social media

Measuring the mid-buying journey on social media would be an engagement activity on your content. If they are sharing your content, they are definitely considering you in some form.

Other consideration metrics would be likes and comments, which indicate whether they are taking more interest in your business.

Website

If visitors are coming to your website, there is a good possibility they are already considering you, but some other metrics help define that they are engaging you, such as repeat visits, pages or session timings, and downloads.

Email

As most emails are to named individuals, and normally based on capturing the email address as part of lead capture, emails are one of the bigger channels used in this stage.

We are interested in understanding which prospects are more engaged than others, so email open rate and CTR are key metrics to help us understand the level of engagement and consideration.

Measuring the late buyer journey

Activities and steps within the final stages, including the purchase stage, can also last a long time. However, this part is probably easiest to measure, precisely because it is the closest to purchase. We could define the initial part of this late buying stage as when leads are handed to sales or when sales start to qualify the lead, and the end of this stage as the lead converting to an actual sale.

Some of the metrics associated with the late buying journey or purchase stage can be linked to higher engagement of content, cost per lead, lead conversion, opportunity conversion, etc. Other examples could be overall conversion rate, opportunity conversion, revenue per visit and retargeting.

Lead and opportunity conversion

Depending on your business, lead conversion can mean those leads which converted to revenue or leads converted to an opportunity, where the opportunity is usually linked to a level of revenue expected (pipeline). Pipeline is used as a metric for some businesses where the sale occurs much later, and the business needs a metric to understand the potential business opportunity. Opportunities are usually described as pipeline until they are closed.

Opportunity conversion can be an outcome metric or process metric depending on what you define as the role or scope of the mid-buyer journey and late buyer journey. If the role of marketing is to deliver high-end leads to sales as the ultimate step, you would measure how many sales-ready leads converted to an opportunity.

Cost per lead

Cost per lead (CPL) is defined as the sum of associated costs in obtaining a lead. Usually only marketing-related costs are counted, rather than the costs of overheads or headcount. CPL also needs to be clearly defined in the context of what type of lead is being referred to. The quality and costs involved can differ greatly, for instance, between marketing-ready leads and sales-ready leads.

The cost of generating a lead is highly variable; factors which impact cost include targeting of marketing, marketing channel and content used. The creative can also be a huge factor.

CALCULATING CPL

Let's assume a marketing campaign included an event, a webinar, some advertising and some paid social posts and the sum of the costs was £5,000. Then let's assume 50 leads were generated. This would make the CPL £5,000/50 = £100.

At this point we have no idea whether these are marketing-ready or sales-ready leads. Let's use the BANT qualification terminology from Chapter 10. Turning to those leads captured, we notice that all we have is a name and email address, which is the 'A' in the BANT. This would indicate that these are marketing-ready leads.

Post-purchase measurement

Marketing in the post-purchase phase is sometimes called retention marketing. The great news is that measuring engagement and purchase activities should be a lot easier in the post-purchase phase, as you will have more data at hand. Post-purchase engagement can therefore be measured by applying some of the mid-buying stage and late buying stage metrics above, as the customer is already aware of you and potentially considering your company for their next purchase.

Aside from these, there are a number of marketing or business metrics that digital marketing professionals can use to measure the effectiveness of retention marketing. These include churn rate, which refers to the number of customers leaving a group of customers. Other metrics could be purchase metrics, as well as engagement metrics through our retention marketing channels and content.

Absolute marketing metrics

Now we've covered different metrics according to stages of the buyer journey, we can turn attention to overall marketing metrics which demonstrate the value of marketing or the overall marketing contribution. We call these absolute marketing metrics.

One way to think about marketing investment is to understand the return the company gets from investing in marketing. Treating marketing as an investment stream and understanding these metrics shows that marketing truly adds value financially to the business, and if this value-add is not according to expectations, then marketing can take action to improve the metric or to look for another way to reflect the value-add.

Return on advertising spend

Return on advertising spend (ROAS) is also used to define the return on marketing spend – even that which is not technically advertising.

In B2B, ROAS can be difficult to define in financial terms, as the sale is typically much further down the line – maybe as much as one year after. It is calculated as total campaign revenue divided by total campaign cost.

Return on marketing investment

Return on marketing investment (ROMI) has a number of potential definitions. Here, we'll define it as any form of return based on marketing invested, either in revenue or margin terms.

ROMI can be used as a metric to understand the effectiveness of marketing or a marketing campaign. It is usually used as a total number to cover a collection of marketing activities.

Marketing contribution

The best practice for determining your marketing contribution is to capture the primary source of each marketing-sourced or marketing-influenced lead. Then you can track qualified leads through technologies such as CRM through the journey, until these leads are converted to pipeline or won sales.

Pipeline contribution

Pipeline contribution measures the number of opportunities generated by marketing that convert into sales opportunities. This metric helps identify which marketing campaigns contribute to business pipeline, and the relative contribution vs non-marketing contribution activities. It is also a good metric to highlight the value-add of marketing.

Vanity metrics and actionable metrics

Vanity metrics highlight volumes or high numbers, but don't actually mean much in relation to your business goals. This is a particular concern for digital marketing as vanity metrics show off positive results, but don't provide context for marketing decisions. Examples of vanity metrics might include impressions, keyword rankings and overall website traffic, without any understanding of background or more detail behind the metric.

This is where actionable metrics come in. These metrics help marketers take action and make decisions. Much of what has been covered relating to

FIGURE 15.3 Marketing hierarchy of metrics

the above stages can be regarded as actionable metrics, as they provide indication of effectiveness (or ineffectiveness) and can provide clues to where we need to take further action.

Hierarchy of metrics

Once goals and KPIs have been identified for marketing activities, one good approach is to build a hierarchy of metrics as illustrated in Figure 15.3:

- Tactical metrics, sometimes called execution metrics, can refer to spend metrics based on tactical marketing activities, and marketing channel-based metrics.
- Strategic marketing metrics relate to how marketing is delivered according to strategic goals such as penetrating a customer segment or growing the business. Compared to tactical metrics, these are often more cross-marketing channel metrics, as strategic initiatives can involve multiple aspects of marketing.
- Business impact metrics measure overall marketing contribution to the business in terms of revenue, margin and pipeline.

Attribution modelling

The final method of measuring marketing effectiveness acknowledges the changing customer journey and the changing dynamics of using multiple pieces of content and channels, often simultaneously. Due to this increasingly enmeshed way of using digital channels and consuming content, a different way of calculating marketing and understanding how different channels and content contribute to outputs is needed.

This is where attribution modelling comes in. Marketing attribution provides a more cohesive measurement approach across the different marketing communication channels.

An attribution model is the rule, or set of rules, that determines how to credit a sale, by assigning credit to touchpoints in a given customer journey. Credit here refers to the return on investment: this could be pipeline, revenue, margin; essentially, it is the measurement you have chosen to focus on. Figure 15.4 shows five different ways to carry out attribution modelling:

1 Last-click or last-touch attribution gives credit only to the last channel which was interacted with or used before purchase. Whilst it is very simple to apply, it doesn't provide an accurate attribution.

2 First-click or first-touch attribution is similar in that only the first touch is provided all credit.

3 The position-based attribution model gives 40 per cent credit to the first and last interaction of the entire conversion journey, with the rest being split between the ones in the middle. This lets you optimize for the important touchpoints, while still acknowledging and preparing for the middle steps.

4 Time-decay or time-based attribution assigns more credit to touchpoints closer to the conversion stage, based on the rationale that the closer the touchpoints are to the conversion stage, the more influence the touchpoint has on the conversion.

5 Linear or non-weighted attribution provides credit equally to each touchpoint. First, last and intermediate events are all treated with the same importance. With linear attribution, a journey with 10 touches would give 10 per cent of the credit to each; a journey with five touches would credit each with 20 per cent.

FIGURE 15.4 Attribution modelling

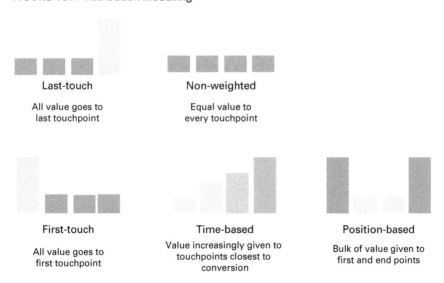

Last-touch

All value goes to
last touchpoint

Non-weighted

Equal value to
every touchpoint

First-touch

All value goes to
first touchpoint

Time-based

Value increasingly given to
touchpoints closest to
conversion

Position-based

Bulk of value given to
first and end points

PRACTICAL TIP
Communicating marketing metrics

When communicating marketing and digital marketing metrics, try to think of the recipient of the metric. This could fall into three key audiences.

Marketing

When communicating to marketers, think of removing vanity metrics, but understanding what they are. Also consider the efficiency and effectiveness in communicating.

Frame the metric within a context, and highlight whether it is an outcome or process metric. For each different goal, you'll want to come up with the top three to five metrics to communicate; some metrics will communicate the output, while others might convey context.

Sales

When communicating to sales, keep to things which interest them. In a pure digital and B2B transactional environment this may be more related to traffic and clicks. Also consider the context – is this lead-related, final pipeline, or revenue-related?

Senior management

Finally, when it comes to senior management and senior executives, think of how it all ties to revenue, margin and units. Even when referring to brand awareness activities, we should be showing how they link to top-level goals.

For example, if the business goal is to grow in new areas, then brand awareness initiatives could talk about making this new segment first aware of the brand and its offerings, with the subsequent step to engage further to support building the business.

This brand awareness initiative could be measured by reach, awareness before and after and other relevant metrics.

EXERCISE

Put it into practice

1 Create a dashboard by buyer journey phase before and after purchase, highlighting the process and outcome metrics.

2 Identify the most suitable absolute marketing metrics for your marketing department out of ROMI, marketing contribution and pipeline contribution, and establish KPIs for the next period.

3 Create a hierarchy of metrics view for your marketing team or area.

References

Interactive Advertising Bureau (2014) [accessed 3 August 2019] State of Viewability Transaction 2015, *IAB* [online] www.iab.com/guidelines/state-of-viewability-transaction-2015/ (archived at https://perma.cc/6B7R-GBHP)

Further reading

Gregory, S (2018) [accessed 3 August 2019] 19 Important Metrics for Measuring Digital Marketing Success, *FreshSparks* [online] https://freshsparks.com/digital-marketing-success/ (archived at https://perma.cc/98M2-LLQZ)

Isaacs, N (2017) [accessed 3 August 2019] Know Your B2B Marketing Metrics: Measure Your Way to Success, *act-on* [online] www.act-on.com/blog/know-your-B2B-marketing-metrics-measure-your-way-to-success/ (archived at https://perma.cc/Y356-FP9F)

Packer, J (2019) [accessed 3 August 2019] The cyclonic buyer journey – Going from funnel to flywheel, *B2B Marketing Lab* [online] www.B2Bmarketinglab.co.uk/blog/the-cyclonic-buyer-journey-going-from-funnel-to-flywheel (archived at https://perma.cc/W7GM-NJHT)

Weiner, G (n. d.) [accessed 3 August 2019] The 6 Ways to Measure Awareness Campaigns, *Whole Whale* [online] www.wholewhale.com/tips/measure-awareness-campaigns/ (archived at https://perma.cc/8K3X-AUU9)

Digital for retaining customers

Most marketing material today focuses on how to acquire customers – but there is less advice out there relating to retaining customers once acquired.

Part Five looks at some of the specific aspects of retention marketing, such as how to retain customers, how to develop business with customers using digital marketing and digital technologies, and how to improve loyalty, as well as the digital channel mix for retention marketing.

16

Types of digital retention marketing

WHAT YOU WILL GAIN FROM THIS CHAPTER

After reading this chapter, you will understand:

- retention marketing and the role of digital;
- customer journeys beyond purchase;
- core retention marketing;
- development retention marketing;
- lapse prevention marketing;
- contact strategies.

Introduction

Retention marketing vs acquisition marketing

Customer retention marketing refers to actions, activities and strategies leveraged by marketing to look after existing customers.

One big change in the past decade has been the increasingly changing responsibility of B2B marketers with regards to marketing to existing customers. It is now not uncommon to hear of B2B marketers splitting their time and budget equally between acquiring and retaining customers. Some even put most of their marketing resources, time and budget into existing customers.

So why is this? The simple reason is that existing customers are easier to target, and probably easier to engage. Existing customers may also be quicker to generate profitable business, considering that in most cases the very first purchase is a fraction of their potential purchase, and especially compared to what they typically spend in the subsequent purchases.

The customer journey beyond purchase

As discussed earlier in the book, the customer journey has multiple stages, and this continues beyond the purchase stage. In fact, the need to educate, nurture, inform and update, as well as many other interactions, are equally important beyond purchase.

So what are the differences with retention marketing? For starters, in retention marketing we know the names of our customers, and of people in the company. We have contact details and we know what they've bought, their industry, and more.

Digital technologies and retention customer insights

Digital marketing and technologies play an important role in retention marketing, and provide us with capabilities and insights into customers which would have been challenging or even impossible to acquire 20 years ago.

Marketers are now able to track customers and understand what they're doing, what they view and what interests them, all without even speaking or interacting with them. As has been discussed before, this allows marketers to gather more information with which to target and approach customers.

Digital word of mouth

Digital enables digital marketers to leverage their most satisfied customers. Digital plays a role in making customers happy by providing them with content, when they need it, and in the way they need it.

Customers interacting with one another on peer-to-peer forums leads to a greater transparency in how businesses engage customers. Happy customers are also more vocal and can show prospects what they could expect from an organization.

Segmenting customers

One key success factor in effective retention marketing is segmenting out existing customers. Segmentation can be done using different bases, for example their location, size of business or industry.

Aside from that, it's good to think of customers based on the stages they occupy in the post-purchase stage. We could define those stages as follows:

- recently acquired;
- core retention customers;
- customer to develop (or development customers);
- advocates and champion customers.

For each of these different retention stage customers, a different approach will be needed for selling and marketing to them. For example, a recently acquired customer might be hungry for information about using their product or services, and they probably need help with understanding these new products and services through vendor content and information.

For those accounts to develop further, considering how to help them in their business would be beneficial, so you may want to capture insights into their needs, their business and their next stages of business with you. The type of information would probably revolve around suggestions on marketing, thought leadership, marketing on areas they're interested in, or suggestions related to purchasing.

You may also want to provide opportunities for sales account managers to meet, engage and consult with them.

Champion customers probably expect a different level of engagement from your team. They may want special treatment in terms of access to information, or even access to a separate website or website area. They may also want reports and more strategic information such as longer-term plans from the organization or roadmaps.

Predictive analytics and retention marketing

Predictive analytics is a form of advanced analytics used to make predictions about unknown future events. In marketing, it is about predicting future sales using data mining, statistics modelling, machine learning and other techniques.

Predictive analytics in marketing can be used for:

1 Predicting customer behaviour: as mentioned, it can be used to identify likely next purchases, and customers with a propensity to buy.

2 Better lead scoring: through predictive analysis, leads can be scored better based on predetermined criteria and as a result can support better nurturing.

3 Improved sales performance and forecasting: by identifying patterns and predicting patterns of customer behaviour including likely future purchases, forecasts should become more accurate and sales performance should improve.

4 Audience segmentation for ideal account selection: using more detailed and accurate analytics can also mean better and more sophisticated segmentation models.

5 Content marketing: predictive intelligence helps marketers tailor their content marketing strategy to fit each customer's needs and preferences.

There are different approaches to predictive analytics, which include the following:

- Cluster models (segments) are used to segment customers and define target groups based on different variables. These variables can range from demographics to average order total. The typical cluster models are behavioural clustering, product-based clustering and brand-based clustering.

- Propensity models are about giving predictions relating to customer behaviour. This could involve predicting the lifetime value of a customer or their propensity to unsubscribe, convert or churn (which we will discuss later in this chapter).

- Collaborative filtering is the third approach, and is used to recommend products and services based on variables including past buying behaviour.

The journeys beyond purchase

Beyond the first purchase there are several activities related to different customer stages. We could call these micro journeys, involving customer activities and a set of steps or actions they take to complete a task.

Examples of activities could include how customers onboard, how they first deploy the product or service, how they search for additional information, how they resolve issues and how they make follow-up purchases.

Let's look at the main stages post-purchase as shown in Figure 16.1.

Onboarding

This journey is how customers first interact with the company they've purchased from, and how the vendor engages its customers. It includes welcoming customers to the relationship, which may just involve a simple email, but could be an opportunity to host a webinar to introduce them. A more personalized onboarding experience for customers can make a difference in successive interactions with them.

The onboarding process can involve customers finding and accessing information related to using the product, and may mean providing information in real time.

Deployment

Deployment of the product or service can be a journey in itself, but it often overlaps with onboarding. Whereas onboarding can involve a lot of operational activities, deployment can relate to marketing, service and sales interaction.

Marketing's role is in providing content related to using the product and maximizing the product usage. They can also play a role in providing information via the web or via social channels to support deployment.

FIGURE 16.1 Post-purchase journeys

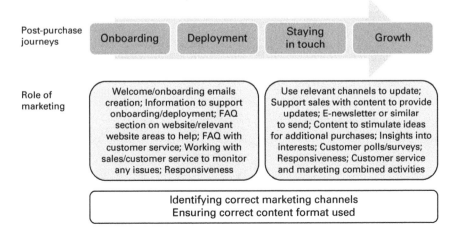

Staying in touch

Even after customers have made their purchase, staying in touch is often a very important step in the eyes of the customer. The first purchase could be a pilot test of your products or services, and their decision to make the final 'real' purchase may be based on this.

Growth

Beyond staying in touch, customers may look to information or support relating to the growth of their business. This could mean, for example, needing more of the product, a different scale of service or a different type of product or service as a result of being a larger or faster-growing company.

Identifying post-purchase journeys

We've identified some of the key stages or activities beyond purchase. Now the key is to understand what the touchpoints are in terms of vehicles and content, so we can shape the right experience for the customer.

Figure 16.2 summarizes these and other key steps in defining post-purchase touchpoints.

Some methods for utilizing touchpoints beyond purchase could include webinars, email, website and social media. The key is to understand:

- the sequence used for different requirements;
- how they are used, ie their role.

FIGURE 16.2 Identifying post-purchase touchpoints

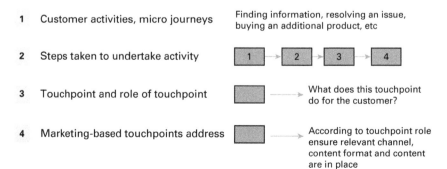

Types of content will vary in the post-purchase phase depending on needs: for example, webinars, blogs, brochures or downloads, feedback, email newsletters, contact forms, events, social media sites, feeds and SlideShare can all be examples of different content used.

As we look at the welcome and onboarding stage, this can be accomplished by email, although using embedded video might make this more engaging and effective. Also, in this stage it might be worthwhile to use push messaging via the browser or an app to remind customers about things.

As customers look to engage further, perhaps around an event, it might be more interesting to offer more personalized email and more possibilities in receiving communication via social media, such as different forms of content.

Marketing's role in post-purchase touchpoints

We need to differentiate between customers who are account-managed and those who are non-account-managed, or between customers where account managers own all communication and those where they don't. It will depend on how media and content is sent to or provided on behalf of sales. Other times, marketing departments agree with sales to populate email with sales account manager details and simply add in the contact name in emails.

Different levels of email and different level of 'personal' touches can go a long way to help with the authenticity of the content and in building relationships with customers.

Core retention marketing

Core retention marketing is the marketing content and activities which address the fundamental needs of existing customers. Let's look at the main elements in a core retention marketing approach. We can break this into types of communication channels and types of content.

Communication channels

In terms of communication channels, you should have an understanding of whether customers are satisfied with the current way they are being communicated to. The obvious channel used is email, but there is a percentage of customers who don't like to receive information in this way.

For those that are happy to receive email, there should be further detailed understanding of the types of email preferred. Do they prefer to receive summary emails in a newsletter form, or more embedded video-based emails? You should also seek to understand if they use social media or whether they may need to access parts of your website.

Answers to the above can be found out based on buyer persona and engagement metrics (as has been covered in Chapter 4). You might also do a check and ask them directly or via their account manager. Other ways to find information could be to conduct a poll or survey. Google Analytics can provide information through tracking a cookie ID or the IP address of the company, from which you can understand whether the website is working for and engaging the customers.

Finally, email engagement rates such as open rate, clickthrough rate and other metrics can tell a similar story as to the effectiveness of your core retention strategies for emails.

Content formats

Turning to content formats and the content itself, there will be differences in terms of customer preferences and response rates – ie, how content is being interacted with, whether it is clicked on, how many times, and so on

Here you might be interested in offering a portfolio of content types, from which you can understand the type and form of information that works best. Some may like interactive content such as video, SlideShare and webinars, while others may prefer blogs, articles, thought leadership pieces and reports.

Also, consider what type of information your existing customers prefer. This can be obtained by asking them directly, or by using tick boxes on a website, email or in some other form which customers can use to log their preferences.

Development customer marketing

Development customers marketing means marketing to customers with the objective to grow your business with them – essentially, to sell them more. One of the bigger challenges is knowing to how use digital marketing and technologies to support both your business and the development customer's business.

The first step comes down to understanding your customers, and understanding the differences between using CRM, data analytics and digital technologies.

Identifying opportunities for next sales

There are different approaches and techniques we can use to understand customers and identify the best opportunities for developing business, as per Figure 16.3.

GOOGLE ANALYTICS / WEB ANALYTICS

Through these technologies you can see what pages your customers view, and what content they download. You can also prompt customers by understanding their content preferences, what they're interested in, and the pages they view.

PURCHASE HISTORY AND FUTURE MAPPING

Using your CRM systems and data, you can understand your customers' purchase history. By knowing what they buy and matching their purchase evolution to that of other customers, you will be able to know their likely next purchases and needs.

FIGURE 16.3 Identifying next opportunities

What	Activity	Technology
Website and Google Analytics	Pages views, number of pages viewed, content viewed, bounce rates	Website analytics, eg Google Analytics
Purchase history analysis	Purchase history analysis Trends in past purchases Purchase evolution map to matched customers	CRM
Portfolio gaps	Portfolio gaps	CRM
Buyer power potential	View buyer power vs current purchase level	CRM and data import from a B2B customer data provider

GAPS IN PORTFOLIO PURCHASED

Quite simply we can view customers' purchases and potential gaps in their purchases, ie products they could buy, but haven't bought. This may be one of our options when we don't have advanced analytics technologies at our disposal.

BUYING POWER POTENTIAL

By importing data from data companies, you can understand customers' potential buying power for your types of services and compare that to what they buy, to get an indication of your share of wallet by customer.

Types of analytics

According to McKinsey, those executive teams which make extensive use of customer data analytics across business decisions see a 126 per cent profit improvement over companies that don't (Mahdavian *et al*, 2016). While the intention to use AI and analytics is there, according to Forrester, 'only 15 per cent of senior leaders use customer data consistently to inform business decisions' (Ramos *et al*, 2017).

In Chapter 5, I introduced the different forms of analytics in terms of diagnostic and predictive analytics. Other types of analytics include portfolio, channel and text analytics:

- portfolio analytics help you understand the different products that are viewed on your website;
- channel analytics help you understand the channels through which a customer generally buys online, eg whether they purchased from a resellers, and, if so, which products and services;
- text analytics help you understand wording, using sentiment analysis to spot customers' pain points.

Cross-selling and upselling

Developing business with customers most often involves cross-selling and upselling. Cross-selling is the action or practice of selling an additional product or service to an existing customer. Upselling is a sales technique whereby a seller induces the customer to purchase more expensive items, upgrades or other add-ons to make a more profitable sale.

Figure 16.4 shows that the development of customers can follow three different paths:

- selling to a higher-margin product or products;
- selling a wider range of products in general;
- a mixture of both.

Tiering / focusing

Most B2B companies operate in an account-based business. This means that they should prioritize or tier accounts to focus on. Some companies may only have very few accounts they focus on generally, and therefore this tiering is unnecessary – however, the majority of customers don't have the necessary resources to approach all their customers at once, and therefore need to find a way to select customers to build business with.

This tiering can be based on highest buying power, lowest share of wallet, most lucrative bid size based on industry, most eligible customer, easiest to grow in industry or any other factors relevant to individual companies. More context can also be gathered from the account manager regarding the potential to grow business within the account.

FIGURE 16.4 Cross-selling/upselling

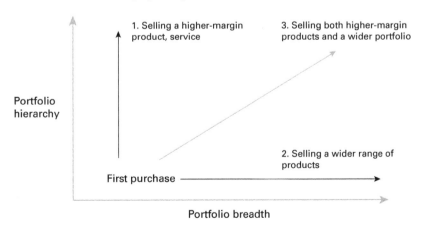

Lapse prevention marketing

We've heard the statistics: it costs much more to acquire customers than to sell to existing customers. Yet customers still lapse, often for no good reason. What if it's possible to predict the lapsing of customers, and use that information to do something about it?

Let's first define what lapsing means: this is when customers stop doing business with you, for whatever reason. Essentially, they are no longer interested or happy with you. This lapsing of customers has different names: customer churn, customer attrition, or customer defection.

The fact is that lapsing has a significant impact on business, as it lowers revenues and profits.

Why do customers lapse?

Customers can lapse for different reasons. These include:

- you failed to deliver against an original need;
- the onboarding process was less than optimal;
- the product wasn't up to standard;
- the customers' needs changed;
- the customer no longer had funding to continue to purchase;
- the competition intercepted and were able to offer better conditions and/ or a better product.

Understanding a bit of context as to why customers lapse can go a long way to improve chances of re-engaging as well as re-acquiring them.

One way to potentially decrease the possibility and effect of churn is to define a set of signals which could indicate lowered engagement, potentially leading to a customer lapsing. Each industry will have different signals, but some of the common ones are infrequency of purchases, lower email open rates and order cancellations. Examples of attrition signals can be seen in Figure 16.5.

Such signals can be identified through CRM software, website analytics and even social media analytics. This view and signal rating could be created to show the bigger picture in terms of attrition, eg higher bounce rates on your website, lower social media engagement, lower-value purchases or more infrequent purchases. Where the charts are bigger, this could require more urgent attention.

FIGURE 16.5 Attrition signals

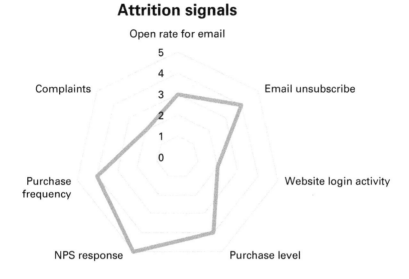

Calculating customer churn

To calculate customer churn, identify the number of customers at the start of a period and end of a period. Divide the change in the number of customers by the starting amount.

From this, you get a decimal, which is your customer churn rate. If it's below 1.00, or 100 per cent, you're experiencing customer churn.

You can also use technologies such as Qualtrics Predict iQ or Churnly, which leverage artificial intelligence to identify those customers or accounts which have a propensity to churn.

Digital marketing strategies to decrease churn

There are different strategies for decreasing customer churn. One approach involves better integrating marketing and customer service. Together, the two areas can monitor dissatisfaction or agree on a set of signals to monitor.

Other activities could involve not only responding to customers faster and in a more relevant manner on social media channels or other marketing channels, but where necessary taking action to adapt marketing accordingly. This might be where marketing statements could be misleading, or if there are product and service issues needing to be addressed.

Other strategies to decrease churn are to use predictive analytics together with segmentation to reach out to customers ahead of lapsing. Customers may be segmented based on types of dissatisfaction comments, allowing the response to be dealt with more appropriately. For example, comments about how products are delivered can be sent to operations, whereas dissatisfaction with responses to sales queries can be routed to customer service or sales.

CASE STUDY
Vodafone

Vodafone, a mobile telecommunications network provider, experienced a particular challenge relating to billing. They could see that customers receiving phone bills churn twice as much as other customers. This is down to a few things, such as confusion over the bill amount, as well as needing to go through multiple pages to understand where the different charges come from.

Vodafone decided to address this issue. They did this by looking at how to remove some of the aspects which were driving churn. One main issue was surprise over the amount, so they empowered customers with more immediate access to information about their bill. They also offered a choice of communication channels with which to receive information, such as the My Vodafone app, the website or via SMS.

The results were a 12 per cent reduction in churn, and a +7 per cent reduction vs the set target (Fraser, 2018).

Contact strategy

The next thing is to consider how to contact customers. This may seem a strange question as they are existing customers, and you may think that sales and account managers are the obvious answer. However, B2B marketers can play a key role in the contact strategy.

The different ways to contact existing customers could include sales contacting the customer directly using phone, email or other channels, or marketing contacting the customer by providing reasons to engage with the company through email, social media, webinar, face-to-face activity, or by offering compelling forms of content such as video or reports.

Customer loyalty and digital

Much of what has been covered across this and the previous chapter should help to improve customer loyalty in general. Customer loyalty can be understood as the gravitational pull a company has on a customer, or the bond or attachment a customer has with a company or brand. Customer loyalty can be shaped by many things including sales engagement, salespeople, customer services, operations and both direct and indirect marketing.

When we think of elements that impact loyalty, much of it comes down to marketing, meaning B2B marketers can do a great deal to shape and improve customer loyalty for their organization.

As we learned earlier in this chapter, the cost of marketing in re-acquiring or acquiring customers is significantly more than the cost of marketing to existing customers. Hence, it pays to market to existing customers.

There are some exceptions to the rule: it can sometimes be beneficial for a business to move their focus away from certain customers who have become unprofitable, and require a disproportional amount of resource to manage or serve them.

Loyalty types

Customer loyalty marketing or programmes to support customer loyalty typically need shaping a bit more, compared to standard retention marketing. Loyalty marketing should involve identifying and segmenting for different types of loyalty, identifying more specifically what shapes loyalty per segment, and then providing or addressing loyalty inhibitors as well as tracking and monitoring.

The following are different types or segments of loyal customers:

1 **Spot customer:** A customer with low degree of loyalty, looking at your company as a provider – a short-term and tactical means to support their business. They may decide to purchase again, but are not to be relied upon.

2 **Repeat customer:** A customer who comes back to purchase more from you. The loyalty is restricted to re-ordering or purchasing a second time.

3 **Customer advocate:** If contacted by another customer or potential customer, they would rate your organization positively overall, and can be relied on.

4 **Customer champion**: A customer who champions your products and rates them very positively. If impacted by a negative experience, they may quickly shift to a lower degree of loyalty.

5 **Strategic champion**: A customer who has demonstrated strong customer loyalty, who champions your products and who has a strong bond with your company. This could be due to collaborative ties, or even family associations. They are typically not put off by one-off negative experiences.

Building customer loyalty through digital marketing

STEP 1: DEFINE WHO YOUR CUSTOMER IS AND WHAT THEY VALUE

The first step a vendor should take to achieve loyalty is to understand exactly what a customer values, largely by considering the diversity in customers and the variety of stakeholders in the buying journey. Defining the segment and stakeholders is key to determining what aspects they value most.

STEP 2: RANK AND PRIORITIZE LOYALTY DRIVERS

The next step is to rank and prioritize loyalty drivers. Is price the key thing, or is it a timely response or quality of information? Is it being up to date with market trends or research reports?

In this respect, the vendor needs to split out the core and expected elements in their offering and combine them with those aspects that drive loyalty. For example, a timely response is probably expected, but the speed of response – such as a one-hour or 24-hour turnaround – may not be.

Marketers can use this qualitative research to rank the information into 'core' or 'expanded' loyalty drivers, where 'core' reflects the main loyalty driver and 'expanded' is a supporting element in driving customer loyalty. For an example of this, see Figure 16.6.

STEP 3: ALIGN YOUR DIGITAL MARKETING CHANNELS, CONTENT AND STRATEGY

These loyalty drivers might determine several things for the retention strategy selected (see Figure 16.6), the content used, and the channels used. Additionally, other departments may need to be involved, depending on the loyalty driver – a timely response might involve sales and customer service as well as marketing.

FIGURE 16.6 Loyalty drivers

When considering how to communicate to your customers, B2B marketers should look at the themes that customers prefer to hear about and the channels they prefer to receive the information on. The frequency of communication may also factor highly in a customer's satisfaction. Some customers may prefer not to receive email at all, whereas others may prefer to receive updates via an online information page, social media or direct mail.

Here it is important to offer alternative forms of communication for your customers. As well as diversifying the types of channel used, vendors can set up communication preference systems. Once implemented, these media consumption habits should be tracked and reviewed through digital and analytical methods.

STEP 4: TRACK CUSTOMER ENGAGEMENT AND SENTIMENT

Before digital, one area vendors found difficult to track was customer sentiment. Previously, companies would rely on account managers or ad-hoc conversations to understand the mood and sentiment of their customers. Now, sentiment can be captured in a much more structured way, be it via digital surveys or social monitoring and listening to track keywords.

As well as tracking sentiment, companies can look at the context of the sentiment and create responses to address it. Providing customers with an outlet to voice their opinions can be powerful, as the customer feels listened to. This can be more than just a monitored customer services Twitter handle, and may include online surveys or events.

EXERCISE
Put it into practice

1 Considering the potential customer needs in the post-purchase phase for your organization's products and services, identify your customers' key micro journeys.

2 Conduct a short survey or poll of your existing customers to understand their communication channel usage and content requirements. If you're using email or other preference centres, you may already have such information available.

3 From the possible routes to identify next customer purchases and opportunities for sale, which ones are you using today? Which ones could you implement in the short term?

4 Create a short list of three to five signals which point to customers becoming disengaged with your organization, and which could eventually lead to customers lapsing.

References

Fraser, C (2018) [accessed 3 August 2019] Awards case study: How Vodafone turned the shock of expensive bills into a positive experience, *B2B Marketing* [online] www.b2bmarketing.net/en-gb/resources/b2b-case-studies/awards-case-study-how-vodafone-turned-shock-expensive-bills-positive (archived at https://perma.cc/V9WT-9DQ4)

Mahdavian, M *et al* (2016) [accessed 3 August 2019] The sales secrets of high-growth companies, *McKinsey* [online] www.mckinsey.com/business-functions/marketing-and-sales/our-insights/the-sales-secrets-of-high-growth-companies (archived at https://perma.cc/FEK7-SJN4)

Ramos, L *et al* (2017) The B2B Marketers Guide to Benchmarking Customer Obsession Maturity, *Forrester* [online] www.forrester.com/report/The+B2B+Marketers+Guide+To+Benchmarking+Customer+Obsession+Maturity/-/E-RES129562# (archived at https://perma.cc/6VNH-6M73)

Further reading

Gleantap (2017) [accessed 3 August 2019] Top 6 Best Customer Retention Statistics 2018 You Need To Know, *Gleantap* [online] https://gleantap.com/6-statistics-highlight-importance-customer-retention/ (archived at https://perma.cc/BTH7-VK88)

Klingelhoefer, U (2018) [accessed 3 August 2019] How to use Big Data to stop customer churn in B2B | Predicting Customer Churn, *Qymatix* [online] https://qymatix.de/en/customers-analytics-B2B-predicting-customer-churn/ (archived at https://perma.cc/R6XM-GLZA)

Loest, D (n. d.) [accessed 3 August 2019] 10 B2B Marketers' Customer Retention Strategies to Decrease Churn, *Campaign Creators* [online] www.campaigncreators.com/blog/10-B2B-marketing-experts-killer-customer-retention-strategies-to-decrease-customer-churn (archived at https://perma.cc/8X8J-LZVZ)

Miller, G (2018) [accessed 3 August 2019] 21 Surprising Customer Retention Statistics For 2018, *AnnexCloud* [online] www.annexcloud.com/blog/21-surprising-customer-retention-statistics-2018/ (archived at https://perma.cc/Q683-EGRU)

Tidey, W (2018) [accessed 3 August 2019] Acquisition vs Retention: The Importance of Customer Lifetime Value, *Huify* [online] www.huify.com/blog/acquisition-vs-retention-customer-lifetime-value (archived at https://perma.cc/J4XF-L5DC)

17

Digital retention marketing channels

WHAT YOU WILL GAIN FROM THIS CHAPTER

After reading this chapter, you will understand:

- the digital channel mix for retention of customers;
- the key digital marketing channels used for customer retention;
- how email is used in retention marketing;
- how webinars are used in retention marketing;
- how websites are used in retention marketing;
- how social media is used in retention marketing.

The digital channel mix for retention marketing

In the previous chapter, I discussed types of retention marketing, including core, development and lapse prevention. This chapter will focus more on the digital channels and channel mix used for retention of customers.

Digital marketing and the use of digital technologies for retaining customers allow you to understand named customers, and to do a better job of marketing and selling to them. Where retention customers are account-managed, you can also use digital to support sales.

Digital technologies will allow you to anticipate needs, but also respond better to them. The difference is that with retention customers you will already have some form of relationship with your customers.

Channel mix: retention vs acquisition

So why talk about digital channel mix for retention customers? There are a number of differences compared to acquisition marketing. In acquisition marketing, we're using a set of channels, content and digital technologies to capture interest and generate awareness among potential customers.

In acquisition marketing, we don't know our users. We don't know with 100 per cent accuracy which channels are the right ones (we can use buyer personas and matched customer techniques to do a job of getting a fairly accurate view, but there is always some deviation), and we also need to include some form of generalization, as there is less capability to fully personalize marketing channels.

How to define the channel mix

One way to think about the right channel mix and use of content is to use the efficiency and effectiveness grid according to specific goals, as seen in Figure 17.1. For example, if the goal is to generate new business from existing customers, then website, email, and potentially social media can be cost-efficient as well as effective in achieving goals. Other channels and content efficiency and effectiveness will depend on how exactly they are implemented.

FIGURE 17.1 Defining the retention mix

Where the objective is to engage customers in deeper discussions, you may need to be explaining complex issues. In this case, email and texting would be ineffective, as they are less suited to long explanations and visual complexity, whereas videos, webinars or illustrations might be more effective.

Though you could technically use advertising to reach existing customers, this involves investing sums of money to reach customers you can already reach and engage with without paying. Therefore, this would not be an efficient way to communicate with your own customers.

Email in retention marketing

As email is mainly an owned channel that you don't have to pay to use, it is a low-cost form of communication, and will be effective for most customers.

It is highly likely you'll have their email address, though of course, you need to ensure you're compliant with all e-privacy and GDPR laws when using emails.

Types of retention emails

As we saw in the previous chapter, there are different activities that existing customers carry out, and for those activities there are different types of email to consider sending. Figure 17.2 gives some examples of these, including onboarding emails, emails to support with deployment of an offer or service, reminder emails, update emails, suggestion emails and welcome back emails.

With so many possibilities in terms of email, you need to be planning accordingly and personalizing where possible, according to where customers are in their post-purchase journey. This in turn will typically lead to higher email response rates.

Email triggers

In the post-purchase stage, such email triggers are generally more possible than in the acquisition stage. These can be set up depending on which content customers view on your website or other areas.

FIGURE 17.2 Types of retention emails

Function-based emails	Customer lifecycle-based emails	Topic-based	Audience-based emails
• Operations emails	• Welcome	• Relevant to customer's industry	• Audience function-based, ie procurement, finance, C-suite
• Customer service emails, eg warranty	• Onboarding	• Theme related to organization	• Personalized to customer specifically
	• Deployment	• Themes related to products/solutions	• Suggestion emails related to customer
	• Reminder emails		
	• Loyalty and recognition emails		
	• Update emails		

There are many types of email triggers, largely to support operations and customer service, but some of the key marketing-based email triggers are products viewed, new products, price changes, preference changes and upcoming purchases.

Segmenting your email database

Email efficiency and effectiveness can be greatly improved by segmenting out your database, and differentiating the emails sent out according to types of customers, stages or preferences in terms of what they'd like to receive. Doing this has the potential to improve the response rates you get from this form of marketing.

You can segment emails based on email behaviours such as open rate or clickthrough rate, or based on customer purchase behaviour – for example, purchases in the last month, or purchases made more than 12 months ago. The customers who have just made a purchase are probably interested in learning how to use the product/service and its potential, whereas as those who purchased 12 months ago are probably more interested any new products, services or updates. They certainly don't need to know how to get started with the product or service.

Frequency of sending emails

How many emails is too many? Some companies believe that email being sent twice a week is fine for their customers, while others believe the maximum is once a month.

So what are the risks associated with getting the frequency of your email communication wrong? By sending too few emails, you may be underserving your customers – some customers may be expecting more frequent engagement, and when it doesn't happen decide to move away from you as they feel neglected. On the other hand, you could send too many emails and customers can become overwhelmed by your organization's communications, or even get annoyed. They may eventually request their email address to be suppressed and removed from your system.

There are a number of options you could consider to find that middle ground:

1 Test and learn: Try providing email at the frequency you think and review the open rate and engagement rate on emails. As you change frequency, do any of these factors change?

2 Ask your customers: Do a quick poll to understand what is best for that segment.

3 Update the buyer persona, and ask for a survey to be conducted specifically about communication channels usage and frequency.

Improving email engagement

Email engagement can be gauged with any metric or indicator which highlights how recipients of email interact with the email.

B2B email engagement can be improved through changing the text, headers and subject lines which speak to your segment. Though personalizing the content may not be necessary in every case, tailoring the topic for the segment you're intending to send to would be valuable.

Using visual images can also improve clickthrough rates, as they can help make the email more interesting and compelling compared to text-only emails. Dynamic videos can work in a similar way, either by embedding a link, embedding the video itself, or embedding an image of the video with a link for the customer to follow.

More recently B2B marketers have also been revamping the whole idea of what an email newsletter is. Some people can be put off by a wall of text, but more modern forms of newsletter condense down messages into a short overview of paragraphs, embedded with images, videos, and links to some compelling and longer-form content.

A B2B e-newsletter can include third-party content, videos, short information on thought leadership statements, links to key areas relating to the topic you mention, and opportunities to engage further.

Webinars in retention marketing

The technical definition of a webinar is a web-based seminar, but today they are used for any situation where you want to provide information and have some form of interaction. One-way webinars are typically turned into webcasts. As these are pre-recorded, they don't have the interaction levels that webinars do.

Webinars today support a great deal more functionality than they did 10 years ago. Ideally webinars include an interactive component with customers. This is usually where the webinar provider listens to questions from the audience, although some webinars today also allow for three-way conversation where participants can speak amongst themselves.

For these reasons, webinars are particularly helpful for resolving the various needs of existing customers. You can use them to offer advice on using one of your products or services, to explore the latest thought leadership topic, to listen to customer feedback, to understand how to deal with certain challenges, or to talk about a new product or solution.

Below are some considerations for using webinars:

- Customer stories: Use webinars to talk about customer stories, and approach webinar attendees as future customer stories.
- Use compelling speakers: Look for speakers who can share valuable insights or high-quality content. Using guest speakers in general can be more compelling than companies pushing their own messages.
- Set up webinars in parts: Have a theme broken into parts to engage customers more.

There is often the challenge of driving attendance to webinars. To deal with this, you could, as an example, target particular customers for whom the webinar content is most relevant.

Another approach is to use build-up notifications, which are short messages via email, SMS or other channels which build up as the webinar date approaches. These could be countdown-type messages. You could also share small pieces of compelling information or insights which they'll hear more about in the webinar.

Webinar structure

Another area often debated is whether webinars should be delivered as a one-way or two-way medium – should the webinar be purely to provide information, or a forum to solicit input and feedback or to encourage questions relating to a topic?

A webinar can be one-way if you only intend to educate and provide information. However, in these cases, you should consider why it needs to be a live webinar instead of a webcast.

For two-way webinars, you should ask some key questions. What are you trying to do with the webinar? Do you want to find out anything, or understand specific responses? If that is the case, then carefully construct the webinar to allow for questions or prompt questions on areas you are interested in hearing about throughout the webinar, so that customers are ready.

You will need to think about how the time should be divided between presenting information and allowing audience questions or interaction. A typical split is to allow two-thirds of the time for the vendor or speaker to talk, and the remaining third for customers to ask questions.

Websites in retention marketing

So, what are the differences in website marketing between acquisition and retention? The first aspect is that retention customers know you and probably know your website. They also know your products or at least one of them, and have probably viewed your product/solution pages a number of times.

So, as customers already know you, your website and your content, the next thing to consider is whether you offer them a different area of the website or a different website to cater for their different needs as retention customers.

A lot of thought goes into website design and architecture for acquisition customers in terms of where traffic will land on a homepage or a dedicated landing page. Unfortunately, the same effort isn't always applied for existing customers.

For existing customers, think of how you can differentiate the website for them, and offer them different paths to navigate. For this, go back to your buyer personas and customer micro journeys, and understand how you can support customers with needs which go beyond their initial purchase.

These can be such issues such as needing to learn more about the product, needing to talk to someone about a specific query, wanting information about accessories and services for the product, hearing from other customers and their experiences, connecting with other existing customers or wanting to buy something additional.

Where we have challenges emailing customers or contacting them directly, we have the possibility to engage them through other channels – for example, we can provide a separate website page dedicated to them, and communicate with them that way.

Mobile in retention marketing

Mobile marketing is another great vehicle to retain customers. Under mobile marketing you might want to consider SMS, QR codes, mobile texting, and use of mobile applications. It can also include mobile polls to engage customers, both by asking questions and by sharing results from short polls.

Mobile marketing can be used to support other activities such as events, and can target customers or prospects with specific messaging according to their location.

Mobile email design

In designing emails, it's important they are responsive. This means they dynamically change size, layout and format to fit the screen of the person opening the email.

For example, this may mean that a three-column email you send will be reformatted into a single-column design for a person opening it on a mobile device, but remain a three-column design if the next person opens it on their desktop.

Mobile marketing tactics

B2B companies such as CA Technologies and Okta have found unique ways to interact with their customers and prospects by creating mobile communities of peers. Whether it's adding an extra channel on Facebook Messenger or developing an advocate community via Slack or other means, these brands are building unique case studies with text-based conversations.

Mobile apps

Mobile apps can help B2B customers through sharing information relating to events or upcoming activities. They can be used by organizations to encourage networking within the industry. Mobile apps also serve more operational purposes, such as delivering key updates relating to account information, inventory and supplies.

According to statistics, SMS has very high open rates – up to 98 per cent – which means that this channel is an effective way of ensuring messages are read by customers (Esendex, 2018).

Mobile beacon and mobile push technology

With mobile beacons, B2B marketers can use smartphone device data to reach and target customers better. These beacons can also be used to attract customers to booths at a trade fair, for example.

Mobile push notifications are good technologies to improve customer engagement. A push notification is a message sent by an application to a mobile device. Push notifications are possible once the mobile app has been installed on the customer's device and they have opted in to receiving messages.

Mobile push notifications come in different forms including reminders, personalized messages, new information, or any call to action. They are great for delivering relevant and timely content and for improving engagement.

PRACTICAL TIP
Get the timing right

A key success factor in push notifications not only being opened, but welcomed, is the timing of the message. Understanding the best time of day and frequency of send will impact open rates, in the same way that email open rates are impacted by their send time.

When thinking about timing, consider that your customers may be on the move or even in different time zones. Additionally, watch out for the number of push notifications you send in a given period – too many, and this could lead to customers opting out.

Social media in retention marketing

Social media can be used for all areas of retention marketing, but is particularly interesting to use in supporting personalization – creating user-generated content (UGC) which in turn engages customers. Social media can also coordinate customer service and marketing activities.

We've already covered personalization in Chapter 4, so in the following section I'll look at UGC and customer service to improve engagement with existing customers.

B2B UGC

UGC is content that has been created by the customers themselves, on an online platform. Although this has been happening for a long time in the B2C space, it is coming more and more into the B2B arena due to increased usage of social media. UGC includes content such as pictures, videos, testimonials, tweets, blog posts and more.

So why is UGC so interesting for B2B marketing? UGC is regarded by consumers as more credible and effective. What's more, according to research, 68 per cent of B2B companies find third-party review sites are an effective way to generate leads (Woodbury, 2018).

A typical approach for developing UGC is to invite customers to participate in some form of engagement activity, and subsequently ask them to share or upload content.

CASE STUDY
Intuit

Intuit, a provider of accounting software, has leveraged UGC for some time and uses it to connect their business segments with expert advice. They run a programme known as QuickBooks ProAdvisors, the participants in which are accountants who have passed one or more exams administered by Intuit.

As part of the programme, they encourage QuickBooks ProAdvisors to provide advice on blogs, social media networks and so on. In turn, these participants can enhance their reputation with their own clients.

This programme benefits the participants as they gain access to new connections as well as expert advice, and benefits Intuit as they can establish their brand further in the industry.

Intuit also hosts a live community forum, the TurboTax Live Community, which houses UGC in the form of tax advice, questions, updates, and other customer-centric content.

UGC social media strategies

We can identify five main strategies in developing B2B UGC on social media (see Figure 17.3):

1 Create a programme which acts as a platform for your customers to engage. This can be a gamified campaign which incentivizes participation.
2 Develop surveys and run these through social media. The responses and output from the survey can subsequently be used as UGC.
3 Create a platform for experts to share opinions or experiences.
4 Create user-generated FAQs, inviting customers to answer questions.
5 Leverage video testimonials from customers, allowing customers to showcase their brand as well as yours.

Social customer service

Another area where social media has been prevalent is in customer service. We could argue that Twitter has been a playing ground for customer service for some time.

There are a number of benefits of using social media for customer service activities. The first is that organizations can respond quickly to incoming

FIGURE 17.3   Social media UGC strategies

communication via social media. Customer sentiment can also be tracked more easily. Another aspect is that it is transparent, which can be both a benefit and a disadvantage depending on how companies deal with potentially explosive situations.

PRACTICAL TIP
Using social media for customer service

Make sure your customers know where you are on social media. As soon as you can, find a way to let customers know where they can find you, propose that they follow you and also show them where to ask questions or raise issues.

This active approach provides a better service for customers, and can improve retention.

CASE STUDY
Caterpillar

Caterpillar is a 90-year-old company which produces heavy-duty construction and mining equipment. Caterpillar has invested efforts over the years in developing marketing focused on the users or purchasers of their equipment. They also go one step further in their effort to create communities and to use content to reach a B2B and B2C audience.

One example is Caterpillar's series of videos and content on YouTube. In one popular video, they created a Jenga-like tower using their own construction equipment. This not only showed off their equipment in an engaging manner, but also helped create excitement around the brand.

Aside from these videos, they also leverage social media to create a community around their B2B business.

Customer retention marketing strategies

In the past chapters and throughout the book we've covered a number of strategies and approaches which can be used in customer retention marketing. Here are the main retention marketing strategies summarized (also see Figure 17.4):

- **Personalization:** Use personalization of channels, content and messaging to create strong relationships with customers.

FIGURE 17.4 Retention marketing strategies

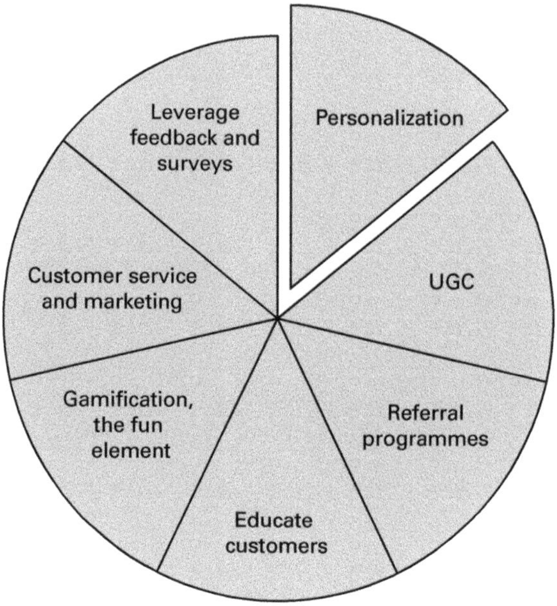

- **UGC:** Support or facilitate customers to share content and information, which in turn influences other customers.

- **Referral programmes:** Set up initiatives which specifically encourage or reward customers recommending and providing feedback and referrals.

- **Educate customers:** Through thought leadership and other forms of content, educate customers related to your firm's areas of expertise.

- **Gamification:** Use gamified marketing initiatives which encourage participation and interaction, whilst using gaming methods such as points systems and earning rewards. These encourage customer loyalty.

- **Customer service and marketing combined:** These strategies focus on improving customer service response to customer queries, or providing easy access to information. This can be through information provision, better forms of updates and chat technologies.

- **Customer feedback and surveys:** Use feedback from customers to improve customer experience as well as sharing it with other customers. Feedback could be on a specific customer experience issue, or related to specific topics which other customers are interested in.

- **Manage communication:** This strategy is focused on governance around communicating to customers, to ensure communication is effective, relevant, timely, consistent and delivered at a regular cadence.

EXERCISE
Put it into practice

1 Create an overview to show customer engagement by channel. Establish which metrics highlight customer loyalty or customer engagement, and which would indicate low engagement and loyalty.

2 Review the different ways of using marketing channels for retention marketing. Which ones are you using today, and which activities would be suitable to implement or trial?

References

Esendex (2018) [accessed 3 August 2019] What is the open rate for SMS in 2018? *Esendex* [online] www.esendex.co.uk/blog/post/what-is-the-open-rate-for-sms-in-2018/ (archived at https://perma.cc/3FQQ-5BTK)

Woodbury, A (2018) [accessed 19 December 2019] 5 Easy Ways to Create User-Generated Content for B2B Audiences, *Precision Marketing* [online] www.precisionmarketinggroup.com/blog/B2B-user-generated-content (archived at https://perma.cc/MP2B-EDZS)

Further reading

Fernandez, M (2019) [accessed 3 August 2019] The Best Time to Send Emails (Here's What Studies Show), *OptInMonster* [online] https://optinmonster.com/the-best-time-to-send-emails-heres-what-studies-show/ (archived at https://perma.cc/9GZG-D5UU)

Hoch, D [accessed 3 August 2019] (2015) In-App Messages Drive 3.5X Higher User Retention, *Localytics* [online] http://info.localytics.com/blog/in-app-messages-drive-higher-app-usage-and-engagement-benchmarks (archived at https://perma.cc/76VG-AFFA)

PART SIX

B2B social media and digital marketing platforms

In this last part of the book we look at key aspects of social media marketing not yet covered, such as social media advocacy programmes, the use of social media in lead generation and nurturing, influencer marketing and the role of social media, social media listening, and how to measure social media by applying a measurement framework.

In the final chapter we examine different areas of B2B marketing technology, new emerging B2B marketing technologies and how to assess marketing technology's needs.

18

B2B social media marketing strategy

WHAT YOU WILL GAIN FROM THIS CHAPTER

After reading this chapter, you will understand:

- key B2B social media channels;
- how to use social media for different B2B goals;
- social media advocacy;
- social media listening;
- key metrics to use across the customer journey.

Introduction

How social media marketing has changed in B2B

In B2B social media has evolved in different ways over the past decade, in terms of the number of customers using social media, and how customers use it for different areas of business.

The volume of customers using B2B social media has changed, and we've seen this grow over time. LinkedIn has grown from a platform of 17 million users in 2008 to 610 million users in 2019. Twitter was projected to reach 326 million monthly active users worldwide in 2019 (Omnicore, 2019).

As such, the ways it is applied within marketing, sales and other functions have changed substantially.

How customers use B2B social media marketing

Customers now use B2B social media in almost every area of business – for example, social media is used to help in purchasing and to research markets. Organizations are using social media to market and sell to customers, and to communicate with customers.

The range of social media channels used in B2B markets is also expanding and changing. For example, in B2B we're seeing more and more use of Instagram as part of B2B marketing initiatives.

Social media platform providers have evolved their functionality to support organizations for a full range of tasks. LinkedIn calls this 'full funnel', meaning it covers all aspects of the marketing funnel. Twitter and Instagram have moved to offering more advertising possibilities that B2B marketers can make use of, while Facebook have introduced Lead Ads, making it easier for convert ads to leads.

Millennials as an influence on B2B social media

We saw in Chapter 1 that Millennials are growing as a percentage of the workforce. With this increase in numbers, there is undoubtedly an influence not only on digital adoption and usage, but also in social media channels. Millennials can also have an direct and indirect influence in the workplace: directly they represent a growing portion of the workforce, but they are also indirectly educating their parents and relatives in using social media platforms privately – and, as a result, in the workplace.

According to a study featured in the *Harvard Business Review*, around 73 per cent of 20–35-year olds are involved in product/service purchase decision making at their companies, with one-third reporting that they are the sole decision maker for their department (Almquist, 2018). It's also interesting to note that approximately 50 per cent of B2B product researchers are digital natives, according to a Google/Millward Brown digital survey of buyers (Prodanov, 2019).

What these statistics tell is that Millennials can no longer be ignored in B2B marketing. They are now a substantial part of the target customers for most industries, and, if you haven't already, you need to think about adapting your social media activities to be relevant for Millennials.

B2B social media channels and goals

It's important to define your goals so that you can understand what you need social media channels and platforms to do for your marketing strategy. To help in understanding the range of channels, refer to the B2B social media navigator in Figure 18.1.

How to increase reach

Depending on the platform, there are different ways to maximize your reach. You could maximize reach by sharing topics with targeted audiences. Twitter is an ideal platform to do this on. You could, for example, use Reddit for reaching and engaging specific B2B audiences.

In reaching customers, we're not yet talking about whether they respond or engage with our content or us, but simply how we ensure our messages arrive at their destination. Twitter has a metric called Twitter reach, which represents the size of an audience and impressions as a proportion of the total number of views of a conversation. Twitter reach takes into account those that share, and promote further your tweets to them so that they find a bigger audience.

FIGURE 18.1 B2B social media navigator

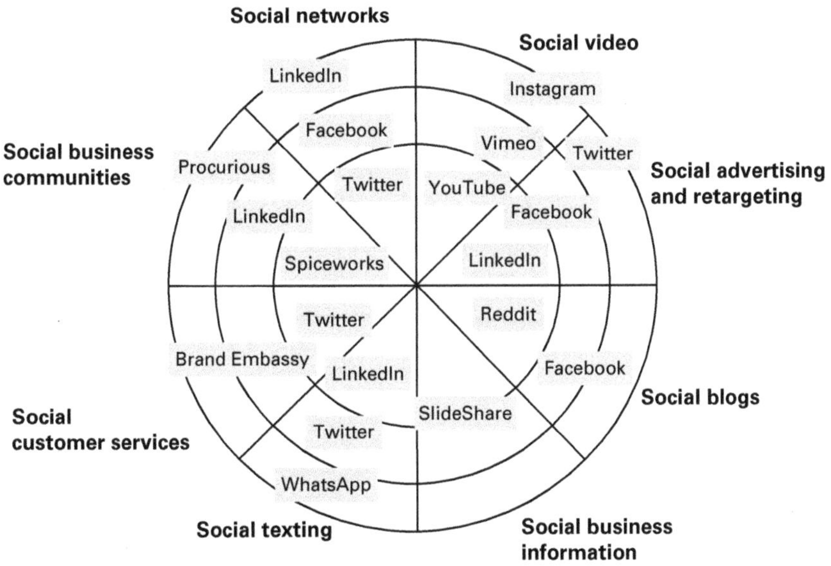

Generating awareness through advertising

The main activity to generate awareness is advertising. There are a number of social media advertising options for B2B marketers: companies can advertise on all the major networks such as Facebook, LinkedIn, Twitter and Instagram, As covered in Chapter 7, the use of social media channels to advertise will depend on the audience you're targeting.

As we go into some more specific advertising functions such as ad targeting, there are a number of companies offering this, such as Twitter, Facebook and LinkedIn. They also offer different forms of ad targeting, such as by geography or demographic.

Retargeting

Retargeting can help convert your social audience from casual viewers to more engaged prospects. As discussed earlier in the book, there are two main types of retargeting: pixel-based and list-based.

Most of the social platforms offer a form or multiple forms of retargeting. For example, Facebook, Twitter and LinkedIn offer targeting based on website visits as well as customer lists.

Reaching and engaging social business communities

Social communities come in different forms. Social business communities can be provided by the social media network providers – eg LinkedIn and Twitter have multiple business forums and groups – but there are also dedicated stand-alone social media communities, such as Spiceworks for IT decision makers and Procurious for purchasing managers.

We can also find such communities by looking at business or vertical associations, who have in the past 10 or so years built an online version of their memberships.

CASE STUDY
The CIO WaterCooler

One interesting example of a social business community is the CIO WaterCooler. This is a community set up to support CIOs and leading technologists to interact and network internationally, to share views and discuss challenges from the industry.

The CIO WaterCooler community online provides articles, blogs, ideas, insights and webinars as well as opportunities to meet up physically.

Sharing videos or visual content

If video sharing features highly in your strategy, you need to know which platforms are the most appropriate for this. Which ones encourage the sharing and commenting of videos? YouTube, Vimeo and Instagram are the obvious choices, though more recently LinkedIn has improved its functionality to offer more video sharing and viewing.

Other interesting visual content platforms include SlideShare from LinkedIn, which offers the opportunity to show content on slides.

Providing customer service

Some platforms are more dedicated to supporting customer service departments. They are typically paid-for services, but offer a connected cross-media channel view of customer service transactions.

The best social media customer service software offerings include Brand Embassy, Bold360, Freshdesk, Brand24, Sprout Social, Conversocial and Sprinklr Care.

Sending messages and text via social media

A number of platforms offer alternatives to email. LinkedIn offers InMail, and Twitter's short-form text messaging is a nice text alternative to communicating via email. Outside of that, WhatsApp and other messenger applications serve as alternatives to sending emails.

CASE STUDY
Reddit

Reddit is becoming increasingly used by marketers. Reddit is an American social news aggregation, web content rating, and discussion website, which also has a number of subreddits or subgroups. You can find a subreddit for most B2B specialisms.

The interesting aspect of Reddit is that people can become members of groups based on interest, and hear about the latest trends. For prospects it is a way to keep on top of things, ask questions and learn about specific areas, while vendors can target content and ads according to different topics.

Reddit offers different subreddits for even very specialized B2B areas. For example, if you're in pharmaceuticals, Reddit have an r/pharma; in fact, there are three different groups.

Tracking business news

Aside from the business news feeds on LinkedIn, Digg, Reddit and Pinterest are platforms where news is shared. They can be used to follow business topics and business-relevant news as well as comment and interact with others in relation to news topics.

Blogs

Social business blogs are professional information or articles online, most of which is unpaid media. Most industries will have a number of credible blogs they can subscribe to, to stay up to date – for example, if you're working in marketing, you could turn to SocialExaminer, QuickSprout or Marketing-sherpa.

Of course, B2B companies can create and use their own blogs to distribute and share their own content.

B2B social media and generating awareness

The following are the main social media channels for generating awareness.

Twitter

When we think of generating awareness and related activities, Twitter can cover a number of key goals. Today many businesses and their employees now actively use Twitter for business purposes – according to statistics, 75 per cent of businesses now market on Twitter (Cooper, 2019).

Let's define the possible different awareness goals:

1 supporting a marketing campaign;
2 amplifying content;
3 targeting specific prospects;
4 reaching as many businesses as possible in a given region.

Twitter offers a set of options for promoting or advertising under Twitter Ads, where you can choose from simple promotion or to launch a full Twitter ad campaign. The choice depends on your goals – for each goal Twitter provides an easy-to-follow set of steps. Note that under Twitter ad campaigns they divide up goals based on reaching audience and increasing followers.

Even though the service is called Twitter Ads, some of the activities and goals might be suited to an early buying phase, and some for a mid-buying journey phase.

PRACTICAL TIP
Retweeting the same content

Marketers often concentrate on generating fresh, quality content rather than being repetitive. However, with Twitter I would argue that there needs to be an exception. There are scenarios which would support the need to retweet the same post multiple times.

Firstly, given the rapid way in which Twitter adds posts and tweets to a recipient's Twitter feed, it's very likely that your target audience will not see a tweet the first time it is posted.

Another key point to remember is exposure to tweets. If a person views your tweet once, it might not register or be remembered. If they see it a few times they're more likely to react.

LinkedIn

On LinkedIn there are the following ways to generate awareness:

- increased reach;
- increased follower numbers;
- higher engagement.

LinkedIn offers multiple advertising possibilities including sponsored InMail and sponsored ads, which now have evolved to include video, text, dynamic, carousel and display. LinkedIn also supports ad targeting, which comes in two main forms – precise targeting and customized targeting to matched audiences.

Under precise targeting LinkedIn offer a number of criteria to narrow down by, including demographics, company type and size, and interests. For customized targeting, there are three options to choose from: website, contact and account targeting.

Instagram

Instagram has only relatively recently been taken up by B2B companies, even though around 70 per cent of B2B companies in the US now use Instagram (Clarke, 2019).

Instagram is all about visuals and short videos. It's the ideal platform for brand storytelling, and is an invaluable tool to add to your awareness-generating toolkit. Companies like Intel, Morgan Stanley and General Electric have embraced Instagram and now we're seeing a number of large enterprise B2B companies also having a presence.

So where should you to start? Instagram can be used to share and capture customer stories, to share company stories which connect with customers and to share visual information.

Instagram Stories are particularly useful for creating a visual dashboard to create a narrative. For instance, where you've helped a customer resolve a challenge or overcome an obstacle, you can talk about this through that platform.

Facebook and B2B advertising

Facebook does have a role to play for some B2B organizations. As mentioned earlier in the book, the use of Facebook depends on type of industry, power or influence of customer over the buying process and also how Facebook is used in general, regardless of your industry.

In short, if you're a lifestyle-type company, or in an area of general interest for consumers, then Facebook can work to promote your company. It can be an ideal platform to tell compelling stories which engage consumers and the general public. Companies like Caterpillar and Maersk are purely in the B2B space, but don't use Facebook to talk about their technical operations or products and services – they use it to connect and engage audiences with key themes, games, fun videos and stories.

Facebook advertising works very much like Google AdWords: your ads will appear to those meeting certain criteria, and you can use custom audiences to upload email lists to target ads to those prospects or customers. This can be done using some of the following criteria: app installs, brand awareness, conversions, engagement, lead generation, or reach.

Based on your goals, there are then a number of different advertising options such as lead generation ads, video ads or carousel ads.

The important thing to consider with Facebook ads is that they are typically quite cheap and provide good reach, which can be useful if you're using Facebook in the right manner, and your audiences are using Facebook for business purposes.

Lead generation and social media

Social media can support the goal of generating leads using different approaches. A lot of social media channels claim to support lead generation, though for B2B there are some that are more effective. Facebook offer Lead Ads, which are more than just adverts, but serve to capture information. LinkedIn also offer a number of options to generate leads.

Lead generation tactics on social media

Special offers on social media can take the form of services, calculators or free reports. These can be great ways to engage, and fall under the heading of 'compelling content'.

Short surveys can be a way not only to engage audiences on a topic, but to generate valuable content to share back. By using results from the survey or poll, you can engage, acquire followers and potentially leads.

Lead capture mechanisms

Content can be gated on social media platforms and can be facilitated through the use of WordPress plugins such as Google +1, Tweet to Unlock, Content Locker and WP Share to Unlock.

An alternative approach is to use links on social platforms which direct the audience to an owned web property where further gated content is provided. That way you're offering ungated content on social media, but separating out the audiences who are particularly interested or engaged.

These are the ones that will make the effort to view more about your company and its products, and potentially be more likely to share some of their details.

Targeting

Use targeting options such as Twitter Audiences. On LinkedIn, you can target posts without paying for the service – under 'post options' you can send to people based on different criteria such as location, job or industry.

If you're targeting, remember to think about tailoring or even personal-izing posts to maximize engagement.

Integrate social media

Including hashtags in Instagram posts can help you move prospects to the next stage. You can also include LinkedIn links in Twitter texts, and so on.

Of course you need to understand the natural sequence of steps between social media platforms. In this respect, you'll need to have a good under-standing of the customer journey steps and touchpoints for your intended customer segment.

Lead generation by social media platform

TWITTER AND LEAD GENERATION

Twitter has different options for supporting the lead generation space:

- **Create prospect lists:** Within Twitter, you can create private lists of users to be used for B2B marketing and lead generation purposes. This segmenting of prospects into lists allows for a more effective sales strategy.

- **Follow prospects:** Following prospects means they become aware of your company, and may communicate directly with you.

- **Inclusion of prospects:** Include prospects on key messages and compelling content, or links to compelling content. This way, they have more of a chance to see what you're doing.

- **Track which customers your competitors are following:** By identifying customers through competitors' distribution lists, you can identify potential customer opportunities.

- **Track industry trends via Twitter Search:** Use advanced Twitter Search to analyse conversations in detail and find out what experts from your industry are talking about, and when and how your competitors are being mentioned. Through this you can improve your Twitter content and lead generation activities.

- **Campaign creation:** Use your most effective Twitter posts to support your campaigns. From your stock of posts there will be those that particularly resonated and drove interest. These posts are the ones which will in turn connect with your prospects.

INSTAGRAM

Using Instagram for lead generation is relatively new, but an increasing phenomenon. Some ways to generate leads could be:

- monitoring and staying on top of the comments;
- using video: this is the most engaging form of visual content;
- creating unique hashtags.

Nurturing leads on social

As we saw from the lead nurturing chapter, nurturing is about helping the customer through their buyer journey by providing relevant and timely information. That means that nurturing can encompass many stages before and after purchase.

Some interesting ways to help progress customers further in their journey are to provide suggestions, and nudges, to facilitate finding the next relevant piece of information. Suggestions can be made through posts and text messages, while nudges come in the form of social calls to action, promoting fresh content to the same audiences and/or embedding links within social media posts.

You can use social widgets in communication. In emails, these can help people connect by providing an easy link point for the social platform.

Social media advocacy

Social media employee advocacy refers to employees of an organization using official social media channels to communicate or share content from the company. In B2B marketing, social media advocacy initiatives are important as customers use social a lot more today to engage or interact with organizations. As social media is about building relationships and improving customer experience, different departments need to understand how to best use them.

Social media advocacy programmes are also there to help guide employees on how to use social media for business. For many businesses the view is that if an employee mentions that they work for a company, they then are representing the company, and therefore need to conduct themselves according to company guidelines.

The benefits of social media employee advocacy are based on the network effect, where people can potentially have an extensive reach through networks. As employees are likely to have more direct connections than the company would have (as followers have many followers), their sharing of content would improve brand awareness.

Another benefit is improved content engagement – clickthrough rate is higher when content is shared by employees (Lessard, 2018).

Who should be an advocate?

Some companies make it their policy to encourage all employees to be active on social media. There are pros and cons to this approach. The main advantage is the sheer number of employees on social media, but a potential disadvantage is whether the posts and activities come across as genuine.

With any advocacy programme, one should look back to the core purpose of social media and what the company wants to achieve through it. Some companies will only promote internal news through social media.

Another consideration is that not all departments or employees are a natural fit for using social media for marketing or business purposes. Clearly marketing, sales and potentially purchasing see real value in using social media for business purposes. However, other areas such as legal or finance may not find social media appropriate.

How to set up a social media advocacy programme

The main phases in a social media advocacy programme set up are in Figure 18.2.

The first step is to ensure that employees are adequately trained in using social media. This doesn't have to be extensive training, but should cover the fundamentals of using particular platforms, as well as general dos and don'ts of using social media.

The next phase is about setting up sharing mechanisms – that is, how the organization will share the latest information which can be posted to social media platforms.

Once the training is in place, the next part is to ensure content and information is provided as well as to support certain employees in writing their own content in accordance with company guidelines.

Finally, social media advocacy activities should be monitored. This can be done through technologies such as Oktopost, GaggleAMP, Hootsuite or Amplify. These technologies can also help gamify the activity of employees using social media through scoring of activities.

FIGURE 18.2 Steps in setting up a social media advocacy programme

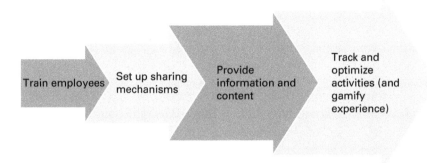

PRACTICAL TIP
Making content more shareable

One way to facilitate social media advocacy is doing small things to improve shareability of information. For example, you could provide links in the information sent, add social widgets links to emails, and/or add social widget links to content.

Having structured email and communication with content structured by theme can improve shareability of information, as employees can find content more easily.

B2B social media listening

Social media listening is the monitoring of a brand on social media to understand customer response, feedback, and mentions of your brand. It is about monitoring keywords, topics, competitors, industries.

Some key areas where social media listening can help are:

- uncovering pain points: by listening, organizations will hear conversations about products and services, which may provide context and insights into pain points;

- understanding how you're positioned: through monitoring conversations, you can understand how customers view you in relation to the competition;

- identifying influencers: who has the largest following, and what influencer content is being shared the most;

- identifying topics and content – for example, monitoring industry-specific hashtags can help you understand what terms and types of content are resonating with your audience;
- getting feedback on products and services: know whether customers are satisfied with products and services, and take appropriate action where needed.

Social listening technologies include Tweet Reach, TweetDeck, Hootsuite, Cyfe, Crowdfire, Twitonomy, Buffer and SocialMention. Some of these are paid for, while others offer free versions.

Keyword tracking on social

Keyword tracking could help to improve content by updating it with relevant keywords.

Examples of technologies include Talkwalker, Keyhole, which offers a real-time hashtag and keyword tracker for Twitter, Instagram and the news, and Followerwonk for its basic version which provides word clouds based on conversations.

Social media sentiment

Social sentiment describes how social media users feel about a particular brand. This sentiment is typically tracked with scraping technologies, and interpreted using natural language processing.

Sentiment analysis is a fundamental social media monitoring tactic that analyses conversations on social and the web quickly and effectively. It presents an instant overview of all mentions in the monitoring stream, regardless of one's level of experience with analytics software.

The social media listening process

To implement social media listening, one can follow the steps outlined in Figure 18.3. It's important to first establish goals and expectations from the listening initiative, and then have a process in place to do something with the results.

For example, what will you do if particular conversations or keywords arise that are not included in your current content or marketing? What if those conversations contradict your messaging?

FIGURE 18.3 Social media listening steps

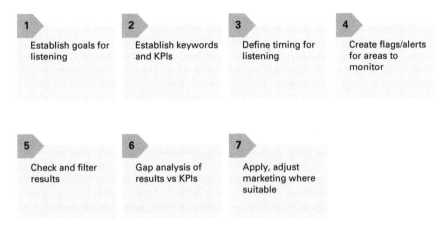

B2B social media measurement framework
==

Social media in B2B has also come a long way in being able to provide measurement. For the mentioned social media activities and strategies in this book, B2B marketers can look to different ways to measure effectiveness. For this we can refer to the social media measurement framework, as per Figure 18.4.

In measuring social media, it is important to define what you are aiming for and how you will measure your success. Goals are the broader desired outcome of your social media efforts, whereas metrics are the way you measure their success.

FIGURE 18.4 Social media measurement framework

	Generating awareness	Lead generation and nurture	Post-purchase
Metrics	Followers Impressions Reach Video views	Engagement Clickthroughs Interactions Page views	Reviews, ratings Recommendations Mentions
Business objective and goals	Brand awareness SOV Brand uplift	Lead generation Lead conversion	Customer retention rates Reduced attrition rates

Awareness

There are different ways to measure awareness or the early buyer stage through social media. Metrics include the following:

- reach: how many people saw your posts;
- new followers: how many new followers you gained;
- mentions: how many times you have been @mentioned;
- ad impressions: the number of impressions from a social media advert;
- video views for social media-based video;
- unique visitors;
- number of earned activities in the awareness phase, such as organic impressions and reach.

Engagement – consideration

Social media engagement is when a member of your community (or anyone else) takes some sort of action around your social posting. Examples of engagement metrics include website traffic from social media, likes, comments or SlideShare downloads of branded content

In the B2B pre-purchase stages, this probably best aligns to the mid-buyer journey, as this is where prospects engage but are not yet customers. Through engagement metrics, they are conveying their consideration of the brand (or lack of if these are negative engagement metrics).

Purchase stage

Some of the metrics to use in the purchase stage include:

- downloads of paper or app of content aligned to the purchase stage;
- attendance at a event, webinar or other activity related to the purchase stage;
- sales-ready form submissions: examples include quotes, demo requests, product evaluation requests and sales inquiries.

Post-purchase stage

Here we can use metrics such as content downloads, customer likes or shares of information to measure aspects such as customer satisfaction. We can also track customer sentiment through polling customers directly or using social listening.

FIGURE 18.5 Social media marketing strategies

Strategy type	Aligned activities	Strategic focus
Pre-purchase	Social media to target/reach Social media for lead nurturing	Support customer journey
Post-purchase	Building community Engaging Regular updating	Improve retention
Social media listening	Listening for sentiment for feedback on products and services/trends	Improve quality and responsiveness of marketing
Social media UGC	Incentivize customers/partners to generate content through different tactics	Content creation, customer engagement
Social media for Influencer marketing	Establish thought leadership, increase reach	Increase reach, increase relevance/acquisition, generate awareness
Social media advocacy	Social selling	Increase reach, support sales in selling

B2B social media marketing strategies

B2B social media strategies

Through the book we've covered a lot of ground in terms of social media marketing and its applications. The different social media activities can be summarized along the following key areas of strategy (see Figure 18.5).

CASE STUDY
Danfoss and Capclub

The Danfoss Group manufactures products and provides services used in cooling food, air conditioning, heating buildings, controlling electric motors, gas compressors, variable-frequency drives and powering mobile machinery. Within their heating division they have been running a programme known as Capclub, which up until recently was a sales tool used to win large contracts.

Capclub is about offering heating installers the possibility to badge their radiator caps with their logos and contact details, or something related to the customer's own brand.

In early 2018, Danfoss decided to move this programme to social media and generally digitize the programme. The objective behind this move was multi-fold; on the one hand, this move was to generate more awareness about Danfoss and their presence in this area of the market. Additionally, the idea was to generate more of a community of heating engineers which in turn would improve retention. Since the shift to social media in early 2018, Danfoss on Twitter have branched out to Facebook and Instagram.

In just over a year, Capclub has built up a membership of 200 companies who have asked for tailored radiator caps. They now have the twitter handle #Capclub. To support Capclub, Danfoss also included other merchandise to promote the programme such as polo shirts and baseball caps.

Capclub has also facilitated user-generated content amongst the heating engineer community as customers post pictures of radiators, caps and so on, and this content has in turn featured in awards programmes such as the sponsored Heating Installer awards.

Danfoss have worked with their PR company, trade magazines and the company behind the annual Heating Installer show, which has further helped to promote the initiative and improve reach.

The Danfoss Capclub has also since come to feature as part of prize draws at events, in games such as 'guess the number of caps in the jar'.

This is a great example of how for very operational products or services, organizations can build communities, gamify the experience and generally humanize their brand with the support of social media.

EXERCISE
Put it into practice

1 Using the B2B social media navigator, check which social media channels you are using for different digital marketing goals. Do you see gaps or areas where social media could be better applied?

2 Create a social media advocacy plan and process for your company. If you already have one in place, consider areas which could be optimized.

3 Create a social media framework for your marketing department, adapting the one in this book.

4 Create a plan for capturing and using user-generated content on social media channels, aligned to a recent or up-and-coming marketing campaign.

References

Almquist, E (2018) [accessed 3 August 2019] How Digital Natives Are Changing B2B Purchasing, *Harvard Business Review* [online] https://hbr.org/2018/03/how-digital-natives-are-changing-b2b-purchasing (archived at https://perma.cc/D9EQ-GC8S)

Clarke, T (2019) [accessed 1 August 2019] 22+ Instagram Stats That Marketers Can't Ignore This Year, *Hootsuite* [online] https://blog.hootsuite.com/instagram-statistics/ (archived at https://perma.cc/TDZ8-2VBV)

Cooper, P (2019) [accessed 1 August 2019] 75% of businesses now market on Twitter, *Hootsuite* [online] https://blog.hootsuite.com/twitter-statistics/ (archived at https://perma.cc/AB8C-9QZY)

Lessard, K (2018) [accessed 3 August 2019] How the Network Effect of Employee Advocacy Amplifies Your Brand Reach, *LinkedIn* [online] https://business.linkedin.com/marketing-solutions/blog/linkedin-elevate/2018/how-the-network-effect-of-employee-advocacy-amplifies-your-brand (archived at https://perma.cc/DW47-J47Z)

Omnicore (2019) [accessed 3 August 2019] Twitter by the Numbers: Stats, Demographics & Fun Facts, *Omnicore* [online] www.omnicoreagency.com/twitter-statistics/ (archived at https://perma.cc/5DYZ-EDAM)

Prodanov, G (2019) [accessed 3 August 2019] Millennials – The B2B buyers of the future and what this means for your business, *uppB2B* [online] www.uppB2B.co.uk/insights/B2B/millennials-the-B2B-buyers-of-the-future-and-what-this-means-for-your-business/ (archived at https://perma.cc/G5WP-7HW7)

Further reading

Masek-Kelly, E (2018) [accessed 10 November 2019] How to Use Social Media to Build Thought Leadership, *Social Media Today* [online] www.socialmediatoday.com/news/how-to-use-social-media-to-build-thought-leadership/542035/ (archived at https://perma.cc/DJZ5-WGNF)

19

B2B digital marketing technologies and platforms

WHAT YOU WILL GAIN FROM THIS CHAPTER

After reading this chapter, you will understand:

- how to identify key marketing technologies;
- how to evaluate marketing technology needs;
- how to select marketing technologies;
- the role of artificial intelligence in B2B digital marketing.

Introduction

Defining marketing technology

The merge of technology and marketing has been happening for some time, and the number and types of marketing technology have significantly accelerated recently.

Virtually all B2B marketers today are dealing with some form of marketing technology, and potentially multiple marketing technologies. Marketing technology, or martech as it is sometimes called, is all about activities and initiatives which leverage technology in achieving marketing goals.

Marketing technologies evolution

Today there are multiple types of technologies which come under the umbrella of martech, even if they support the wider organization.

The marketing technology landscape coverage has been captured in the martech landscape documents produced by Scott Brinker. According to his research, the number of marketing technology vendors has grown from around 150 in 2011 to about 5,000 in 2017 (Brinker, 2017).

The importance of marketing technologies

Marketing technologies support a number of roles for today's B2B marketers, as follows:

- Enabling small businesses to compete: Marketing technologies for CRM and account-based marketing make things possible for smaller companies that 15–20 years ago only large companies could do. Essentially, digital technologies can help to level the playing field, allowing smaller companies to be able to compete with larger enterprises.

- Improving efficiencies: Marketing technologies can facilitate faster capturing of information, analysis and implementation which can improve responsiveness, while also requiring fewer people to carry out tasks.

- Automation of tasks: This can include the automation of sending messages, and of viewing and managing marketing channels.

- Data assimilation and analysis: Marketing technologies support data assimilation, data crunching and data interpretation, which only large enterprises could do before with analysts or data specialists.

- Integration: Marketing technologies can facilitate the integration of marketing channels or content – for example, leveraging QR code technologies to integrate marketing channels, or using NFC technology to capture data at events and load it to a digital database.

Ownership of marketing technologies

For most companies, marketing technologies are left to the marketing department to manage, understand and roll out. The good news is that a lot of these technologies don't require technical people or IT people to understand and integrate. Many are intuitive and ready to use straight out of the box.

That being said, it does mean that B2B marketers may need to step out of their comfort zone to understand these technologies.

Marketing technology requirements

Deciding which marketing technologies you need is an important task. To help you get started, look at the following core areas of digital marketing (also seen in in Figure 19.1) to assess your needs in terms of urgency and importance:

- Channel-based marketing: Technology specific to marketing channels, whether this is mobile, email, social media, print, webinars or advertising.
- Cross-channel-based marketing: Technology to manage marketing across multiple marketing channels.
- Content management and testing: Technology to create, manage and schedule content.
- Internal marketing, social advocacy and sharing: Technology to roll out social media to wider teams in the organization.
- Media placement technologies: Technologies to support the buying and placement of media, often described under the umbrella term of 'programmatic technologies'.
- Social media marketing: This includes social media analytics, social media advocacy and social media influencing software.

Another aspect to discuss relating to needs assessment is whether the technology should be owned in-house, or can be subcontracted to an outside third party. For example, in the area of programmatic technologies, this is typically not something companies buy in-house even in larger enterprise companies, but would be outsourced to an external supplier.

Figure 19.2 outlines the key steps in evaluating marketing technologies.

FIGURE 19.1 Areas of marketing technology

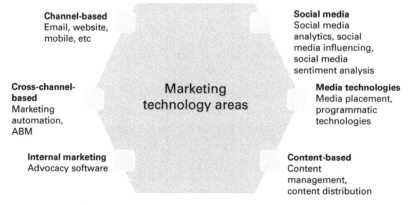

FIGURE 19.2 Steps in marketing technology assessment

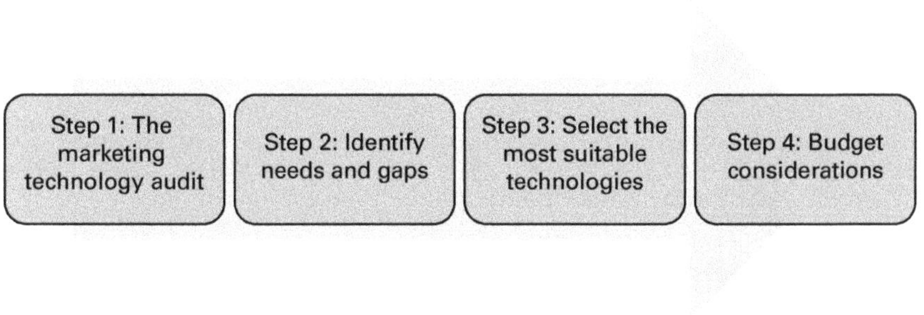

| Step 1: The marketing technology audit | Step 2: Identify needs and gaps | Step 3: Select the most suitable technologies | Step 4: Budget considerations |

STEP 1: THE MARKETING TECHNOLOGY AUDIT – IDENTIFY WHAT DO YOU HAVE

The first step is to do a technology audit. It might be the case that the company has various licences at hand to use technologies. Here the first thing to do is to view what you have access to directly and indirectly, and where you may still have valid licences.

STEP 2: IDENTIFY NEEDS AND GAPS

The next stage is understanding your needs. There are a lot of technologies out there, and you don't need all of them. It also needs to be considered that some technologies now integrate multiple functionalities and play the role of different separate marketing technologies. For example, cross-channel social media analytics platforms include analytics for multiple social media platforms.

The way to identify your needs is to think about where process improvements are required. Another approach is to consider technology requirements by stage in the customer journey eg in advertising, content or lead generation, or by specific marketing channels. It's important to understand which technologies are nice to have, and which are more critical to the business.

In considering resource requirements think of any additional skills or resources required for using the technologies. Depending on the answer to this, you can consider whether to buy the technology in-house or use an external company.

STEP 3: SELECT THE MOST SUITABLE TECHNOLOGIES

Once you have specified an area in which to invest in marketing technology – for example, CRM, marketing automation, advertising or social listening – it's now about selecting the right solution. For each area you probably will find multiple technology options.

But how do you know which ones are good, and which ones work best for you? Some ways to evaluate your options are to read reviews from reputable companies, which describe the technology and provide an assessment.

You could also use websites dedicated to marketing technology, such as Capterra and G2crowd.

STEP 4: BUDGET CONSIDERATIONS

Marketing budgets are not limitless, and today they can quickly get used up in purchasing technologies. According to Gartner's 2018 CMO survey, marketing technology accounts for about a third of marketing budgets (Cannon, 2019).

Here are some considerations when allocating budget for technologies:

- Will they support critical marketing goals?
- Is there a free version or alternative you could use?
- Assuming you do need to pay for the marketing technology, how specifically does it address the goal? Some marketing technology companies offer technology suites which encompass extensive functionality, but you may not need it all.
- How many of you need a licence? Can one person use the licence and share the findings across the team?

Artificial intelligence and digital marketing

Artificial intelligence (AI), sometimes called machine intelligence or machine learning, is intelligence demonstrated through machines as opposed to humans. AI is evolving rapidly – only a few years ago this technology was regarded as somewhat in its infancy, and used by a limited amount of B2B companies.

In the area of B2B digital marketing AI has become an interesting technology, as it not only supports roles but enhances productivity and, in some cases – such as chatbots and email management – may replace the need for marketers.

Aside from the roles that AI supports and enhances, it goes a long way to help B2B marketers reduce costs, particularly in the case of repetitive tasks which can take up time.

Key areas and roles of AI in B2B digital marketing

We can define four main areas where AI supports B2B digital marketing: analytics, lead generation, advertising, and customer experience.

AI FOR MARKETING ANALYTICS

Key applications for AI in the field of marketing analytics are:

- **Data filtering and analysis:** Marketing is increasingly becoming a data-driven area. The key is to use data effectively to improve the customer experience through targeting, tailoring marketing better and analysing it to determine patterns. As a result of demand, data analysis can consume a large amount of people's time, which is where AI can help. One example is ABM software, which can take care of a number of data management and filtering tasks related to marketing to organizations.

- **Social listening and sentiment analysis:** AI in social listening is used to conduct sentiment analysis. Potential negative issues can be spotted more rapidly, allowing organizations to respond faster.

AI FOR CUSTOMER EXPERIENCE

In addition to providing customer insights, AI can help marketers with improving and optimizing customer experience:

- **Chatbots and conversational AI:** Unlike previous bots or basic technologies which provided automatic responses to queries, AI-based chat bots learn how to resolve issues and answer questions, and can initiate genuine conversations.

- **Speech recognition:** Voice-activated devices and their potential improved due to advances in speech recognition technology, as well as things like natural language processing. In 2017, Google's level of speech recognition accuracy reached the coveted 95 per cent threshold (Sentance, 2018).

AI FOR LEAD CAPTURE AND GENERATION

AL can be used here as follows:

- **Lead management:** It takes time to find leads, to contact them, and to nurture them. AI technologies can help to manage this sometimes very long lead generation and lead nurture process. For example, AI applications like Conversica can follow up in an authentic manner.

- **Email messaging:** Companies can use AI products to improve their marketing emails by creating subject lines and calls to action that generate the most customer clicks or higher responses. This is not fully fledged content, but content in the form of messaging. AI can analyse a prospect's personal information to create the best tone and communication, which in turn yields higher response rates.

AI FOR ADVERTISING

Finally, AI can support advertising in the following ways:

- **Audience targeting and segmentation:** Dynamic segmentation is an application of AI that takes into account the fact that customer behaviours are rarely fixed or unchanging, and that people can take on different personas at different times for different reasons.

- **Programmatic ad targeting:** AI has been used for quite some time already in programmatic advertising and ad targeting, and has resulted in bidding and targeting becoming more efficient. AI when applied can determine the best time of day to serve an ad, or target users who are likely to engage with the ad. AI can also be used to adjust bidding strategies based on customer lifetime value (CLV), and invest more in potentially higher-value customers.

CASE STUDY
ServiceMax

ServiceMax, a field service technology vendor, was acquired by GE a few years ago and wanted to use the GE name and brand to expand its customer base. As part of the focus, they worked with DemandBase to leverage a programmatic ABM solution technology. Their challenge was to support better and relevant journeys for their website visitors.

To do so, they used DemandBase's Site Optimization solution, which uses AI to capture and aggregate all information about visitors, such as firmographic and intent data, to predict the pages they will go to.

By using this solution, ServiceMax were able to decrease bounce rates by 70 per cent whilst increasing time on site and pages per session by 100 per cent (B2B Marketing/LinkedIn, n. d.).

The future of B2B digital marketing

In terms of trends and technologies, this book has already covered a lot of different areas which will influence and impact the future of B2B digital marketing. Such trends and technologies covered earlier in the book include personalization, podcasts, user-generated content, advertising targeting technologies, sales enablement applications, new functionalities incorporated into social media, predictive analytics, marketing automation and many more.

Below are some further technologies and trends which deserve a mention.

Long-form content

Up until recently, there has been a view that digital content should be digestible, snackable and in short form. In the area of SEO, companies and agencies creating content are now seeing high engagement with long-form content in the most unlikely of situations and audiences.

Long-form content appears to be better researched and thought through. It may be that a lot of long-form content is regarded as high value and therefore people receiving it will take the time to read through it.

Video marketing

This has probably been influenced a lot by social media-based video marketing in the form of YouTube and Vimeo. About 80 per cent of users prioritize live videos over blog posts (Schools, 2018). Additionally, mobile video is being promoted through B2B social network LinkedIn, as it develops new video solutions for advertisers.

Video is seen to drive leads, and B2B marketers state that they produce more video content than any other content type (Marshall, 2014).

Augmented reality and virtual reality

Augmented reality (AR) technology adds graphics, sounds, haptic feedback and smell to the natural world as it exists. Augmented reality in the B2C space has been around some time, for example with reality gaming technologies such as Pokémon Go.

Accurate computer vision is important for the sophisticated development of AR, and particularly for its applications in marketing. So far, AR has been deployed to great effect in a marketing context by home improvement and furniture companies such as Home Depot, Lowe's and Ikea, although there have been more recent interesting examples of it in B2B industries such as Lloyd's Register. Lloyd's Register, an international provider of engineering and technology-centric professional services, created a virtual reality safety simulation allowing engineers to test in a safer environment. This was subsequently used as part of their training services.

In the B2B marketing space, AR can be used in a number of areas. By previewing products before purchase, customers are able to look at what they are about to purchase in detail. AR can be used where customers are not able to physically attend a B2B event, and so are provided with a virtual environment. AR can also be used to show real-life business scenarios.

B2B organizations sell a variety of products, solutions and services, all of which change and evolve over time. As technology transforms every industry, the way B2B organizations engage with their customers changes as well, providing them with alternate ways to reach their audience and present their products, solutions and services.

B2B voice marketing

Voice-based B2B marketing is an emerging trend, and one major area is voice-based search. According to 2018 statistics, 50 per cent of all search queries were set to become voice-based by 2020 (Sentance, 2018).

The growth of voice marketing in B2B through aspects such as voice-based search means that mobile should be prioritized, as we see an increasing use of mobile devices for purchasing. Forty-two per cent of B2B customers use mobile devices in the purchasing process (Snyder and Hilal, 2015).

Live video

Live video can be popular with larger organizations who use it to demonstrate product solutions, and highlight how products are made. Through live videos organizations are able to connect directly with followers in real time using smartphones and an application. The result is that they can potentially be more authentic and engaging compared to polished and previously edited videos.

Live videos can capture situations in real time such as events, meetings, interviews or behind-the-scenes views of the company. Live videos can be promoted through most of the main social media platforms today as they now support this functionality – for example, on Facebook, Instagram and Twitter it is now possible to promote live video. LinkedIn has also introduced LinkedIn Live, which allows individuals and organizations to broadcast videos in real time.

Messenger applications

Messenger applications include WhatsApp, WeChat, Facebook Messenger and Viber. In recent years, usage of them has increased dramatically – for example, as of July 2019 1.6 billion people worldwide were using WhatsApp (Clement, 2019).

Messenger apps offer additional compelling opportunities in B2B marketing. According to Nielsen, messaging ranked second out of nine possible communication forms for business, and 53 per cent of B2B customers are more likely to purchase from a business they can message directly (Liffreing, 2016).

Additionally, 29 per cent of respondent to a 2016 HubSpot survey selected messaging apps like WhatsApp or WeChat as their preferred business communications channel (O'Brien, 2017). Through messenger applications we can personalize content distribution according to different target groups.

CASE STUDY
WhatsApp

WhatsApp launched its WhatsApp for Business service in 2018. This includes ad services to engage and retain customers. WhatsApp can be a great tool to distribute content. It may be that after a customer has purchased your product, they return to your website to read content.

Through WhatsApp, organizations can share blogs and industry news, inform customers of up-and-coming activities such as webinars or events, or inform customers about related products or offerings.

EXERCISE

Put it into practice

1   Using Figure 19.1, create your own view of the technologies that you're using today, and look at where there are gaps. Are any of these gaps important areas or key needs?

2   If yes, consider how you can access and use the technology, eg by purchasing a low-cost version or a limited licence of the technology. If there are no budget challenges, use online evaluation sites to select the most suitable one for your organization and industry.

3   Of the four areas of AI in marketing, which areas would be most interesting for your company to test and trial?

References

B2B Marketing/LinkedIn (n. d.) [accessed 3 August 2019] AI in B2B: Going beyond the hype, *LinkedIn Business* [online] https://business.linkedin.com/content/dam/me/business/en-us/marketing-solutions/case-studies/pdfs/AI-in-B2B.pdf (archived at https://perma.cc/XM69-SGN2)

Brinker, S (2017) [accessed 3 August 2019] Marketing Technology Landscape Supergraphic (2017): Martech 5000, *chiefmartec.com* [online] https://chiefmartec.com/2017/05/marketing-techniology-landscape-supergraphic-2017/ (archived at https://perma.cc/PE3B-V8UU)

Cannon, J (2019) [accessed 3 Aug 2019] Marketing technology grabs 29 percent of 2018 CMO budgets, survey says, *MarTech Today* [online] https://martechtoday.com/gartner-cmo-spend-survey-29-percent-of-2018-marketing-budget-allocated-to-marketing-technology-232633 (archived at https://perma.cc/X5UR-EU3C)

Clement, J (2019) [accessed 20 October 2019] Most popular global mobile messenger apps as of July 2019, based on number of monthly active users (in millions), *Statista* [online] www.statista.com/statistics/258749/most-popular-global-mobile-messenger-apps/ (archived at https://perma.cc/KQU2-PR6P)

Liffreing, I (2016) [accessed 20 October 2019] Facebook study: 53 per cent of consumers more likely to shop with a business they can message, *Campaign Live* [online] www.campaignlive.com/article/facebook-study-53-consumers-likely-shop-business-message/1404632 (archived at https://perma.cc/ZF4A-84QP)

Marshall, C (2014) [accessed 11 December 2019] 76 per cent of B2B Marketers Use Video Content Marketing, *Tubular Insights* [online] https://tubularinsights.com/B2B-video-content-marketing/ (archived at https://perma.cc/CLD4-7QQV)

O'Brien, C (2017) [accessed 20 October 2019] How B2B brands can use social apps to market & sell, *Digital Marketing Institute* [online] https://digitalmarketing-institute.com/en-gb/blog/19-07-17-how-B2B-brands-can-use-social-apps-to-market-sell (archived at https://perma.cc/3UAH-EYSW)

Schools, D (2018) [accessed 11 December 2019] Live Video Scares Me, But This Small Instagram Poll Revealed a Confidence-Building Lesson, *Inc.Com* [online] www.inc.com/dave-schools/why-live-video-is-so-scary-how-you-can-go-live-with-confidence.html (archived at https://perma.cc/CWW2-GLXH)

Sentance, R (2018) [accessed 3 August 2019] The future of voice search: 2020 and beyond, *eConsultancy* [online] https://econsultancy.com/the-future-of-voice-search-2020-and-beyond/ (archived at https://perma.cc/CZ3E-Z3HF)

Snyder, K and Hilal, P (2015) [accessed 3 August 2019] The Changing Face of B2B Marketing, *Think With Google* [online] www.thinkwithgoogle.com/consumer-insights/the-changing-face-of-B2B-marketing/ (archived at https://perma.cc/HH2V-3XBK)

Further reading

EverString with Heinz Marketing (2018) [accessed 3 August 2019] The State of Artificial Intelligence in B2B Marketing, *EverString* [online] www.everstring.com/resources/report-the-state-of-ai-in-b2b-marketing/ (archived at https://perma.cc/G3RT-5V54)

Lister, M (2017) [accessed 3 August 2019] 37 Staggering Video Marketing Statistics for 2018, *Wordstream* [online] www.wordstream.com/blog/ws/2017/03/08/video-marketing-statistics (archived at https://perma.cc/78AJ-XUXF)

INDEX

Note: Numbers in headings are filed as spelt out; acronyms are filed as presented. Locators in *italics* denote information in figures/tables.

CPSIA information can be obtained
at www.ICGtesting.com
Printed in the USA
LVHW022025131021
700323LV00002B/4